Gardens of Italy and the Western Provinces of the Roman Empire

From the 4th century BC to the 4th century AD

Linda Farrar

BAR International Series 650
1996

Published in 2016 by
BAR Publishing, Oxford

BAR International Series 650

Gardens of Italy and the Western Provinces of the Roman Empire

ISBN 978 0 86054 837 9

© L Farrar and the Publisher 1996

The author's moral rights under the 1988 UK Copyright,
Designs and Patents Act are hereby expressly asserted.

All rights reserved. No part of this work may be copied, reproduced, stored,
sold, distributed, scanned, saved in any form of digital format or transmitted
in any form digitally, without the written permission of the Publisher.

BAR Publishing is the trading name of British Archaeological Reports (Oxford) Ltd.
British Archaeological Reports was first incorporated in 1974 to publish the BAR
Series, International and British. In 1992 Hadrian Books Ltd became part of the BAR
group. This volume was originally published by Tempvs Reparatvm in conjunction
with British Archaeological Reports (Oxford) Ltd / Hadrian Books Ltd, the Series
principal publisher, in 1996. This present volume is published by BAR Publishing,
2016.

Printed in England

BAR titles are available from:

	BAR Publishing
	122 Banbury Rd, Oxford, OX2 7BP, UK
Email	info@barpublishing.com
Phone	+44 (0)1865 310431
Fax	+44 (0)1865 316916
	www.barpublishing.com

Dedicated to the memory of Pamela Handley, my first tutor in Classics

CONTENTS

	Page	
LIST OF ILLUSTRATIONS		iv
FORWORD AND ACKNOWLEDGEMENTS		v

CHAPTER ONE: INTRODUCTION   1
    Notes
CHAPTER TWO: EVOLUTION OF THE ROMAN GARDEN   4
    The *Domus*, or town house
    Villae rusticae, Urbanae and *Suburbanae*
    Notes
CHAPTER THREE: NONRESIDENTIAL GARDENS   9
    Gardens in association with dining establishments
    Market gardens
    Funerary gardens
    Portico gardens
    Public parks
    Notes
CHAPTER FOUR: THE ARCHITECTURE AND LANDSCAPING OF GARDENS   13
    Paths
    Decorative fencing
    Pergulae
    Summer dining couches
    Garden seats and tables
    Walling
    Sunken gardens
    Terraced gardens
    Maritime Villas
    Gardens of Large and Palatial Villas
    Notes
CHAPTER FIVE: WATER FEATURES   20
    Features of water basins
    A suggested typology, following archaeological evidence
    Type A, B, C, D, E, F & G
    The position of water features in a garden
    Different forms of water feature: *Euripi*
    Caves and grottoes
    Nymphaea, of basilica form
    Aediculae nymphaea
    Facade nymphaea
    Notes
CHAPTER SIX: GARDEN ORNAMENTATION   28
    Table I
    Table I: A sample of Ancient Roman sites as an indication of the
        range and frequency of garden sculpture   30
    Table II: Examples of statue types less frequently found in Roman gardens   32
    Catalogue of sculpture found in Roman gardens:
    Altars - Venus - Priapus - Cupid - Children - Mars and Amazons -
    Apollo - Hercules - Bacchus and his entourage - Muses -
    Nymphs and River Gods - Rustic genre (mortals) -
    Ephebes, athletes, wrestlers etc - Herms - *Oscilla* - *Pinakes* -
    Sundials - Urns & Bowls - Water Stairs - Fountain outlets - Automata
    Notes
CHAPTER SEVEN: FLORA & FAUNA IN GARDENS   41
    Frescoes used as confirmation of plant species
    Archaeological evidence of plant species grown in gardens
    Fauna in gardens
    Notes

CHAPTER EIGHT: ROMAN HORTICULTURE 50
    Garden technicians
    Gardening tools and equipment
    Horticultural techniques
    Notes
CHAPTER NINE: CONCLUSIONS 55
    Survivals of the Roman garden
    Interpretative Archaeology and Roman gardens
    Notes

APPENDIX I: Museums and archaeological sites visited to
              collect material for this study 60
APPENDIX II: Pliny's *Hippodromus* garden 61
APPENDIX III: Garden plants mentioned by Pliny in his *Natural History* 62
APPENDIX IV: Archaeological evidence of Roman garden flora 64

ABBREVIATIONS 66
BIBLIOGRAPHY 66
FIGURES 72
PLATES 100

LIST OF ILLUSTRATIONS:

FIGURES:

1a. Plan of a basic Roman town house with an *atrium tuscanicum*.
1b. A peristyle house.
1c. Later form of peristyle house.
2. Plans of houses with gardens in Pompeii.
3. Plan of the house & garden of Loreius Tiburtinus Pompeii.
4. Plan showing the *hortus* at a *Villa Rustica*.
5. Plan of the *Villa Urbana* of Poppaea, Oplontis, with findspots of plant material & sculpture.
6a. Marble plan of a funerary garden.
6b. Reconstruction drawing of the Mausoleum of Augustus.
7. Plans of portico gardens from fragments of the Severan Marble Map of Rome.
    a. Porticus Pompeii.   b. Forum Pacis.
    c. Divus Claudius.   d. Porticus Liviae.
    e. Adonaea.
8. Decorative fencing as depicted in frescoes.
9. Miniature frescoes of gardens.
10a. Plan of Hadrian's Villa at Tivoli.
10b. Serapeum and Canopus at Hadrian's Villa, Tivoli.
10c. Hadrian's Villa: Central areas.
11. Garden plan: House of the Thunderbolt, Ostia.
12. Cross section of part of a water basin.
13. Cross section of the Euripus.
14. Type C basin.
15. Type D basin
16. Plan locating type E basins (demi-lune).
17. Type F basin.
18. Type G basin.
19. Model of a grotto.
20. Plan of a basilica type of nymphaeum.
21. Multiple fountain niches.
22. Fresco depicting garden statuary.
23. Fresco depicting an urn in front of a decorative marble wall.
24. Plan and view of the garden sculpture at the House of the Golden Cupids, Pompeii.
25. Plan and view of the garden statuary at the House of Marcus Lucretius, Pompeii.
26a. Bronze balustrade with janiform herms as posts.
26b. Water basin at Welschbillig, Germany.
27. *Oscilla*.
28. *Pinakes*.
29. Sundial.
30. Owl automata.
31. *Coronariae*, garland and chaplet makers.
32. Plan of the garden at the House of the Chaste Lovers, Pompeii, with findspots of plant material.
33. Plan of the garden at Fishbourne, Britain.
34. Horticultural tasks, from a mosaic rustic calendar.
35. Mosaic of the 'Lilygrower' from Carthage.
36. Horticultural tools and equipment.

PLATES:

1. Plants grown in raised containers, in an *atrium*.
2. Plant containers in a later form of peristyle garden.
3. Fresco of a *Villa Urbana*.
4. Fresco depicting a grotto.
5. House of the Hunt, Pompeii.
6. Villa of Poppaea, Oplontis.
7. Decorative stone wall from Welschbillig.
8. Reconstructed pergola, House of L.Tibertinus, Pompeii.
9. *Triclinium* under a *pergula*, at Vienne, Gaul.
10. Mosaic of Lord Julius, Carthage.
11. Schola from the Triangular Forum, Pompeii.
12. Garden bench and matching water basin, Sousse.
13. Sunken garden at the House of Ancora Nera, Pompeii.
14. Terraced garden at the Villa of the Mysteries.
15. Plumbing to water features.
16. Type E, demi-lune basin.
17. Type B basin, Schola of Trajan, Ostia.
18. Type D basin, House of Meleagro, Pompeii.
19. Type F basin, with caissons, at Conimbriga.
20. Gutter basin, along three sides of a garden, Vienne.
21. A Euripus basin, House of L.Tibertinus, Pompeii.
22. Island-like nymphaeum, Domus Flavia, Rome.
23. Aedicula nymphaeum, House of the Little Fountain.
24. Facade nymphaeum, House of Cupid & Psyche, Ostia.
25. Venus (from Ostia).
26. Fresco depicting a statue of Mars.
27. Putto carrying urn.
28. Bronze Amorini carrying duck, House of the Vettii.
29. Pan & Satyr statue group.
30. Silenus & Maenad statue group, from Carthage.
31. Reclining nymph fountain figure.
32. Rustic genre, old fisherman.
33. Draped herm of Mercury.
34. Janiform herm heads, of Bacchus & Ariadne.
35. *Oscillum*.
36. Small decorative water stairs.
37. Garden scene, fresco from the House of the Wedding of Alexander, Pompeii (with key to plants depicted).
38. Fresco from the Garden Room at the House of Livia, Primaporta, Rome.
39. Garden fresco from the House of the Marine Venus.
40. Fresco on a low wall at Oplontis.
41. Roman flora & fauna depicted on a *pluteus*.
42. Row of five tree root casts, Oplontis.
43. Mosaic depicting a garden technician.
44. Plant beds as described by Pliny the Elder.

FORWORD & ACKNOWLEDGEMENTS

This study, with the exception of minor additions, is my thesis submitted (October 1995) for a degree of M.Phil. in the Classics & Ancient History Department at Warwick University. Since this date new work in the fields of Garden Archaeology and Landscape studies, such as that by Jashemski in Tunisia, and MacDonald & Pinto on Hadrian's Villa at Tivoli, have recently appeared in print. To save delaying the publication of this thesis, I have only referred to them briefly in the notes, but have included them in the Bibliography.

All the figures that were not drawn by myself have been fully acknowledged, and (with the exception of Pls.19,37 & 38) the photographs were taken by the author.

I would like to thank numerous people for the kindness shown to me, and for supplying information for my research, especially the following:
B. Conticello, Soprintendente scavi di Pompei, for permission to view gardens not open to the public. Christian Dewez (from the Villa at La Malagne) who kindly gave an impromptu detailed tour, in the pouring rain, of the villa and its valley setting, and giving details of the research programme that is being undertaken. Vincent Jolivet and Catherine Virlouvet, from the French School at Rome, for information on their excavations at Rome. Lisa Moffett (from Birmingham University) for material on plant remains at Alcester, included into ch.7. Eddie Price, excavator of the Villa at Frocester Court. Claire Ryley (Education Officer at Fishbourne Palace) for information regarding flowerpots found on site, and of a survey in progress on the Roman flora of Britain (mentioned in ch.8 & 7 respectively). Christopher Tuplin (from Liverpool University) for information on Persian gardens included in ch.2. Prof.W.J.H.Willems (excavator of the Villa at Voerendaal) for information on the pathway and Jupiter column included in ch.3. Hilde Smith, who translated some passages from the German. Dr. Lance Smith for producing plans for fig.1 & of Hadrian's Villa (fig.10). Pauline Wilson in Computer Services who printed the camera ready lasercopy.

I thank my three thesis examiners, Prof. Barry Cunliffe, Dr. Martin Henig and Dr. Stephen Hill for their pertinent comments and suggestions which have been incorporated in the text. However, any errors that remain are my own.

Most of all, I give many thanks to my supervisor Dr. Stanley Ireland for the kindness shown and his never ending patience.

CHAPTER ONE: INTRODUCTION

This research is a study on aspects of horticulture, or the culture of the *hortus* (the Roman word used to denote a garden) as distinct from work in the fields, agriculture. Different forms of garden will be discussed, such as the rustic *hortus* which often included an orchard and an area for growing vegetables and herbs, country gardens and those of the town, down to the humble window box or balcony garden that was equally important to city dwellers living in apartments. However, because of the nature of evidence available my main focus of attention will be on decorative gardens, domestic or public, used as an amenity.

As gardens are usually associated with dwellings, a study of Roman housing was also needed; for the development of houses and villas often appears to run parallel with a change in the concept and use of the garden. During my research I consulted many plans of ancient towns and villas to discover the layout of garden features in all of the provinces so that I would be able to ascertain similarities or differences in the areas concerned. However, many town plans identify public buildings but tend to simplify areas of housing. Often streets are shown but the location of housing is coloured in or sometimes merely an outline is given. Gardens, if they can be identified, are usually left blank. Roman gardens have been overlooked for years, with excavators mostly tending to concentrate on structural remains, such as walls and mosaics. Many books on mosaics, however, do produce a detailed plan of dwellings locating each mosaic and indirectly they show the existence of a garden that is otherwise not referred to.

In excavations the garden area is often overlooked because of restrictions in funding and time available. Large-area excavations, which would be most informative, are time-consuming and therefore expensive, and may not produce significant results as opposed to the areas occupied by buildings. Compromises such as a trench cut within the garden may indicate the existence of a metalled surface, as at Verulamium,[1] but without further evidence this should not be accepted as meaning that this surface extends across the whole area. Evidence of Roman gardens is slight and ephemeral, yet sometimes a mechanical digger is used to determine if a path led to the entrance of the villa (as at Easton Maudit);[2] and at Eccles a swathe was cut across the large courtyard and revealed, but luckily did not destroy, a centrally located fishpond.[3] This brutal method will always furnish incomplete data, but if carefully used it could reveal the existence of some garden structures that have the good fortune to be in the path of the digger; it will however destroy traces of cultivation.

On multi-period sites, a garden (like a house) could be redesigned a number of times, which might complicate its later interpretation. And when a house/villa falls into decay, the garden would soon become overgrown. Weeds and seedlings of wild trees would colonise the space and confuse any remaining traces. Later when the site has reverted to agriculture deep ploughing could then inflict further damage, as at Frocester Court where half of the garden details were lost in this way.[4] Therefore on many sites preservation is slight, and a matter of chance survival, but at Pompeii the catastrophic eruption of Vesuvius that engulfed the city with a thick layer of ash and lapilli sealed the surface of AD79. This has protected traces of cultivation and many of the gardens' furnishings; also a date can be allocated for this style of garden art. Because of the quantity of garden areas here[5] they remain a major source of comparable material against sporadic survivals elsewhere. However, structures in Pompeii, such as water basins, will never be removed to determine earlier phases of gardens. At a few locations (such as Vienne or Ostia) a partial stratigraphic record of structural elements in a decorative garden exists; but traces of previous bedding trenches for instance are rarely encountered. It is hoped that this will now be remedied by the greater use of garden archaeology. For in general houses are often dated by the style of their mosaics, and the garden, if discussed at all, may correspondingly be said to have features of that period also, whereas what survives are traces of the last period of cultivation.

Many sites were excavated a long time ago, when standards of archaeology were not so stringent as they are today, and therefore study is seriously hampered by the scant records of earlier excavators and the fact that once the soil has been removed from site vital information is lost for ever. Where a garden area was examined, all that remains are the structural elements. With the increasing use of scientific methods of archaeology, however, more details can be uncovered than were looked for in the past. Recording techniques have greatly improved in the last fifty years and modern excavations often include an environmental archaeologist who studies questions such as land use and its effect on the economy of the area. When such methods are applied to the garden, its flora and fauna can sometimes be revealed. The more specific, relatively new, science of Garden Archaeology has primarily been used in Britain to uncover lost parterres and garden features of 16th-19th century AD country houses, yet these techniques can also be used in Roman gardens. When applied to the Roman period this field is interdisciplinary, for it will include a study of paleobotany, palynology, geology, classical art and architecture, ancient literature, ancient religious practices, the Roman diet, culinary and ornamental plants grown, and those for medicinal purposes, also aspects of Roman domestic life and society. The information that can be accumulated is therefore extremely diverse.

There are few modern works on Roman gardens from which I could extract information. Lafaye (in Daremberg & Saglio) contributes articles under *Hortus*, and *Topiarius;* and Gothein has chapters on Greek, Roman and Byzantine gardens. Both were useful as a background study, but like many were written at the turn of the century and are now quite out of date.

Grimal's study (first published in 1943) is the standard history of Roman Gardens but is in many ways limited, for it is concerned only with the period up to AD138 and aims to illustrate Roman gardens at the peak of their perfection. He includes material from the area of Pompeii but to a large extent he concentrates on the gardens of the city of Rome

INTRODUCTION

itself. He includes a survey of Ancient Roman literary attitudes to gardens, and in a philosophical manner he constantly aims to show how Rome's love of nature was made manifest in the garden. His archaeological sources for Rome included Platner-Ashby, Lugii and Lanciani (the last two were archaeologists in Rome) which I was able to consult at first hand. Grimal believes that there were three styles of Roman garden which are likened to the last three of the Four Styles of Pompeian Frescoes. He names these the Ciceronian, Augustan, and Flavian, the first being a period of imitation of Hellenism; the second includes natural elements as introduced by the paintings of Ludius; the third was baroque in flavour. I feel that this is incorrect, for gardens of all periods were diverse, and this classification omits earlier and later periods which also need to be taken into account. Jashemski (1979,341,n.1) states that 'the author's major conclusions have been questioned by other scholars' and that they are often quite different from those in her own book.

Jashemski pioneered the use of scientific archaeology in gardens at Pompeii, and her works are clear and informative. Her first volume, in 1979, contained data on various aspects of Roman gardens, and the second, being an appendix of the first, is a source book for all the details of gardens excavated under the area covered by Vesuvius. It also includes the extant frescoes and mosaics depicting scenes of a Roman garden. These books have been widely consulted, but as these are concerned with the region of Campania, I still needed to find comparative material for other provinces within the Roman Empire.

Articles, archaeological reports, and guide books to numerous sites were sought in order to ascertain the extent of horticulture in the provinces. During my research I also visited many archaeological sites and museums to collect material for this study. At these sites I have personally inspected a number of Roman gardens to see for myself the variety that existed, and to observe and record details, which have given me a better understanding of my topic. I include a list of locations visited in Appendix I.

A variety of books were consulted for information on the flora of the Mediterranean region, of which the most useful was that by Blamey & Grey-Wilson. Some research which produced negative results was Godwin's *History of British Flora* which focused on how the glacial periods affected our flora, and is only useful in that it shows which plants existed before the Romans came. Other sources that were consulted but have not been used for this study are the works of Dioscorides, who was primarily concerned with medicinal plants and does not give details of their cultivation or other uses.

Of the ancient literary authors the agriculturalists Cato (2nd century BC), Varro (c.36BC), Columella (c.AD60) and Palladius (4th century AD) wrote manuals on farm management and husbandry. A great deal is not relevant to this study, but they do include sections on the culture of the *hortus*, as part of the farm or villa estate. Much of this is of a practical nature, and would appertain to methods used on a smallholding or in market gardening, but some passages could be said to inter-relate to practices used in decorative gardens and are thus very informative. The manuals were used to extract data on how the climate and seasons affect planting and the growth of certain plants, arboriculture, especially of fruit trees, and the management of fishponds and aviaries housed in gardens.

The agriculturalists acknowledge their debt to earlier writers such as the Carthaginian Mago, whose works were considered so worthy that all twenty-eight books were translated from Punic into Latin (but unfortunately have not survived). They also cite Greek authors, but these wrote on individual aspects of agriculture rather than a combined manual, which was the Latin aim. All of these may, however, have been influential in the development of the science of agriculture and horticulture in Rome.

Cato's work is brief and succinct but is nevertheless worthwhile, for he is informative on early practices. Varro contains less horticulture but in the course of giving advice on profitmaking occupations such as beekeeping, and the management of fishstocks, aviaries and game preserves, he is also informative about those who preferred to include such areas in pleasure gardens on their domain. Columella provides a thorough manual on all aspects of agriculture and horticulture, and is later used extensively by Palladius.

The many volumes of *Naturalis Historiae* by the Elder Pliny are a mine of information on items grown in gardens. Trees, flowers and vegetables are discussed for their medicinal or culinary properties, and he includes those used for decorative purposes. His wide-ranging source-material covers the cultivation and distribution of numerous plants with, in some cases, notes on their origins. He also gives details of notable examples of flora and fauna, and in the process provides snippets of information on private and public gardens.

A number of poets and other authors were also used to glean relevant passages (e.g. Martial, Ovid, Seneca, Horace, Statius, Luxorius); they are often quite brief, and in general comment on urban parks at Rome or large estates rather than the small private garden of a town house. This omission is understandable though, for the small and ordinary were less remarkable, and overlooking them reflects attitudes of the society in which these authors existed.

In Varro, and the letters of Cicero and Pliny the Younger details are given of features in several extensive properties which are thought to be typical of their type.[6] The latter provides two lengthy descriptions of gardens which are an extremely important source of material. Many features described in ancient sources have their existence proven by archaeology, and investigations show that small gardens share a number of similarities with those of their larger counterparts, with many items reproduced on a smaller scale to suit a more restricted area, a space that was no less important to the owner of a small or large garden.

Besides descriptions we also have contemporary illustrations in frescoes, which depict plants of the period in a somewhat idealised form that includes ornamental garden

INTRODUCTION

sculpture. Similar garden furnishings are also documented archaeologically, and the painted versions give an impression of a real garden. Miniature landscape frescoes are also an important source to ascertain different forms of garden landscaping, such as parterres, terracing, and the use of trelliswork enclosures. Such paintings show an intrinsic love of nature, and the naturalistic rendition of an abundant flora and fauna enables an analysis of species to be undertaken. They are to me illustrative of the actual appearance of elements in a Roman garden.

My objectives were:

1. To ascertain if the gardens seen at Pompeii were representative of those throughout the Empire, or particular to that area.
2. To discover the effect of regional customs, and differences in climate, on the appearance of a garden.
3. To uncover the range of characteristic elements found within Roman gardens.
4. To determine if it was possible to find a chronological sequence for any of the garden features.

All these points will contribute to our understanding of Roman gardens and their place in society.

NOTES TO CHAPTER ONE

1   Frere, 1983, 159.
2   Unpublished. Towards the close of the excavation, but prior to my visit, a digger had cut down to the clay subsoil in the hope that the remains of a pathway would be revealed in the section of the trench. However no trace had been found on this occasion.
3   Detsicas,1973,77.
4   Gracie & Price, 1979, 10.
5   Jashemski (1979,25) states that of the area excavated so far in Pompeii 450 gardens have been found.
6   Littlewood,1987,9,n.1.

CHAPTER TWO: EVOLUTION OF THE ROMAN GARDEN

From the earliest of times a garden (albeit a simple one) had been considered an important part of the Roman family home, which was in the early periods a rustic farm. The population at that time was largely agrarian and therefore farms or smallholdings would include a kitchen garden to supply salad greens, etc, for the table. The garden would be the means by which the family could be self-sufficient and through tradition the area held a certain sanctity.[1] It was generally placed beside the home, making it convenient for the womenfolk to attend to between chores inside;[2] whereas agriculture was usually practised by the stronger male population. An *area* defined beds or plots for plants,[3] while the word *ager* was applied to the cultivated fields on a farm.

In the 5th Century BC one of the Twelve Tables, Table VII,[4] concerned land rights and the ancient *heredium* (the inheritable portion of the property). The term appears to have been used when referring to the vegetable garden; and the word *hortus,* which came into use later, was applied to an enclosure but could also mean the farm as a whole. *Hortus* may have derived from the Greek *hortos* which was used when referring to an enclosure of cultivated greens. In our earliest surviving Latin agricultural treatise Cato lists the subdivisions of a rustic farm, and places the watered *hortus* (meaning the vegetable garden) as the 2nd most important, first place being reserved for a vineyard.[5]

Latin bucolic authors such as Virgil, Tibullus and Calpurnius Siculus,[6] can be used when considering the form of early Roman gardens. Also the Homeric Poems appear to show similarities, and they all describe what appears to be a *potager*, an area arranged as a vegetable garden or orchard, the most descriptive being the gardens of the mortal Laertes, the father of Odysseus; and those of Alkinoos, the King of the immortal Phaeacians.[7] The latter became proverbial for the ideal qualities in a garden, that of being ever fruitful and plentiful, on land that was fertile and well watered. This type of garden, especially those with orchards, features in several ancient myths, such as the Garden of the Hesperides.

The rustic type of garden remained popular throughout the Roman period for humble properties and in places solely committed to farming. The Virgilian story of the 'Old Man of Tarentum'[8] portrays the simplicity of this good humble way of life.

The *Domus*. or town house

In urban environments dwellings needed to fit into a restricted network of streets, and therefore in the Roman world the form of *domus* most often encountered in early times appears to be those with an *Atrium Tuscanicum*, which were thought to have derived from Etruscan prototypes.[9] These were of an axial form, comprising an entrance passage, *atrium, tablinum* and generally with the *hortus* to the rear of the dwelling (see fig.1a). This type can be detected in the early phase of dwellings at Pompeii and date to the end of the 4th or the beginning of the 3rd century BC.[10]

In built up areas an adequate supply of water would be difficult to obtain, and this type of house in many ways helped to overcome this problem. The closely built houses were of necessity inward facing, the street frontage often being occupied by shops, and properties had a party wall between each other. Therefore roofs of this type of house were given an inward slope to direct falling rainwater through the opening of the *compluvium* into the *impluvium* basin below. From here water was channelled into a cistern, usually located to the side of the *impluvium*; the water could then be drawn up for the use of the household and to water plants in the garden.

A later development was the introduction of a peristyle garden, placed to the rear of the *tablinum* (see fig.1b). The earliest of those at Pompeii date to the 2nd century BC.[11] The peristyle is believed by some to have been adopted from the Greeks, but I feel this is misleading. Firstly, Diodorus Siculus (V,40,1) states that the Etruscans invented the peristyle. The Etruscans were believed to have influenced the Romans on a number of points, and were considered as being responsible for the introduction of the early form of *atrium*, so perhaps his authority can be trusted here also. The Etruscans were, however, influenced by the Greeks, and Romans had contact with Magna Graecia, but after the Roman conquests in the East, Rome in general was very much inspired/corrupted by the spoils of war and what was seen in these lands. So if a comparison is to be drawn, we need to inspect forms of Greek housing.

We have already noted the rustic garden of the Homeric Age, but in the Classical Greek period incessant warfare encouraged the majority of the populace to live behind city walls. Excavation, and literature of the period, shows that there do not appear to be gardens in Greek town houses, but rather market gardens situated outside of the city walls. A different tradition had been established where citizen and slave would go out to tend the fields by day and return at night, or when alerted to danger. Carroll-Spillecke and Wycherley[12] show that the entrance of a Greek home opened directly onto an open court that was either of beaten earth or paved in some manner.[13] The rooms were disposed around the yard in an irregular fashion. Even the towns built on a grid system (such as at Olynthos or Priene)[14] were not provided with house gardens. This is partly because of a lack of space; for urban housing was built to a high density. There was also no direct water supply; townspeople relied on water from communal cisterns, wells, and fountain houses. Also laws may have forbidden the planting of trees close to walls[15] which, if they were of mudbrick, would be damaged by roots. Vatin gives instances, including a Law recorded by Aristotle,[16] where provision was made for all household refuse to be carried out of the city by civic dungcollectors to be used as manure on extramural market gardens. However, within the *polis* public areas were sometimes provided with shade trees, such as the planes in the Agora at Athens, planted by Cimon in the 5th century BC and there may have been plantations or groves around shrines (as was the case at the Hephaistion)[17] but if so these were usually located near a spring or stream.

Later, after contacts with Persia, Xenophon describes some of the gardens of the East.[18] Theophrastus made a study of plants and was known to have a garden, but its whereabouts (in or out of town) is not certain. Pliny (*NH*,XIX,51) however, informs us that Epicurus (c.250BC) was the first person to introduce a house-garden in a Greek city, but unfortunately its form is not mentioned.

In the Hellenistic period, we hear how the sight of Persian paradise gardens and game parks had a great impact on Alexander and his friends,[19] and how later the Hellenistic rulers and their followers adopted many of the trappings of the east. Little has been discovered archaeologically to prove this, but at Pasargadae (in Iran) Stronach has revealed the orderly plan of the royal park or *paradeisos* of Cyrus, constructed some time after 546BC. This shows a well laid out enclosure with rows of trees, and columned pavilions opening onto a symmetrically planned irrigated garden at its heart. This type of garden is believed to have been emulated by the Hellenistic rulers and possibly the wealthy landowners. At Pergamon, Aigai, Pella, and Demetrias[20] the royal abodes incorporate a vast open area surrounded by the colonnades of various wings of the palace. These gardens however have not been studied in detail, and therefore we lack knowledge of any internal features. The addition of porticoes to the Hellenistic garden may have been simply to enclose the garden inside the building, within the city, whereas the Persian garden appears to have been enclosed by bands of trees (many perhaps fruit bearing)[21] and ultimately the boundary wall, and the palace was set inside this forested garden landscape.

I therefore believe that the Roman peristyle garden, was not borrowed directly from the Greeks, but was a mixture of Hellenistic/Persian and Etruscan ideas. The Roman peristyle was imprinted onto the old *hortus* at the rear of the house and did not replace the *atrium*, which for many centuries held the sanctity of tradition. In accordance with this we find that rooms associated with the atrium retain their Latin names, but paradoxically those facing onto the new garden area were given Greek names, the *exedra*, and *oecus,* as was the *peristylium* itself. These might suggest an origin in the Greek world, but might equally refer to the increasing Hellenization of the Roman world at large. Where possible the axiality of the Roman *domus* was preserved, and through their love of nature we find that the Romans preferred to include, even on a small scale, a living tapestry of plants into their colonnaded courts.

This form of house with atrium & peristyle (fig.1b), became highly popular, and is found in numerous dwellings at Pompeii (fig.2 shows just one region of the city but illustrates many houses which, before additions, have as their nucleus the basic features of the 'Italic house'). Three appear on a fragment of the Severan Forma Urbis, the marble map of Rome commissioned under Severus,[22] and is a testament to the longevity of this type. Its popularity lay partly through its being a means of enlarging the house, and the open area was used as a light well for surrounding rooms, but in addition the garden and its shady porticoes also provided an extra living space where there would be fresh air. Vitruvius shows to what extent these qualities were valued:

> 'the air from greenery is rarefied and removes the thick humor from the eyes, thus improving vision, as well as removing other humors from the body' (*De Arch*,IV,9,5)

Vitruvius (ibid,VI,5,1) mentions that *vestibula* courtyards and peristyles were areas of the house that were open to the gaze of others, therefore the proportionally larger area occupied by the peristyle would become an ideal location in which Romans could display their wealth and love of ostentation.

The possession of a garden becomes another status symbol, and therefore when opportunity allowed garden areas were enlarged (as at the House of Obellius Firmus, Pompeii) or a second garden was installed (as at the House of the Faun (fig.2h). The increasing importance attached to gardens is shown by a later development where the *atrium* is altered to allow plants to be grown there also. The open space of the *compluvium* was widened and became almost another peristyle. The *impluvium* was then turned into a water basin surrounded by planters. Examples can be seen in the *atrium* of the House of the Relief of Telephus at Herculaneum, and at the House of Loreius Tiburtinus at Pompeii (fig.3 & Pl.1).

Later developments which can be seen at Ostia (in the House of Fortuna Annonaria (V,ii,8) dating from 1st century AD),[23] saw the reduction of the *atrium* into little more than a passageway. In some cases (as in fig.1c) this area was widened and then acted as a *vestibulum* before entry into the peristyle itself. Variations of earlier and later peristyle houses are found throughout the Roman Empire, in North Africa, the Iberian peninsula, Gaul, and at Caerwent in Britain.[24] At Volubilis[25] rows of the later type of peristyle house (suggested in fig.1c) were constructed, showing how standardized the form had become by the 3rd century AD. Even in dry hot countries, in areas with limited water supplies, the court could be provided with stone plant containers, or long troughs, as in the '*Maison aux Jardinières*' at Timgad, and the House of '*Omnia tibi Felicia*' at Dougga[26] (see Pl.2). In the Romanized Greek East, however, large palatial properties appear to have gardens, but many of the town dwellings (such as the terraced houses at Ephesus, Apamea in Syria, Daphne near Antioch or Side)[27] retain the Greek preference of having a paved court. However they admit garden elements such as a Roman style nymphaeum, and perhaps plants were grown in pots although none are recorded archaeologically. Local traditions, as well as the climate, were influential in determining the design of housing.

The population increase in many cities led to the introduction of *insulae* or apartment blocks. In general these were arranged around a court or light well which contained little more than a cistern, and a *dolium* for the night soil. In Ostia there are a number of *insulae*, which show the restrictions in space and comfort especially on the upper floors. Literary references indicate that even here Romans could bring nature into their confined living area by having plants in pots either on balconies or on window ledges. Martial (XI,18) describes his efforts at growing plants on his window ledge; and Juvenal (*Sat*,III,270/1) reminds us of the dangers of walking in streets beside these blocks; for you needed to beware of projectiles (perhaps also the occasional flower pot) falling from above. Wall paintings of street scenes from Boscoreale show balconies with pots, but as these appear to be broken ones they may have contained Adonis gardens.[28] However, they would be difficult to find archaeologically, for in most cases only the foundations or lower storey survives. Pliny (*NH*,XIX,59) records how plants in window boxes were felt to be an expression of a longing for a view of the country, but burglaries now 'compelled them to bar out all the view with shutters.' There are also references by Seneca to roof gardens but again these cannot be found archaeologically.[29]

The most spacious *insulae* at Ostia, called the Garden Houses, however, were given a communal garden with decorative fountains.[30] Tenants would have no doubt paid a higher rent for the amenity of the gardens which would have made their outlook more pleasant.

Villae rusticae, Urbanae and *Suburbanae*

The living accommodation of a large country farm (or fundus) was often called a *villa rustica*, and like humble cottage-type small holdings also possessed a *hortus*. Several have been excavated in Campania, and were studied by Carrington, but it is only more recently, at the Villa Regina at Boscoreale, that details of the *hortus* area have been identified,[31] fig.4 gives its form and shows its proximity to the living quarters of the villa. Individual vegetable plots can be discerned, and a cistern placed off-centre would have enabled the gardener to 'quench the garden's ceaseless thirst'.[32]

With the advent of a more luxurious lifestyle, the rustic farm or *villa rustica* for some became more and more inappropriate and many were modernized to conform to new fashions. Many villas were simply given a new wing, thereby separating the owner's accommodation from work areas, such as at the villa of Sette Finestre.[33] Varro (c.36BC) speaks of changes in country life, and how some of the new fashions could be made to turn a profit for the owner, instead of being merely decorative[34] a trend of which he disapproved, but which was clearly becoming prevalent.

For the commencement of villas for pleasure, rather than farming, a passage in Cicero (*De Leg*,II,2,5) may be used to inform us when such alterations were thought to have taken place; for in the space of time between his grandfather's lifetime ('when the homestead according to old custom, was small') and his father's occupancy (when he 'rebuilt and extended' the family home) it was transformed into a *villa urbana*. This period saw the introduction of well appointed and desirable properties, with gardens, and suggests a date of late 2nd-1st century BC. Varro (*R.R.*,III,2,3/10) shows that the term *villa* was then used when speaking of a farmhouse, country mansion, or luxurious town house.

Of the suburban villas, the term *villa suburbana* referred more often to the building, whereas the property as a whole was usually still referred to as the *hortus* of a particular person; and as such sixty-seven at Rome have been recorded by Platner & Ashby.[35] These gardens became landmarks in the city and were sufficiently well known to be useful when locating a person's address.[36] Vitruvius states that the homes of men of substance both in town and country should be suitable to their station, they should contain:

> 'princely vestibules, lofty halls, and very spacious peristyles, plantations and broad avenues finished in a majestic manner.' (*De Arch*,V1,5,1)

The land associated with *villae urbanae* was remodelled into extensive gardens. Pleasant and attractive gardens became desirable. We hear of colonnades opening onto ornamental terraces called *xysti*; those of Pliny's Laurentine villa were 'scented by violets'.[37] He however retained a *hortus rusticus*, showing that perhaps there was still a place somewhere for the needs of the table. Promenades and shady groves were popular, and are thought to have been a recreation of the famous walks in the Academy at Athens that were admired by Roman visitors. Many of the new elements in gardens were given Greek names, such as Academy, Lyceum, gymnasium, xystos, hippodromos, and again this points to a growing philhellenism, but in many cases the Roman meaning of the word changes.[38] The Greeks, perhaps because of the war torn nature of their land, focused their attention on enhancing natural sites in the landscape, such as caves with springs, which became the shrines of nymphs in grottoes. They were venerated with the addition of flowers and statuary.[39] As with the Greek appellations, the Romans adapted these basic Greek/Hellenistic concepts but the resulting new garden form was their own invention.

Roman technology, especially of hydraulics, revolutionized the art of gardening. The introduction of aqueducts and plumbing to private houses and estates enabled a wider range of plants to be grown. Also gardens could now be enlivened by water features. The scope that the new technology allowed was enormous.

Extravagance was clearly a feature of the day. For instance, a conspicuous waste of water (which was chargeable and therefore expensive) would serve to show the unlimited wealth at the owner's disposal. It became fashionable to have fishponds.[40] However these and other garden features would no doubt have been affected by changes in taste and fashion during the long period of the Roman Empire (different forms of water features are discussed in ch.5).

Many wealthy Romans, such as Cicero and Pliny, possessed a number of properties.[41] Horace (*Odes*,II,15) notes that near Rome the growth of large villa estates was becoming so great that there was little agricultural land left on which to grow food. This 'progress' would lead to shortages at Rome, thereby affecting its economy, but shows how important landscaped gardens had become. Plutarch recalls that Pompey had chided Lucullus (whose name became a byword for the excesses of a luxuriant lifestyle) for designing his property at Tusculum in such a way that it would be:

> 'uninhabitable in winter. Whereupon Lucullus burst out laughing and said: "Do you suppose, then, that I have less sense than cranes and storks, and do not change residences according to the seasons?" ' (Lucullus,XXXIX,4)

Varro (*RR*,I,137) shows that others vied with Lucullus in size and quantity of villa estates. Pliny (*Ep*,IX,40) favoured his estate at Laurentum in winter, for the climate beside the sea was milder; whereas he could avoid the heat of midsummer when he stayed at one of his properties beside Lake Como.[42] Cool air to be found within mountainous districts, by lake-shores, or beside the sea, encouraged men to favour these localities during the heat of midsummer. Winter and summer resorts soon became well established.

Owners were, however, still dependent on the local climate and soil conditions, and therefore in different regions in the Empire there are variations from the *villae urbanae* mentioned in literary texts. In warm climates the villa opens outwards as well as inwards, and porticoes face onto garden courts or the extensive landscaped grounds. This can be seen in depictions of villas in frescoes and mosaic (e.g. Pl.3). The winged villa in this plate shows similarities to the partly excavated north facing facade of garden A at Oplontis (see fig.5). The meticulously detailed excavation has enabled us here to make a reconstruction of the appearance of gardens associated with *villae urbanae*; but for the more extensive park-like grounds no detailed study has been made, partly because of the expense of such a project, and partly through only small areas being open for excavation at any one time. We do however, have descriptions of Pliny's villa and gardens at Tusculum and Laurentum which give an insight into the wider landscaping of the grounds of such villas. Of especial interest is his lengthy description of a *hippodromos* garden. This is so important in our effort to regain the atmosphere of Roman Gardens that I have therefore thought it necessary to reproduce it in appendix II.

Elsewhere, the Hispanic villas, detailed by Gorges (1979,121,fig.19) were basically of three different types, one is linear, but the other two forms contain garden courts (courtyard villas with a central peristyle, and large complex villas). In Gaul including Germany, there are a number of winged and courtyard villas (as in Britain). Many of these contain garden features such as a fishpond sited so that the owners could view the spectacle from facing rooms or corridors, e.g. at Echternach[43] or Fishbourne, which, although in a cooler climate, have a facade which is reminiscent of that depicted in Pl.3. In Pannonia,[44] where the climate is colder in winter, there were courtyard villas, some with a fortified appearance. Porticoes were less open, and enclosed a central courtyard garden which was in many cases provided with a central water basin.

Rivet (1970,64) believes that the Italianate villa gardens at Fishbourne in Britain are to be seen separately, and he infers that in general others did not follow fashions seen in Italy.[45] Nevertheless, evidence found elsewhere suggests that gardens may have existed, albeit on a simpler scale owing to the differences of climate and taste. Evidence has been found of fish ponds and bedding plots,[46] which increasingly shows that the area enclosed by the wings of villas may well have been reserved as a pleasant decorative area, perhaps a garden. In fact Varro (*RR*,1,23,4) suggests that when planting on a farm provision should be made for orchards and flower gardens, for they 'are profitable for the pleasure they afford'. Some villas would remain purely rustic, but others could be, as Columella describes, of three parts;[47] of these the *villa urbana* is the abode of the owners, while a nearby *villa rustica*[48] the rustic part, was farmed by his manager.

Where walls with gateways enclosed land close to a *villa urbana* livestock would be kept at bay, and the area could be used for plants or plantations. Owners often lavished great care and expense on decorating the inside and outside appearance of the building. Therefore I feel that similar thought and effort would have been expended to decorate the area in the proximity of the building, specifically the area onto which the main rooms faced, if only to demonstrate the social standing of the owner, and provide a satisfactory setting for the building.

NOTES TO CHAPTER TWO

1 'Consequently even a certain sense of sanctity attached to a garden' (Pliny *NH*,XIX,19,50).

2 Pliny (*N.H.*,XIX,4,19) shows that the *matrona* had the responsibility for provisioning the household with produce from the *hortus*. Finds of women's hairpins in garden areas at Frocester Court supports this view (Gracie & Price, 1979,13).

3 Lawson (1950,99). The word *area* is used by Columella (*RR*,XI,3,13).

4 Warmington in *Remains of Old Latin*, Vol. III, XII *Tabulae*, Table VII,4a.

5 Cato, *R.R.*,I,7.

6 Virgil,*Georg*,IV,109/48; Tibullus,1,17; Calpurnius Siculus, *Eclog*,II.

7 Homer, *Odyssey*,XXIV,225ff; & VII, ll2ff, respectively.

8 *Georgics*,IV,130ff.

9 McKay (1975,21) mentions three prototype *atria*, which can be dated to the 5th century BC at the Etruscan city of Marzabotto. Carroll-Spillecke (1992,94) shows that by the 3rd century BC at Cosa, there were houses with a *hortus* inside early Roman cities.

10 Jashemski,1979,16.

11 Ibid.

12 Carroll-Spillecke,1992,86ff; Wycherley,1976, 177/180.

13 Gothein (1966,60) mentions that plants in pots may have been grown in courtyards. Certainly in ancient Greek literature (and vase painting, e.g. at Karlsruhe) there is evidence for the planting of ritual Adonis gardens. Here quick growing seeds were sown in old pots or broken amphorae and then the plants were left to die in memory of the lovelorn Adonis.

14 See note 12.

15 SEG XIII,521.11.158-161, an inscription from Pergamon, cited by Carroll-Spillecke (1992, 100,n.12).

16 Athenian Constitution, 50.

17 Thompson,1963,fig.11.

18 *Oeconomicus*, IV, 13/14; IV,20/21.

19 Arrian,*Anab*,VII,25,3; VII,25,6 for references to a palace garden. For a game park type of *paradeisos* see Quintus Curtius (*Hist. of Alex,*, 8,1,11/19).

20 Cima & La Rocca,1986,figs.5, 8&9; and Catling (1974,21,fig.36); respectively.

21	Information provided by C. Tuplin, at a research seminar on *Greek gardens and Persian Paradeisoi*, at Liverpool University, 12 Nov 1993.		both the front and rear of the main block of the villa (Information supplied by the excavator, E.Price, at the C.I.A. conference 1994).
22	Boëthius & Ward-Perkins,1970,fig.53.	47	*R.R.*,I,6,1. The third part of the villa estate was the *villa fructuaria*, or storehouse.
23	Boersma,1985,198, fig.188.	48	e.g. La Malegne, Belgium, where the *villa rustica* was roughly 200-300m distant from the *villa urbana* and its terraced garden.
24	Wacher,1978,fig.22b. Unfortunately this example (like a number of others) is from a partially excavated site rendering the identification of an entrance way somewhat difficult. I believe that the room with a series of steps may indicate a point of access perhaps even the presence of a vestibule.		

21 Information provided by C. Tuplin, at a research seminar on *Greek gardens and Persian Paradeisoi*, at Liverpool University, 12 Nov 1993.

22 Boëthius & Ward-Perkins,1970,fig.53.

23 Boersma,1985,198, fig.188.

24 Wacher,1978,fig.22b. Unfortunately this example (like a number of others) is from a partially excavated site rendering the identification of an entrance way somewhat difficult. I believe that the room with a series of steps may indicate a point of access perhaps even the presence of a vestibule.

25 MacKendrick,1980,306.

26 Evidence for Dougga was from personal inspection. For Timgad see Ballu (1910,40,pl.12). Pl.13, in Ballu, shows that the balusters of the exterior slabs of the 'jardinaires' (or planting troughs) were ornamented with finials of janiform theatre masks. For this decorative form see chapter six, page 35.

27 Aksit,1994,34/5; Balty,1981,122 & 132; Levi, 1971,167, figs.26&63, respectively. A nymphaeum was noted at one of the two houses seen at Side.

28 Ling,1991,fig.28. For Adonis gardens see n.13.

29 *Ep*,122,8 & *Controv*.5,5. Groves of trees, and fishponds, are mentioned although this may be an exaggeration. Due to the problem of weight, I feel that Seneca may actually be referring to gardens grown on raised terraces rather than true roof gardens.

30 The Garden Houses date c.128A.D. (Watts,1994, 86/9, & fig on p.88),

31 Jashemski,1987,64/71 & fig.32.

32 Columella, *R.R.*10,25.

33 Carandini & Tatton-Brown, 1980, 12/14, & fig.5.

34 *R.R.*,I,13,6.

35 Vol.I,1929,264/273, entry under Horti.

36 Paoli,1990,144.

37 Pliny,*Ep*,12,17.

38 The Roman meaning of *xystos* is discussed by Vitruvius (*De Arch*,VI,7,5). Varro deplores the fact that 'they do not think they have a real villa unless it rings with many resounding Greek names'.

39 Ridgeway, 1981,20.

40 It is noted by Pliny (*NH*,XVIII,1,7) that by his day an ornamental garden of two acres had become insufficient for such as Nero's ex slaves, and 'now they like to have fishponds larger than that'. This perhaps may be an exaggeration, but indicates that water features had become commonplace, and therefore needed to be enlarged or elaborated in some way to make them more noteworthy.

41 Cicero,*Atticus*,4,18; Pliny,*Ep*,III,19. Pliny's mother-in-law had four properties (*Ep*,I,4).

42 Ibid,IX,7. Pliny (*Ep*,V,6,1) also says that his estate in Tuscany is healthy in summer, for it is 'at the very foot of the Apeninnes'.

43 Wightman,1985,111/3 & fig.16. A model of this villa in the Luxembourg National Museum of History and Art shows its appearance.

44 Lengyel & Radan,1980, figs.47; 55; & 56.

45 He cites the following large villas as exceptions, Woodchester, Southwick & Chedworth.

46 At Bancroft (Williams & Zeepvat,1994, Vol.I, fig.101) there was a pond and possibly a flower bed. Zeepvat (1988,fig.19) gives the dimensions of eleven fishponds found in Roman Britain. At the modestly sized villa at Frocester Court bedding plots have been discovered at both the front and rear of the main block of the villa (Information supplied by the excavator, E.Price, at the C.I.A. conference 1994).

47 *R.R.*,I,6,1. The third part of the villa estate was the *villa fructuaria*, or storehouse.

48 e.g. La Malegne, Belgium, where the *villa rustica* was roughly 200-300m distant from the *villa urbana* and its terraced garden.

CHAPTER THREE: NONRESIDENTIAL GARDENS

That gardens played a useful and important role is demonstrated by the fact that they were often incorporated into the design of buildings that served the community and its visitors. In many cases these areas of greenery would appear similar to their domestic counterparts, but the building and garden would have been decorated to a high standard by rich patrons who were often keen to demonstrate their philanthropy and civic pride. In such places statuary (such as figures of Emperors etc)[1] may be of a more monumental nature. At Ostia private clubs and guilds appear to have constructed communal dining halls (*collegiae* or *scholae*) arranged around a garden, such as the Schola of Trajan belonging to the Shipbuilders Corporation, or the House of the Triclinia which is thought to be the Guild House of Builders.[2]

Visitors could be catered for in a *hospitium* (inn), or a *mansio*; these were also situated on main routes to provide shelter for long distance travellers, such as at Wall on Watling Street in Britain.[3] The garden of this coaching inn was furnished by a demi-lune basin (see ch.5).

Gardens in association with dining establishments

Cauponae, tabernae, and inns which made provision for *alfresco* dining used these facilities as a form of advertisement, as modern ones make use of an attached beer garden. The lines of the Syrian Copa (a celebrated innkeeper) reveals their form and appeal:

> 'There are garden nooks and arbours, mixing-cups, roses, flutes, lyres, and cool bowers with shady canes... Come; rest here thy wearied frame beneath the shade of vines.' (Virgil, Minor Poems, Copa, 7f & 31).

Archaeological evidence from such establishments in Campania has largely confirmed the lines above,[4] and the reconstruction drawing by Jashemski (1979, fig.249) suggests their appearance. Here a masonry *triclinium* surrounded by post holes and root cavities attest outdoor dining areas under vine covered pergolas.

Market gardens

Hortus or *Hortuli* were terms that encompassed land used for market gardening. These establishments were, according to Cicero[5] and Varro,[6] to be found on the outskirts of cities. They were thus close to a ready market and the short distances would ensure that produce remained fresh, thereby attracting better prices. Fruit, vegetables and flowers were grown in such districts; Varro mentions violets & roses.

In Pompeii, Jashemski has located several commercial gardens within the walls of the city.[7] However, these were mostly located to the south-east where housing was less dense. Such areas reserved for food production could prove useful in a siege situation.[8]

In Egypt epigraphic evidence survives of leases of garden lands; these are primarily pertaining to land used for commercial purposes, which needed to be registered for taxation. Several indicate a degree of specialization, such as a cucumber garden, narcissus or rose garden.[9] A papyrus from Oxyrhychus[10] reveals that Dionysia had asked a commercial grower to supply her with 2,000 narcissi and perhaps the same amount of roses for her son's wedding. Over 4,000 narcissi but only 1,000 roses could be found at the time, indicating large, or many, areas under flower cultivation.

Funerary gardens

Leases, in Egypt, also included funerary gardens.[11] An inscription on marble concerning the funerary garden of Mousa[12] relates to how the garden was leased, and then illegally sold, later to be returned to the heirs. This indicates that the land concerned was of considerable extent, sufficient to be profitable. Such gardens were almost always sited outside city walls. Cicero[13] recounts the great pains involved in searching for a suitable *hortus* within which he would construct a funerary monument for his daughter Tullia. He required a position outside the city limits of Rome, in a fashionable district to suit his station in life and her honour, but at an affordable price. *Cepotaphia*, were the most developed form of funerary monument, and were designed to provide enough produce from the land enclosed around the monument to sustain the shade of the departed. Banqueting facilities were often included for the benefit of family and friends when commemorating the deceased, and the insertion of a libation pipe or vessel would ensure that the shade could also partake. Inscriptions mention that vineyards were planted to provide wine for libations,[14] or there was a stipulation that profits from the sale of garden produce would be used for specific purposes or occasions e.g.:

> ' from whose yield my survivors may offer roses to me on my birthday forever.' (CIL, v, 7454, Toynbee, 1982, 98)

Trimalchio[15] envisages his own funerary garden, and sees the plot containing fruit trees and vines. He also reveals the plausible extent of a typical *cepotaphia*:

> 'a hundred feet facing the road and two hundred back into the field'

which would be more than sufficient to provide offerings. Any surplus produce could provide an income for the heirs.

Archaeological evidence was found by Jashemski at Scafati.[16] Here the partially excavated enclosure measured 8m x more than 20.5m. As six large tree roots were discovered, she believes that the area under the shade of those trees would have been 'planted with fragrant flowers'. An indication of species favoured in funerary contexts is found in the *Culex*, a satirical poem to a dead gnat:

> 'Here are to grow acanthus and the blushing rose with crimson bloom, and violets of every kind. Here are spartan myrtle and hyacinth, and here saffron,...soaring laurel...oleander and lilies,...rosemary and the Sabine plant,...marigold, and glistening ivy,...amaranth,...and ever-flowering laurestine...' (Virgil, 398-407).

Two valuable maps of funerary gardens survive, engraved on marble. One in Perugia Museum[17] includes a complex of buildings, for the ritual funerary banquets, and also perhaps accommodation for the slaves and equipment to maintain the garden. The second, found at the necropolis on Via Labicana near Rome[18] (see fig.6a) provides a plan indicating the location of the monument and its relationship to what appear to be plant beds and rows of trees or vines.

The most famous funerary garden was the *silvae et ambulationes* associated with the mausoleum of Augustus at Rome. This large circular monument, like ancient tumuli, was surmounted by a mound of earth. Ancient sources mention that a grove of evergreen trees was planted above the tomb, and a bronze statue of the Emperor crowned the summit.[19] The surrounding area was left open to the public.[20] Fig.6b indicates the possible appearance of this monument built in the *Campus Martius*.

Portico Gardens

There were a number of portico gardens in Rome, and maps locating the ancient ruins show their proximity to other buildings. One of these is the first public park in Rome, the *Porticus Pompeii* constructed in 55BC.[21] It was an area enclosed by covered walkways, *portici* designed to give shade from the sun, and shelter from rain, when the audience retired between performances in the adjoining theatre.[22] The adoption of Hellenistic porticoes to enclose the garden within a *peristylium*, was perhaps partly motivated by the need to separate the garden from the surrounding streets and buildings. The porticoes henceforward were united into one entity, and hereafter the term *portico* was used to indicate an enclosed garden of this type.

Propertius (*El*,II,32,11f) describes some of the characteristics of the famous *Porticus Pompeii*. There were shady columns and an 'avenue thick-planted with plane-trees rising in trim rows' as well as water features with statues. Fortunately a plan of this important garden can be drawn from relevant surviving fragments of the Severan Forma Urbis (see fig.7a). Richardson (1992,318) believes that the four centrally aligned rows of squares represent pollarded plane trees, around two large rectangular water basins. However Gleason (1994,14) argues that these two areas form the *nemus duplex* (double grove of trees) mentioned by Martial (II,14,10). A series of *exedrae*, semicircular and rectangular, probably provided seating, *scholae*, on the outer margins of the garden. Lugli (1938,80) however wrongly believed that these were nymphaea. The fountains mentioned by Propertius may have been situated in proximity to larger water features, perhaps in the area marked A, or they may have been placed to the rear of the *scenae*, but any interpretation will have to await confirmation by archaeological means. The *Porticus Pompeii* is thought to have been inspired by Greek or Hellenistic *peristylia*, and Vitruvius' description of a Greek style *palaestra* provides many similarities:

> 'Three of the sides are to be single colonnades; the fourth which has a south aspect is to be double, so that when rain is accompanied by gales, the drops may not reach the inside...On the other three sides, spacious *exhedrae* are to be planned with seats...double colonnade walks in the open are to be planned [*xysta*] ...The *xysta* ought to be so laid out that there are plantations or groves of plane trees between the two colonnades. Here walks are to be made among the trees with spaces paved with cement...' (*De Arch*,V,11f).

The *Hectatostylum* immediately to the north of Pompey's portico provides a double colonnade (like the Poikile wall at Hadrian's Villa, Tivoli), and *exedrae* with seating clarifies their function. Plantations could refer to box, which was a feature of 'sun warmed Europa';[23] laurel that adorned the *Porticus Vipsania*;[24] or vines grown on trellises, such as protected the walkways in the *Porticus Liviae*.[25] Others may have contained combinations such as laurel, myrtle and box-trees.[26]

The components of the *Porticus Pompeii* may be compared with later portico gardens, for which it provided a model. This type of garden was associated with theatres,[27] libraries,[28] baths complexes,[28] temples,[29] or they stood on their own.[30] Such porticoes became fashionable places in which to stroll, or sit, where one could be seen, they also served as a venue for assignations. The plans of porticoes illustrated in figs.7 & 14 reveal a number of similarities, although they were attached to a variety of buildings.

The Portico attached to the Library of Hadrian at Athens (fig.14) had a single colonnade on all four sides, but was provided with a series of *exedrae*.[31] There was a plantation in the open interior, and by positioning the elongated water basin on the central axis a *nemus duplex* was created.

Details of the portico garden of the *Forum Pacis* (fig.7b) are known from fragments of the Severan Forma Urbis. The garden forms a *temenos* of the Temple of Peace. Two rectangular *exedrae* were built into the lateral walls. Two areas of irregularly shaped rows of boxes would suggest a *nemus duplex*, and appears in the reconstruction drawing by Ward-Perkins (1981,fig.30). However, Lloyd (1982,92) suggests that flower beds would be more likely owing to the narrowness of the beds, and that normally there was a convention to drill a hole to indicate a tree or column. Apart from the spoils of the Jewish War, statuary and paintings from the demolished Domus Aurea appear to have been put on public display here.[32] Pliny (*NH*,XXXVI, 24,102) indicates that the whole complex was aesthetically pleasing, and he counted it as one of the three most beautiful buildings in Rome. Procopius (*Bell.Goth*,IV,21,11-12) mentions the existence of a fountain and statuary here.[33]

Another temple portico the *Divus Claudius* was inscribed on the marble map of Rome (see fig.7c). Again there appear to be exedrae, but a series of lines as opposed to holes has been drawn to indicate a planting scheme. Richardson (1992,87) feels that these may be for vines (as in the *Porticus Liviae*). Lloyd (1982,95) however, because of their close spacing and parallelism, sees these features as representative of rows of hedging, perhaps of box, as at Fishbourne in England. The portico was furnished with fountains and nymphaea under Nero, after he extended the Aqua Claudia to supply the gardens, which he altered to incorporate into the domain of the Domus Aurea.[34] Richardson (1992,88) describes how remains of a water channel in the roof of the surviving eastern (rear) portico indicated that water fed a series of niches, in what appears to me to be, a facade type nymphaeum.

Porticoed gardens were often named after their donor; Livia's Portico was one of the most popular resorts mentioned by Ovid, Martial, Pliny & Strabo.[35] This example demonstrates that such gardens are not always connected to public buildings or monuments. As can be seen from fragments of the marble map (fig.7d) it had *exedrae* on the lateral sides and a continuous double colonnade. In the centre there appears to have been a rectangular water basin, and each corner was furnished by a small lobed fountain.

The *Adonaea*, is thought to be located on the Palatine, as a quotation from Philostratus records that the *aula* was in the vicinity of Domitian's palace, it was:

> 'bright with baskets of flowers, such as the Syrians at the time of the festival of Adonis make up in his honour' (*Vita Apoll.Tyana*,VII,32).

This portico garden was also mentioned by Ovid (*Ars Am*,I,75) as a place much frequented, and we are fortunate that a plan survives on the Severan marble map (fig.7e). It appears to have had a wide colonnaded entrance, and the first encircling row of dots could indicate porticoes. After an interval, three further rows of dots are thought to represent vine-covered arbours in the open courtyard.[36] The elongated rectangular feature across the centre of the garden is thought to be a *euripus*, and the series of irregularly shaped boxes that surround it may be flower beds. Four blocks, each of four lines (with serifs) have remained a puzzle; my interpretation would have been that these perhaps detail benches or beds, upon which the pots containing 'Adonis Gardens' could have been placed. After the plants had died they could then have been thrown into water, the *euripus* here, to complete the ritual.[37]

Recent archaeological research has revealed some contradictions.[38] In the Domitianic phase the plan of the garden does not tally with that depicted on the marble map. However, under Severus, some evidence of porticoes exists, and several rows of half amphorae used as flower pots have been discovered on what appears to be alignments similar to the lines engraved on the map. The pots had been set in the ground with marble chippings, and because they were placed so close together, I believe that the pots may have served as receptacles for plants associated with Adonis. A wider spacing would indicate permanently planted pots of flowers or shrubs; in such instances the pots are usually found to be cracked open by root growth, although some pots would be pre-broken so that growth would not be checked.[39]

Evidence shows that planting schemes are arbitrary and ephemeral; details can easily change over the centuries. But it appears that gardens played an important part, as a complementary adjunct to architecture and to beautifying their surroundings. Another aspect revealed by Vitruvius[40] is that such areas could prove valuable as sources of wood during times of siege. At such times these localities could also be used for food production.

Public Parks

The public, from time immemorial, had access to areas considered as sacred woodland, a *nemus* or *lucus*, inhabited by spirits such as a *numen*.[41] As time went by many of these areas were eroded, for land was valuable. As the density of housing increased green areas within cities were correspondingly more important; therefore the creation of parks expressly for the use of the public was seen as a humane act of beneficence to the populace, as well as being good propaganda for the donor. Archaeological evidence for parks is extremely rare; in some instances boundary *cippi* record an edge of the area in question.[42] However, some details survive in literary references. We have already mentioned the first public park, that of Pompey. Not to be outdone Caesar made provision in his will to open his gardens at Trastevere to the public.[43] Augustus planted the *Nemus Caesarum* by the Naumachia,[44] as well as the *silvae et ambulationes* around his own mausoleum.[45] Agrippa also willed his *thermes* with attached gardens to the public,[46] later called the *Campus Agrippae*. Martial reveals that these were much frequented, and Ovid (*Ex Ponto*,I,8,37-38) recalls their beauty:

> '*Campi pulchros spectantis in hortos, stagnaque et euripi Virgineusque liquor.*'

Within the *hortus* was an artificial lake (*stagnum*) which was a location for Nero's revels, mentioned by Tactitus (*Ann*,15,37); and a long water basin, the *euripus*, all fed by the *Aqua Virgo* (mentioned in ch.5). Strabo (XIII,1,19) places a fine statue of a lion, plundered from Lampsacus, between the two water features. There was also a *nemus*, which may have been the grove of plane trees adorned with animal statuary recorded by Martial (III,19,2).

To establish further the possible appearance of these parks, we would need to include paths, and perhaps shrubberies and flower beds, also areas covered by grass. A number of references mention sitting upon flower strewn grass,[47] and the climate would allow for the possibility of a green sward, although in high summer it would have appeared somewhat yellow. Martial (III,20,12/3) indicates that seats were included in such areas. Although parks contained statuary and features of an appropriate monumental nature, they could in many cases be said to resemble large domestic gardens, some had in fact originally been private gardens before being opened to the public.

NOTES TO CHAPTER THREE

1   As in the Schola of Trajan, Ostia, where a large statue of the Emperor of that name was discovered (Cordello,1986,40).
2   Ibid, and Meiggs(1960,fig.8) respectively.
3   Details were given to me during a discussion with the excavators, F. & N. Ball, following a lecture on Wall (1994).

4   e.g. Pompeii (II,viii,5)(Jashemski,1993,94) and Pompeii (VI,i,1) (Jashemski,1979,168, fig.249).
5   Cited by Grimal,1969,109.
6   Varro,*RR*,I,16,3.
7   e.g. Pompeii (VIII,vi,4-5)(Jashemski,1993,219) & Pompeii (I,xv, 1-3) (Jashemski,1993,61).
8   Vitruvius,*De Arch*,V,9,8.
9   Johnson,1975,101/2.
10 Rea,1978,100,letter 3313.
11 Johnson,1975,101.
12 Fraser & Nicholas, 1958,118.
13 Cicero (*Ad Att*,XII,23) mentions an ideal garden belonging to Cotta, but following difficulties with the sale others were considered; such as the *Horti Scapulae* (ibid,XII,37), but these proved unwise to buy (ibid,XIII,33a).
14 CIL,xii,1657 (Toynbee,1982,98).
15 Petronius,*Sat*,XV,71.
16 Jashemski,1979,148.
17 Toynbee,1982,98,fig.7.
18 Toynbee,1982,99,fig.8.
19 Strabo, *Geog*,5,3,8.
20 Suetonius, *Vita Aug*,100.
21 Gleason,1994,26,n.3. Plutarch (*Pompey*, XLII,4) informs us that the design of this portico was based on the theatre complex at Mitylene.
22 Vitruvius,*De Arch*,V,9,1.
23 A portico garden mentioned by Martial (*Ep*,II,14,15).
24 Martial, *Ep*,I,108,3. Martial benefited from a view of this site from his garret window.
25 Pliny,*NH*,XIV,3,11. Other references mention two myrtles in the shrine of Quirinus (ibid,XV,36,120), and a lotus tree in the precincts of Vulcan (ibid,XVI,82,236). Pliny (*NH*,XII,2,3) also reports that
    > 'different kinds of trees are kept perpetually dedicated to their own divinities, for instance, the winter-oak to Jove, the bay to Apollo, the olive to Minerva, the myrtle to Venus, the poplar to Hercules...'

    This could perhaps indicate that each species was planted in different areas within a sacred garden, or that plantations of a specific species associated with a particular divinity could be found in, or as a grove outside, their respective temple precinct.
26 Gordian III c.AD238-244 proposed to include these in a 500ft long portico garden. The project did not materialize, but the brief description is useful in comparison with those built earlier. He also intended to have a statue-lined central path leading up to a Basilica and Bath complex 'so that the pleasure-parks and porticoes might not be without some practical use'. (*SHA*, The Three Gordians, XXXII,6f).
27 Such as at Merida, in Spain (MacKendrick, 1969,138,fig,6.5). My attention was drawn to that of Italica, which is thought to resemble that of Pompey (Prof.J.Richarson,Edinburgh). The site has been surveyed (resistivity) but has not been published, and to date I have been unable to acquire details.
28 e.g. The *palaestra* of the Baths at Conimbriga were augmented with garden features (Alarcão & Etienne,1981,77). Another example, the Portico of the Petronii at Thuburbo Maius in North Africa, exemplifies how a *palaestra* also served as an urban park. Inside this portico I found reliefs of nymphs (standing, and pouring water from a conch shell) which are often found in garden contexts. The interior of the portico gave the impression that it could once have been a garden, rather than being paved.
29 Evidence for plantations (in the Greek Classical period) was discovered in an enclosure that surrounded the Temple of Hephaistos in Athens. Here cracked flower pots have been found in a series of ancient planting holes excavated into the rock. A formal planting scheme was adopted, for care had been taken to align the shrubs with columns of the temple. The garden has today been replanted with myrtle (Thompson, 1963,fig.11).
30 As at Vaison-la-Romaine, in France. The Portico of Pompeius, although only partially excavated, was furnished with *exedrae* and a large, deep fish pond in the middle of which was an island (Goudineau & Kisch, 1984,42).
31 MacKendrick,1981,475,fig.8.18.
32 Pliny,*NH*,XXXIV,19,84. Pliny (ibid,XXXVI,4, 27) also mentions a statue of Venus in the precincts of the Temple of Peace; and a Nile 'with 16 of the river-god's children playing around him' (ibid,XXXVI,11,58). The 'Nile' is probably the recumbent river god in the Vatican, Braccio Nuovo Museum. inv.no. 2300. Such large works of art were suitable for display in gardens of the public sector.
33 Of these, a fountain in the form of a bronze bull is noted as being in front of the temple.
34 Richardson (1992,87).
35 Ovid, *Ars Am*,I,72; Pliny,*NH*,XIV,3,11; Strabo,*Geog*,5, 3,8. Martial (*Ep*,III,20,8) mentions the *Schola Octaviae*, and is thought to allude to part of the Porticus Liviae or Octaviae.
36 Lloyd,1982,98.
37 Gow,1938,195.
38 Morel,1993,434,fig.4.
39 Cato,*De Agricultura*,LII,2.
40 Vitruvius,*De Arch*,V,9,9.
41 Pliny,*NH*,XII,2,3.
42 e.g. Platner & Ashby,Vol.1,1929,266.
43 Suetonius, *Caesar*,83; Cass.Dio.XLIV,35,3.
44 Tacitus, *Annals*,XIV,15.
45 Suetonius, *Augustus*,100.
46 Cass.Dio.LIV,29,4.
47 Martial (*Ep*,IX,40,1); Macrobius (*Sat*,VI,2,5). However grass here might apply to that found in large gardens in the countryside, for in both cases a stream is nearby. Further evidence for grassed areas is found in a number of frescoes depicting villa scenes, such as at the House of M. Fronto in Pompeii (see Pl.3).

CHAPTER FOUR: THE ARCHITECTURE AND LANDSCAPING OF GARDENS

The Roman garden was the province of a *topiarius*, a title given to a gardener of ornamental gardens. The name relates to *topia*, described in the Oxford Latin Dictionary as meaning contrived effects of natural scenery, therefore a *topiarius* could be seen to create landscapes. The Roman concept of a fine landscape was such that they believed it needed to be civilized and decorated by the addition of buildings to make any improvement. Roman gardens would have contained numerous architectural elements, and by looking at the manner in which they were disposed we can ascertain if they were sited in a random fashion, or as part of a particular architectural scheme within an ordered landscaped. In several locations in Campania[1] and at Fishbourne,[2] we find that plant beds and paths were arranged in a symmetrical manner, and paths invariably lead to a special focal point, often of an architectural nature. Therefore the art of a *topiarius*, together with that of the architect would ensure that the natural surroundings would be altered in certain ways (often structurally) to complement and enhance buildings; and architecture in turn would provide the frame behind the picture of nature perfected by man.

As seen in chapter two, the design or architecture of the house or villa was adapted to include gardens. In the developed form of 'Italic' peristyle house the preferred form was a garden surrounded by four covered porticoes. This type became so fashionable that when insufficient space was available architecture and art were manipulated to try to imitate this ideal. In such cases one or two porticoes would be placed as normal and the solid enclosing walls of the garden could be decorated with applied stucco or painted columns to complete the mock peristyle. Garden scenes were often painted in the intervening spaces to break the solidity of the wall, and, by giving the appearance of a garden beyond, the area would appear larger than in reality.

Examples of both peristyle and pseudo-peristyle may be seen at Pompeii. If we examine plans of housing (I have used here maps from *Researches in Campanian Archaeology*, hereafter RICA) we see that the majority of dwellings in the region of the town shown in fig.2 have a garden, small or large. Gardens are of varying size and shape, for house boundaries reflect the fortunes of the various inhabitants revealing that a number of owners, at some date, purchased an adjoining property to create further living quarters and at the same time enlarge the garden, or made space for a second garden. The map also highlights the efforts made by inhabitants of diminished dwellings to retain some form of garden or *viridarium*.

Areas of greenery were in the main separated from the rest of the house by an ambulatory covered by a portico, the columns of which, depending on cost and the availability of supply, were either of marble/stone or brick. In the case of the latter, bricks were manufactured in segments of a circle; then the column was covered with moulded stucco. Many subsequently resembled fluted marble columns, but on inspection I found that a large number had been recoated with a smooth pink finish on the lower portion only (a third) at some later date (as in Pl.5). In some houses holes or slots were visible in columns indicating that a low barrier fence had been inserted between columns,[3] or where they occur at a higher level a curtain pole may have been attached. There are literary references for the latter, for Pliny (*NH*,XIX,6,24) mentions that a red curtain was used to protect moss growing in a peristyle. A curtain could also shade a south-facing colonnade during summer or alternatively help stop draughts in wintertime.[4]

Numerous other abodes were furnished with a low masonry wall, a *pluteus*, in place of a fence. As many appeared to have been a later insertion, they perhaps relate to a change of fashion, or for comfort, such as a need to deflect low level draughts from penetrating adjoining rooms in wintertime. Low walls which are often about 40/50cms high may also have been used as a form of bench seat. A barrier of some kind could also save small children in the household from trampling plants grown in the garden, or knocking over statuary displayed there, and would stop them from falling into fish ponds. Pl.5 demonstrates the form and use of *plutei* in a small garden at Pompeii. Access into this type of garden was more restricted, and we usually find that a whole intercolumniation of the peristyle is reserved for the entrance. The opening more often than not corresponded with that of the main dining room.[5] In a number of houses the space between the pair of columns that framed the entrance to the garden had been widened, so that the outward view obtainable by diners in the *triclinium* would not be impeded.[6] The columns that framed this vision of greenery were sometimes of a monumental nature, such as square fluted columns,[7] which could have had the effect of making the entrance more distinguished.

Clarke (1991,160) discusses how lines of sight appear to be of prime importance.[8] The architecture of the house was in some cases manipulated to create a through vista to the garden, which was often provided with a focal point. When a dwelling was of an irregular plan, corridors and doorways were in many cases placed off centre, and windows were inserted.[9] Rooms that did not directly open onto the garden were often fitted with window openings instead of a door, so that the room could benefit from a view of the greenery, and receive more light and fresh air.

Beyond the peristyle, gardens were further delineated by stone or brick gutters, designed to collect rain water dripping off portico roofs. At the Villa at Wortley (Britain) the gutters had been cut out of massive blocks of stone. In some houses such as the House of Meleagro, Pompeii (fig.2b) the corners of gutters are provided with a concave quarter circle which, during storms, could act as a funnel to direct the precious water down a hole and into the cistern below (see Pl.6). Only one or two would lead to the cistern, others would make ideal locations for large plant pots as at this house. Draw shafts of cisterns are usually placed at the edge of the garden or in the peristyle; they are often in the form of a disc lid[10] placed onto a rebated stone slab (see Pl.5). A more decorative version was the *puteal* which resembles a chimney pot. A number of these can be seen in Pompeii, and again these are plain or carved.[11]

The above mentioned features apply to both small and large peristyle gardens, of town house and villa. For as can be seen in plans of villas, such as at Oplontis in fig.5, the buildings include a number of peristyle or pseudo-peristyle lightwells, usually adorned with greenery. The following features while appertaining to these gardens, also may be seen in the park-like grounds of large villas.

Paths

The Roman garden contained pathways, circulatory or leading to features or beds within the garden.[12] Pliny (*NH*,XIX,20,60) mentions how paths around bedding plots with raised borders were also used to water beds. These are seen on various archaeological plans at Pompeii, such as in the *hortus* or produce garden at the Villa Regina, Boscoreale (fig.4). In the decorative gardens of Campania the composition of paths is not usually revealed, and any accompanying photographs seem to indicate as Ciarallo (1993,110) notes in the recent excavation of the House of the Chaste Lovers, Pompeii (IX,xii,6/7), that the narrow paths were of beaten earth. Paths often become apparent because of a change in soil texture and colour, from hard packed earth (being the path) to the darker enriched soil within bedding areas. Alternatively where circumstances allow, the direction of paths can be traced by rows of holes (fig.32). The form of the cavities can indicate that either fencing or hedging was present. In some cases, as at the *Adonaea* in Rome, paths may be separated from bedding areas by brick edging.[13] Where evidence survives elsewhere materials used to make walkways were dependent on available local sources. Therefore we sometimes find paths consisting of loose or broken stones, sherds of pottery and tile, sand or gravel. In Britain (because of glaciation) gravel is more readily obtainable, and was therefore utilized at Frocester.[14] Pliny and Cicero[15] mention walks (*ambulationes*) in their gardens, and the *gestatio* or drive for litter-borne outings. Vitruvius (*De Arch*,V,9,7) furnishes details on how to construct sand covered *ambulationes* with drains, to ensure that the surface would remain dry.

Decorative fencing

Fig.32 also identifies a simple form of fencing used to surround bedding. Ciarallo (1993,112) had found evidence that two different types of reed had been inserted into the ground in such a manner that a diamond patterned trellis could be achieved. Frescoes may also be used to identify the types of garden fencing current during the Roman period, and the way in which they were used (see fig.8).[16] There are many examples similar to that of Fig.32, as at Oplontis (Pl.40). More decorative versions may be seen at the Auditorium of Maecenas in Rome, or the House of the Wedding of Alexander at Pompeii (figs.8e & f + d & g, and Pl.37) where apertures of different shapes are incorporated into the design. This type of fence, allowed some foliage to peep through, thereby softening any straight lines. At the House of the Fruit Orchard[17] we see a taller construction. This kind of trelliswork would be utilised to partition various parts of the garden. Other frescoes, mainly miniatures, show how trelliswork was used to make little enclosures, arbours and pavilions, access being through plain or arched doorways (fig.9). All of the above mentioned fences appear somewhat fragile, and realistically they would have served to delineate a given area rather than form an effective barrier.

Wooden fencing[18] was of a more robust but open nature, an example of the former is found in a fresco in Naples Mus.inv.no.9705, which has panels in a simple X design above a solid base (fig.8c). Simpler versions have been found on frescoes at Rudston and Wortley in Britain (fig.8a & b). Low decorative stone or marble walls are exemplified by those seen in the fresco from the House of Livia at Primaporta, Rome, (fig.8k and Pl.38) which shows both lattice and wall can exist side by side. The wall has alternating panels of 3 different designs. In many examples depicted in frescoes, walls and fences were furnished with recesses, either rectangular or semicircular (e.g. in fig.8h & i and Pl.38). These served to break the severity of otherwise straight lines, and the niches also became ideal locations in which one could place a fountain, statuary, seat, or specimen tree, for the important object would then be highlighted and protected by the architectural lines of walling. Hedging, as can be seen at Fishbourne (fig.33), was often planted along similar architectural patterns.

Decorative stone walling also appears to have been used to stop people from falling from a height, or into water. The fresco showing a grotto from Boscoreale (Pl.4) illustrates a wall along the cliff above. Similarly such barriers would have protected one from the drop at the edge of garden terraces. Several reliefs portray stone balustrades on balconies.[19] This type often includes a sculptured finial on the baluster, which resembles the herms found in decorative walling around the large water basin at Welschbillig (see Pl.7). Whilst protecting people, such walls allowed light through, and would not obstruct views, but enhance the Roman view of landscape.

Pergulae

Arbours or pergolas are depicted in a number of frescoes, e.g. Pl.4 from Boscoreale, and fig.9. A light framework of lattice or wood is often shown as a support for climbing plants, such as vines or ivy. These shady canopies made pleasant walkways in summer, and were an ideal location for seating where one could 'take the air', or as a place for alfresco dining during clement weather. The nilotic mosaic from Palestrina[20] incorporates a scene in which diners on luxuriously covered couches amuse themselves under a vine-covered tunnel of latticework. Archaeological evidence for *pergulae* has been found in many gardens in Campania, testifying to the popularity of these features. Generally the upper framework leaves little trace, but the position of wooden posts used to support it confirm their existence. At the House of Loreius Tiburtinus (fig.3) rows of post holes were found to have cavities of vine roots nearby,[21] and vine-covered walkways have recently been reinstated by copying designs seen in wallpaintings. The effectiveness of such temporary structures in adding to the beauty of a garden can be gauged in Pl.8.

Summer dining couches

Masonry *triclinia* or *biclinia*, frequently found to be shaded by a pergola, testify to the practice of alfresco dining. Examples have been discovered in several gardens in Campania and elsewhere, such as the House of the Thunderbolt at Ostia and at a house in the North-East quarter of Vienne in Gaul. Summer *triclinia* comprise three couches forming three sides of a rectangle. Each couch was inclined, the tallest part facing towards the centre, where a small circular or rectangular table was usually placed within reach of all reclining diners. A narrow shelf was often incorporated into the couch and would be ideal for resting drinking cups (see Pl.9). The masonry couch was made more comfortable with the provision of covers or mattresses. The less frequent *Biclinia*,[22] are usually placed so that diners face each other, a good example survives at the House of the Thunderbolt at Ostia (fig.11). The curved form *stibadium* or *sigma* is rarely found on excavation,[23] but is well documented in literary sources.[24] Pliny (*Ep*,V,6,37) also mentions the use of a water table (*mensa*) a pool of water placed in front of dining couches. Here trays of food could be floated and food kept cool by the refreshing water. This extravagant idea is found in reality in association with the *biclinium* at the House of Loreius Tiburtinus in Pompeii (fig.3 & Pl.21) and besides the *stibadium* in the so-called Serapaeum at Tivoli (fig.10b). Water *mensae* are often only a small part of interconnected water channels, fountains and pools seen in elaborate water gardens (water features will be fully discussed in the next chapter).

Garden seats and tables

Portable items of furniture, such as tables and couches, were placed in the garden on occasions for the comfort of visitors and members of the family as Statius reveals; he continues to describe the immediate action required to save these costly items from a sudden storm.[25] Some mosaics such as Pl.10 illustrate furniture. Here a wicker seat and couch appear in a garden setting.[26] Martial's garden couches (V,62) may have been a more permanent garden fixture, probably of wood[27] or wickerwork; nevertheless he recounts that they were broken.

A stone or marble seat, such as Pliny's (*Ep*,V,6,40), would be more durable for all year round outdoor use.[28] The appearance of marble garden seats or benches may resemble an elongated version of Greek thrones seen at theatres, or an adaptation of *scholae* found beside some tombs or in public porticoes, such as that in the triangular forum at Pompeii, which has a cantilevered bevelled edged seat with a solid arm rest in the form of a winged griffin (Pl.11). Solid rectangular benches appear to be relatively more frequent on archaeological sites.[29] In Sousse Museum inv.no.MXIX. Ro.110 a stone bench incorporating a back rest, with bands of mosaic, is placed fronting onto a similarly decorated semicircular water basin (inv.no.MXIX.Ro.109). The cement render and mosaic panels were similar, the seat was the same height, and the length matched that of the basin, so they were clearly linked, but there were no accompanying data. However this form of basin was common to that region, so I feel that they would both have originated from a Roman garden, and perhaps their juxtaposition in the museum courtyard reflects how they were found on excavation (see Pl.12). As can be seen the provision of wide ledges on this type of water basin (and in *plutei*) would also serve to invite people to sit on their edge and relax for a moment or two.

Tables found in gardens sometimes have their top missing, for while the support was often of marble, stone or masonry, the top on occasion was made of wood.[30] Tables associated with outdoor *triclinia* were generally fixtures and as such had masonry bases. Others were monopodia, a form having a central decorative carved marble leg,[31] or a type that is in many ways similar to the *cartibulum* usually seen in the *atrium*. These either have two wide solid supports, generally carved, or three slender carved legs which perhaps recall the more portable wooden or bronze varieties,[32] (see Pl.28).

Walling

The confines of *horti* were by necessity functional, to stop thieves, such as at Pompeii,I,xx,5, where the wall alongside the street was rendered insurmountable by inserting on the top jagged fragments of amphora (having the same effect as the modern use of broken glass). However, garden walls could be embellished by frescoes, by the addition of *aediculae* or *nymphaea* (see chapter five), or in larger properties by having decorative brickwork. Bands of different coloured stone and brick, some making a lozenge pattern, were employed in terrace walling at a Villa near Tivoli;[33] while at the Villa del Pastore at Stabiae a photograph[34] reveals how the wall, which was constructed in *opus reticulatum* of alternate bands of dark and light stone, has a crest of semicircular arcs in a wave like design. Another method employed was to place little turrets along the line of the wall, as at Sette Finestre.[35] It may have served as a form of decoration, but it could also have made the wall appear more solidly built, or alternatively because they resembled miniature dovecotes or towers of a city wall they may have been designed to serve as a false perspective to give the illusion of a garden larger than reality. As it is quite rare to find walling surviving to its original height, these examples are therefore extremely interesting for they were meant to be seen not covered. The expenditure incurred in creating decorative walling such as those cited, really implies that the area contained within must have been devoted to a pleasure garden rather than being used for husbandry or vegetables. A further method employed in gardens of large estates was in fact to achieve the reverse effect, that of concealing a boundary wall. At Tusculum Pliny (*Ep*,V.6,17) planted hedges of box to be trimmed in tiers. In the right circumstances, as in this case, they would have an effect of incorporating the adjacent landscape as part of the garden. Tiered hedges could be made to mimic a semi-natural looking belt of shrubbery which would render the boundary almost invisible at a distance.

Various landscaping methods were used to create different effects. One option was to construct a sunken garden.

Sunken gardens

In the peristyle gardens of the Domus Sollertiana at El-Jem, North Africa, the soil level was approx. 80cm below the ambulatory, which would help to conserve moisture for plants grown within the garden. A number of terracotta waste water outlets, still visible in the walls, would have allowed surplus water to be directed straight to the planted area. In such hot and potentially dry countries different techniques or methods were sometimes employed to maintain a garden under difficult conditions.[36]

At the House of Ancora Nera, Pompeii (fig.2g) the garden was reached by descending a flight of nine steep steps. The *hortus* was in effect one story below ground level (Pl.13). A cryptoporticus ran around all four sides of the garden, in place of a peristyle. On three sides some of the arched openings of the cryptoporticus were partly blocked up to provide niches for statuary yet still let light into the covered passageway behind. The fourth, north facing, side was furnished with three rusticated apses, the central containing an *aedicula*. At upper story level a colonnade, presumably with a low protective wall, gave the impression of a two-story dwelling. The height of this structure would certainly help to keep the garden cool and moist and be of especial value in high summer. To the north three dining rooms were placed so that diners could benefit from a view of the verdant scene below, with the *aedicula* at its focal point.

Such deep sunken gardens are also seen in palatial abodes, such as in the so-called 'Stadium' of the Domus Augustana in Rome. At upper storey level a large *exedra* was constructed opening onto the enclosed garden below, so that the Emperor and his friends or guests could benefit from a change of air, and scent emanating from the plants nearby. This arrangement of large rooms placed to overlook gardens below is again found in the 'stadium' of Hadrian's Villa at Tivoli, although in this case the garden was not sunken, but was at a naturally lower level. The architect here made use of the irregular terrain and built on the cliff above; he also cut into the rock to make two large rooms below.

Terraced gardens

The Romans usually preferred to build on level ground, and therefore terraces were constructed to provide a flat platform to work on.[37] Rather than have a completely solid foundation the substructures often comprised cryptoportici. These served to provide extra rooms for storage, or alternatively could furnish cool underground rooms for use in the hot summer months. Ashby (op.cit.) when surveying the countryside around Tivoli located many surviving terrace platforms of villas of Roman date. Several villas were found to possess more than one terrace. Gardens would surround buildings, and lower terraces might be devoted solely to gardens and associated pavilions. The terrace above would also give the necessary height to provide sufficient pressure to supply water features below. Terraced gardens could create an effect to recall the once-famed Hanging Gardens of Babylon.

At the Villa of the Mysteries, near Pompeii. we can see a terrace garden of modest proportions (Pl.14). The substructure was provided with a cryptoporticus, and we can observe that there is still a sufficient depth of soil above in which to grow bushes. At the House of the Stags, Herculaneum, the gardens were extended by building up to the town wall. In this way a second garden became a sunny plant-filled terrace from which one could enjoy a marvellous view out to sea. The inhabitants could also now benefit from any cooling sea breeze in summer.

In Rome vast landscaping projects were carried out by several aristocratic members of society,[38] such as Maecenas, who transformed an area on the Esquiline that was once the unsavoury burial ground outside of the Servian Wall.[39] Sallust incorporated into his gardens the valley between the Quirinal and Pincio. This contained a spring and brook which were enhanced by terracing.[40] These gardens later became the favourite abode of a number of Emperors. The *Horti Luculliani* were constructed in the area of the Pincian Hill, which became known as the *Collis Hortulorum*. They were the first large gardens made in Rome and with those of Sallust were among the most renowned. Fortunately sufficient traces of some of the substructures built to retain soil in terraces remained here up to the 16th century for their inclusion into drawings and maps.[41] These are thought to have been more than 13m high. It is also thought that the 'Muro Torto' was a continuation of the terrace works carried out at this time. These walls were so massive and strongly built that they were included into the Aurelian Wall. Modern excavation in the vicinity[42] has uncovered a long gently curving *ambulatio* of approx. 180m, and in some ways match plans drawn by Ligorio[43] c.AD1553. These show a large semicircular *exedra* that was furnished with niches and flanked by a series of ample sized rooms. They were built on the upper terrace and were linked to lower levels by monumental staircases. The whole is thought to have been inspired by the Temple of Fortuna at Praeneste, or a theatrical scenae frons.[44] With its hillside setting, overlooking the once green and wooded areas of the Campus Martius and the Mausoleum of Augustus, it would have been magnificent.[45]

Literary sources often like to emphasise Roman ingenuity, and the talents of landscape architects. Seneca (*Ep*,LV,6) describes works accomplished at Vattia's Villa, and elsewhere (VII,10,5) he comments on the fact that people were building their lordly structures on bays, lakes[46] and on mountain peaks to obtain a fine prospect. Statius reveals the transformations accomplished by Pollius Felix at Surrentum, and how the natural scene:

> 'was wild and unlovely, now it is a pleasure to go.....Here, where you now see level ground, was a hill...where now tall groves appear, there was once not even soil: its owner has tamed the place...each window commands a different landscape'.   (*Silv*,II,2,33ff).

A fine outlook was most desirable, and the preferred view needed to be of Nature tamed, where architecture enhanced the scene. This is seen in surviving frescoes of landscapes, which according to Pliny (*NH*,XXXV, 37,116/7) were made famous by Studius at the time of Augustus. His subjects included country houses with porticoes and gardens, groves, woods, hills, fishponds, *euripi*, rivers, and coastal scenes. These frescoes emphasise the buildings, the works of man, and the role of gardens is to provide a green and pleasant background. Garden elements are in the main used to unite and highlight various architectural groups.

Maritime Villas

The most famous in this group was the Villa of Lucullus on the Bay of Naples. Plutarch (*Luc*,XXXIX,2f) mentions that here Lucullus had 'built dwellings in the sea' and cut channels through the rock, perhaps to create an island residence that may have looked like a floating palace. Texts indicate that Villas beside the sea were popular as a respite from the summer heat of Rome, when a cooling sea-breeze would be most welcome. Even the practical Columella (*RR*, 1,5,5) advises that 'a villa is always properly placed when it overlooks the sea'. Plants in the gardens, however, could suffer from wind damage and salt spray. Pliny (*Ep*,II,17,14) noted this in the open areas at Laurentum and therefore placed his kitchen garden behind the protection of a cryptoporticus.[47]

Lafon (1981,347,fig.4) identifies and locates around sixty villas lining the Tyrrhenian littoral during 50BC-AD50, which appears to be the greatest period of their construction. Apart from Pliny's description (ibid.) the form of their gardens may be difficult to ascertain. However at Val Catena[48] on the Adriatic island of Brioni Grande, archaeologists have shown the extent of buildings and garden around the bay and their relationship in the general landscaping of the whole bay. However details within these gardens are elusive, and perhaps can be more easily visualised through maps locating the partially eroded remains discovered at the sumptuous maritime villas of North Africa, such as at Silin, Zliten, and Tagiura.[49] These appear to contain one or more large enclosed gardens or terraces with water features, such as *euripi* at Silin and Zliten, also a demi-lune basin in the latter, and a shaped basin at Tagiura. Villas built on the banks of large rivers and lakes would share many characteristics of maritime villas, in that they would open onto the water's edge.[50]

In Britain the closest we have to a maritime villa is the Palace at Fishbourne. Here the south wing, which is today under modern housing, may have opened onto a landscaped area (with pond) down to the sea and harbour.[51]

Gardens of Large and Palatial Villas

The Golden House of Nero, is perhaps the most infamous of this group, for as Suetonius (*Nero*,31) relates, Nero built without regard to others a grandiose palace set in a vast estate in the middle of the city. His landscaping projects included an artificial lake surrounded by pastures and woodland; in fact he wished to create an atmosphere of *rus in urbe*. Of the buildings that have survived[52] we can see that rooms faced into garden courts or out to a wide terrace from which one would have a view of the lake below. The imposition of so huge an estate which blocked previous arterial routes into the city was too abhorrent for the people, and therefore it was broken up after his downfall, with much of the area reused for buildings which would be used by the public. Such vast areas of land occupied by one man were seen as wrong in the heart of the city, but did not cause so much resentment in outlying districts or in the countryside.

Most of the literary documentation on Roman gardens concerns the large or palatial. As most poets and historians lived within the circles of the wealthy, their work would naturally be of a biased nature, for the average is not so remarkable. Likewise we see aspects of an affluent society represented in art, for villas in landscape frescos are also normally large. Many owners appear to have decorated their homes and gardens to resemble somehow those of the aristocracy. Therefore many features in small gardens reflect those of their larger counterparts. In large gardens, however, there was more space; we still find some enclosed courts or peristyle gardens within the building complex, but beyond there may have been acres devoted to landscaped gardens. Large areas could be given names, such as the 'Hippodrome' garden described by Pliny (*Ep*.V,6,32f). Grounds could be dotted with special features such as a tree house. Velletri's was large enough to hold banquets in its canopy. It was particularly favoured by Caligula who called it his 'nest'.[53] One might find garden pavilions, such as a Belvedere or prospect tower, such as described by Luxorius.[54] From Pliny's description of his large garden at his Tuscan villa we learn how special outdoor dining areas could be accompanied by a small *cubiculum* or *diaeta* where people could take a siesta after meals. Pliny believed that this building:

> 'contributes as much beauty to the scene as it gains from its position. It is built of shining white marble, extended by folding doors which open straight out into greenery; its upper and lower windows all look out into more greenery above and below....There you can lie and imagine you are in a wood, but without the risk of rain.' (*Ep*,V,6,38).

This description gives a good indication that garden pavilions would be functional as well as aesthetic. On Varro's estate at Casinum[55] there were bridges crossing a stream, alongside of which a path led up to a *museum* (nymphaeum building), and down to an *ornithone* (aviary)[56] but here the ingenious structure contained nets in the colonnade for 'all manner of birds' and in the centre ponds for fish and wildfowl; a summer dining area was also included.[57] Varro remarks that the aviary of Lucullus was not so hygienic, for there the diners ate amongst the birds, while in his own the birds were confined to the areas in the colonnade and part of a tholos where perches were placed in tiers to mimic a theatre auditorium.[58] Varro and Cicero mention islands in rivers on their properties. The latter[59] talks of his fondness for this spot and how, whenever possible, he would come to sit there and unwind.

At the Villa of Hadrian at Tivoli we are fortunate in that we can see how the numerous buildings are disposed in relation to garden areas (see fig.10). In this figure colonnades, where known, are indicated to show where they open onto garden areas (or open paved courts in the Greek style e.g. the 'Doric peristyle'). The *Historiae Augustae*

(*Had*.XXVI,5) informs us that Hadrian named parts of his villa after places of especial interest, such as Lyceum, Academia, Prytaneum, Canopus, Poikile, Tempe and Hades, with the exception of the Prytaneum[60] these areas are all associated with garden features. Much in this domain is of a monumental nature and is therefore rather *sui generis*, but relatively more modest versions would have existed elsewhere.

The name Hades was given to an underground grotto with a statue of Cerberus located east of the Academy. Grottoes feature in a number of large estates (these will be discussed in ch.5). At Tivoli the terrain was used in imaginative ways; to the north of the Piazza D'Oro a pleasant valley was landscaped to recall the idyllic setting at Tempe. Another valley contains, and serves to isolate from other buildings, the Canopus area where a large water basin and dining facilities recreated that infamous district on the Nile delta. The so-called Greek and Latin Libraries that may perhaps have been associated with the Lyceum had an irregularly shaped garden furnished with a thin shallow *euripus* water basin that had octagonal terminals.[61] The exterior walls of this garden were provided with numerous niches for statuary facing onto what may have been a processional entrance.

The north wall of the Poikile was named after the famous *stoa* at Athens, and overlooks a large garden that has been given the same name. The covered portico was used to exercise oneself in walking *in circuitum*. This type of portico is usually provided with rounded turning points at one or both ends. Inscriptions, found here and in association with similar features elsewhere,[62] state their distance, often showing that a certain number of turns would make a *stade*. These *ambulationes* are often placed to ensure that one side faces the sun, to provide shelter but warmth on winter walks, while the reverse face would have sufficient shade during hot summer months.

Natural phenomena such as waterfalls were, where possible, also incorporated into the landscaping of an estate. We learn of the shrine of the nymphs that was placed close to the much loved Bandusian falls of Horace.[63] Waterfalls were sometimes enhanced by man but nevertheless they remain beautiful in their setting. Several estates included a small shrine or temple, often placed to provide a particular focal point of attention, such as in the grounds of both the gardens of Lucullus and Sallust at Rome,[64] where they had been placed on high ground. Statius (*Silv*,III,1) describes a temple dedicated to Hercules at the villa of Pollius Felix. This appears to have been on a cliff terrace overlooking the sea. Pavilions and shrines would have been included in the landscaping of large domains, but unless there is an inscription, literary reference, or clear signs for its purpose, identification remains elusive.

All of these features should not be seen in isolation, for on many estates nymphaea in the form of caves or grottoes became part of the landscape. In both town and country properties nymphaea, water basins, or fishponds were also constructed in gardens and sometimes in light-well courts. These required the excavation of a considerable amount of earth/rock, the construction of the basin itself and the addition of an hydraulic system. They therefore need to be seen as part of the overall landscaping in the grounds of villas and houses. As these structures are so important to the spirit of a Roman garden I will discuss them in depth in the next chapter.

NOTES TO CHAPTER FOUR

1. Jashemski,1993, appendix I.
2. Cunliffe,1968,pl.XIV.
3. e.g. at the House of the Lovers, Pompeii,I,x,10-11 (Jashemski,1993, 50, fig.59). Jashemski (1979,50) states positions and measurements of fence slots in columns.
4. At Oplontis in garden C, fig.5, a south facing colonnade (highlighted) was partially blocked by inserting doorways. Some had slit windows above, this may also have been a method used to shade a portico (see Pl.6). Presumably such devices were not needed in the other porticoes of this garden, for surviving root cavities show that trees would have given sufficient shade there.
5. As in the House of Adonis, Pompeii (fig.2c).
6. An example is the House of Ancora Nera, Pompeii, (fig.2g).
7. This is seen in The House of the Trifolium, Dougga, North Africa, although, as in this case, water features were often placed in this important position, close to and facing the main dining room.
8. Cf. Wallace-Hadrill,1988,82.
9. e.g. The House of the Bear, Pompeii, which is a very small house. An example in a larger property is the House of the Citharist, Pompeii,I,iv,5/25 (Jashemski, 1993,29). Here the gardens are not in a direct line of sight from the entrance of the house, but with the *fauces* angled and the *tablinum* omitted, a partial view could be achieved, even if this was little more than the columns of the peristyle beyond. It would be, however, enough to show that the owners possessed a garden.
10. They were sometimes carved, for example, a rose pattern at the House of Cantaber, Conimbriga.
11. Cicero (*Ad Att*,I,10) requested his friend Atticus to purchase for him relief carved *puteal,* amongst other works of art.
12. At Voerendaal, in the Netherlands, a Jupiter column was placed in the middle of the main pathway leading to the villa, with the path widening around it (Willems & Kooistra,1987,139,Afb.2).
13. Morel,1993,431.
14. Gracie & Price, 1979,13.
15. *Ep*.V,6,17 & 34; *De Leg*,III,1; respectively.
16. With the exception of D & K, these examples were drawn from an analysis of notes and/or photographs made during my various study tours. Details for D were taken from Jashemski,1993,fig.421. K was based on different versions of the same scene shown in Pl.38 which illustrates the complete irregular repeating pattern of the decorative panels in the marble wall. Fig.8k shows the section to the right of the centrally located specimen tree.
17. Pompeii,I,ix,5 (Jashemski,1993,fig.366).
18. Metal railings were also used, an example in bronze was found in Lake Nemi (Moretti,1940,fig.48) (see fig.26a).
19. e.g. on the obelisk base in the Hippodrome at Istanbul.

20 Whitehouse,1976,Pl.19a & b.
21 Jashemski,1993,82/3.
22 Fifty one *triclinia* as opposed to six *biclinia* have so far been discovered at Pompeii (Jashemski,1993,10).
23 Jashemski (1993,211) states that only one has been found, at Pompeii,VIII,iii,15.
24 Martial (XIV,87); Pliny (*Ep*,V,6,36); Methodius (*Symp*) in Rossiter, 1989,105,n.33.
25 *Silvae*,III,86/8. In this case couches only are mentioned.
26 Another example, also from Africa, is shown in Gothein, 1966,Vol.1, fig.93.
27 Their existence in gardens is confirmed by traces found in the lower garden of the House of Loreius Tiburtinus, Pompeii (Jashemski, 1993,83).
28 Our literary evidence for outdoor seating is strengthened by Cicero (*Acad.Luc*,II,3,9) who also informs us that the walks in the *xystus* at the Villa of Hortensius were provided with a seat (*sedem*).
29 e. g. A masonry bench placed against the interior of the garden wall, at the *Thermopolium* on Via di Diana, Ostia.
30 Pliny mentions circular table tops made out of citrus wood, which was much prized (*NH*,XIII,29,95).
31 e.g. at the House of M. Holconius Rufus, Pompeii,VIII,iv,4, (Jashemski,1993,212).
32 A table with *trapezophori*, two wide supporting legs, was placed beside the draw shaft of the cistern in the garden to the rear of the *atrium* at the House of the Dioscuri, Pompeii (fig.2d). Examples of the three legged form may be found at the House of the Stags, Herculaneum, and at the House of the Vettii, Pompeii.
33 Ashby,1906,190,fig.33.
34 Jashemski,1993,fig.356.
35 Carandini & Tatton-Brown, 1980, 12,fig.6.
36 At Bulla Regia, which is in a very hot dry inland region of Tunisia, houses were provided with an underground suite of rooms for use during the summer. These were arranged around a central light well and were invariably furnished with garden elements such as decorative water basins (Thébert,1993,223).
37 Ovid (*Ex Ponto*,I,8) remembers seeing the porticoes of Rome 'with its levelled ground'.
38 Lucullus being the first, circa 60BC (Plutarch, *Luc*,39,2).
39 Horace,*Sat*,I,VIII,10-15.
40 Richardson,1992,203.
41 e. g. those of Bufalini circa AD1551; and Ligorio, c.AD1553 (Broise & Jolivet,1995,191).
42 By the French School at Rome.
43 Grimal (1969,fig.32). Richardson (1992,195) casts doubt on these features, but recent work has now partially confirmed their existence. Some authors (Richardson, *op cit*, and Platner & Ashby,1929,264) attribute the hemisphere to the *Horti Aciliorum*, but Grimal, Broise & Jolivet, and I, believe they are part of the *Horti Luculliani*. New evidence suggests that the works mentioned are attributable to Valerius Asiaticus who took over the gardens after Lucullus. It was only in the 2nd century when they became the property of the Acilii Glabriones.
44 Grimal,1969,269.
45 One of the dangers in possessing a beautiful garden is that it could invite the envy of the Imperial family. Tacitus (*Ann*,XI,1) reveals how Messalina so coveted the *Horti Luculliani* that its owner Asiaticus was finally forced to commit suicide in order that she could take possession. Other gardens were appropriated through the terms of a will, such as the *Hortis Lamiani*, *Maecenatiani*, and *Sallustiani*.
46 Two different types of lakeside properties are briefly mentioned by Pliny, who gives them names (*Ep*.IX,7): 'Tragedy, because it seems to be raised on actor's boots' - this evidently stood on a terraced site above the lake - while Comedy 'wears low shoes' and was made to curve with the shoreline. The supposed Villa of Catullus, with a large enclosed garden, has come to light at Sirmione on Lake Garda (Siracusano,1969). It was built on a peninsula and was therefore almost surrounded by the sight and sound of water.
47 Van Buren (1948,fig.4) used Pliny's descriptions to reconstruct a plan of this villa, and a model exists in the Ashmoleum Museum. A different version can be found in Ricotti,1987,figs.35-37, which links the buildings and gardens in a more satisfactory fashion. Castell in 1728 (p.17) set the villa into an extensive, fanciful, landscaped setting.
48 Boethius & Ward-Perkins,1970,fig.125.
49 Silin (Rebuffat,1974); Zliten & Tagiura (Rebuffat,1969).
50 e.g. Wittlich, overlooking the Rhine, Germany (Swoboda,1969, Abb.32).
51 Cunliffe,1971,143 & fig.31.
52 Hemsoll,1990,12.
53 Pliny,*NH*,XII,5,3.
54 *Anth Lat*,18. Suetonius (*Nero*,38) mentions one owned by Maecenas, from which Nero viewed the burning of Rome.
55 *RR*,III,5,9/10.
56 Cicero (*Ad Fratrem*,III,9,7) mentions the inclusion of an aviary at his brother's Manilian estate.
57 *RR*,III,4,3.
58 Van Buren & Kennedy (1919,61,fig.1) reconstruct the appearance of this building.
59 *De Leg*.II,3,6.
60 I feel that this appellation could have been given to the Piazza D' Oro area, for the courtyard and associated aristocratic dining facilities could have resembled Greek buildings designed to cater for official hospitality.
61 Before visiting his friend Varro, Cicero (*Ad Fam*,IX,4) asks; '*si hortum in bibliotheca habes, deerit nihil*', this would perhaps imply an enclosed garden within or attached to such a building, where texts could be read in good light outdoors. Elsewhere (*Ad Att*.I,8; I,9) he mentions areas at his various properties that were named after the Lyceum and Academy at Athens. One can imagine that these would also be provided with garden courts. Plutarch (*Luc*,XLII,1) implies there was a cloister garden attached to the library of Lucullus, who opened these for public use.
62 Grimal,1969,255. A similar portico was found at Tarracina (Lugli,1926,142,no.90).
63 *Odes*.III,13.
64 Broise & Jolivet,1955,fig.6, & Lanciani,1897,416, respectively.

CHAPTER FIVE: WATER FEATURES

An adequate supply of water has always been one of the most important features for the well-being of a garden, especially in areas with a hot climate where growing plants need a regular supply of water.[1] Literary sources[2] mention that the *hortus* of a villa (here referring to a vegetable or orchard type of garden) should be sited conveniently close to a spring, or a source of running water, so that water could be channelled from the stream to irrigate the garden. If the property was too far away from such a source, then the gardener would have to rely on water drawn from a well. However, if the garden lacked both of these, then the only recourse would be to install a cistern to collect precious rain water. Palladius (I,61) also explains how to make a cistern, and adds that you could stock fish there.

Varro (*RR*,III,3,5) informs us that at first there were natural ponds which were utilized to supply a stock of water birds for the table as well as fish.[3] Then at around 91-88BC we learn from Pliny (*NH*,IX,80,170) that the Elder Licinius Murena invented the use of artificial fishponds, *piscinas*. What type is not revealed, but that they proved popular is evidenced by comments made by Pliny and Varro that Murena's example was soon followed by Philippius, Hortensius and Lucullus.[4] Murena, was so named for his love of a particular type of fish, the *murena* (believed to be a moray eel).[5] As this is a marine creature the implication is for a salt-water pond. Varro (*RR*,III,17,2) mentions the existence, at that time, of two sorts of fishpond:

1. The freshwater (*dulcium*), which were supplied by Nymphs (meaning spring water).
2. The salt water (*salsarum*), which he implies, were owned by the nobility.

In this experimental stage, we learn from Varro (Ibid,III,17,9) that some of the fishponds belonging to Marcus Lucullus became stagnant, but his brother Lucius, who had a garden in the grounds of a maritime villa near Naples, lavished huge sums on excavating channels or tunnels, to connect his water basin to the sea, so that the tides or currents could freshen the water of his fishpond. Cassiodorus (*Variae*,12,15) although of a later date, describes a rock-cut pool he had excavated at Squillace on the Adriatic coast of Calabria, where the fish were fed by hand. He adds that the sight of the fish 'both refreshes the spirit with pleasure, and charms the eye with wonder'. Columella (*RR*,VIII,17) provides us with information on how tidal fishponds were constructed, and from this we see that the Romans appreciated the importance of a renewal of water in fishponds.

For inland water basins, the precautions made were to have a channel leading into the basin, to feed the basin with water, and then to have an outlet, often at the other end of the basin. Another provision was to install a fountain, so that the water jet(s) could aerate the pond and at the same time introduce a change of water. A fountain while serving a useful function would also decorate the area (many were works of art, and will be discussed in chapter six). To provide enough pressure for a fountain, there needed to be a supply of water at a higher level. Pliny (*NH*,XXXI,57) attests that 'water rises as high as its source'. Therefore, if the property was on a hillside, water could be tapped from a spring nearby, and stored in a tank or cistern on a terrace above.[6] Another method was to use a *tympanum* machine to raise water. Vitruvius (*De Arch*,X,7,3) shows that 'in this way water is supplied from below for fountains by pressure'.

The system of water storage in gardens at Pompeii, discussed by Richardson (1988,51-54), is I feel relevant to a number of other localities in the Mediterranean area. In the early period the inhabitants relied on water from wells, and rain water collected off roofs into cisterns. With the introduction of the aqueduct, in the Augustan period, Richardson (Ibid,63) believes that these cisterns were not abandoned for then the flow of water was mainly directed to baths and street fountains, and in gardens was limited to small jets or trickles of water. Once a basin was filled only a minimal amount of extra water would be needed to top it up, and when features are placed at different levels water would be reused, if by gravity it was allowed to flow to lower basins (as at the House of Loreius Tiburtinus). I feel that Richardson's views are correct; water was no doubt expensive and also in many areas limited; there still needed to be sufficient water in the catchment area to supply continually an aqueduct. Earthquakes or accidents could also disrupt services thus necessitating the continued use of a cistern. It was also noticeable that in Pompeii many water features are placed so that the overflow could run into a drainage channel and from there to a cistern; again a conservation measure was employed to save their precious supply.[7]

Where properties were sited in proximity to major rivers a constant source of water could be relied upon. In such places it might appear that there was a conspicuous and extravagant use of water[8] but if the supply was assured there would be no restrictions excepting the expense of the amount of water used if drawn from a state controlled aqueduct as opposed to a privately constructed supply.

With the introduction of aqueducts there was almost a revolution in the art of gardening.[9] Water could be channelled from distribution points, and directed to holding tanks or piped straight to the water features in gardens.[10] Lead piping was seen at a number of houses in Pompeii.[11] At the House of the Vettii, they were placed in the drainage channel of the garden, in the open, and a stop tap (which was turned by a key) is visible in the south west quadrant of the garden (see Pl.15). The tap could be used to regulate the flow of water to water features, and individual fountains could be switched off or on when required. Franchi (1992,163) provides some information on stop taps found in Pompeii,[12] and explains that they were usually made of a bronze alloy '73.70% copper, 18.53% lead, 7.72% tin', which would give greater strength than lead for a part in regular use.

Features of water basins

The most important material used in their construction was concrete, which helped to make them water-tight. Espérandieu (see fig.12) shows a cross section of a large basin, showing how wooden piles were used to give extra support to the structure above. This was perhaps a necessary precaution when constructing very large pools which would contain a considerable weight of water. Stone slabs lined this pool. Elsewhere (such as at Eccles & Bancroft) stone or tile was used in the first instance, then coats of cement were applied on the inner surfaces making the basin water tight. Detsicas (1974,77) informs us that the thickness of the *opus signinum* at Eccles was 2.5cm on the walls, and 7.5cm on the floor of the basin. He provides details of the various stages of construction in the fishpond, and the procedure used here may have been observed at other Roman sites.[13]

The inner surface of basins were sometimes coated with a painted waterproof plaster. In Pompeii many basins still have their blue interior coating in situ,[14] some have traces of fish and aquatic creatures swimming against a blue background.[15] The blue painted interior would help to make the water look healthy, and would provide a good reflection. The benefit of a lining painted with fish, would be that any rippling of the water would give the impression that fish were swimming inside. Pools were presumably cleaned out periodically, or the decor would have become too obscured by deposits of silt/slime.[16]

An alternative to painted plaster is seen at La Melena, in Spain, where the inner walls of the basin were covered by mosaic depicting fish.[17] In North Africa shallow basins are often completely covered by decorative mosaics, often depicting marine creatures or subjects related to the sea[18] (see Pl.16). They would serve as a catchment basin for a fountain, and in fact one example bears the logo 'Nympharum Domus' which would confirm their use.[19] Splashing water would have kept the colours of mosaic tesserae bright, but this type of basin was largely decorative for these pools have a minimal depth of water making it unsuitable to stock fish.

Shallow water basins may have originated from the *impluvia* seen in *atria*, for it has been noted that the *atrium* in later times came to be regarded as another area to adorn with plants, and or garden elements. The use of such shallow constructions would be to provide a water collection point (from the fountain rather than the draw shaft of a cistern) and to provide a focal point in a courtyard/garden. Also in very hot weather the cooling and refreshing effect of the water would have been particularly beneficial, for the moisture would help to humidify the otherwise dry atmosphere.

Basins with an adequate depth, of roughly 0.50m or more are believed to have been sufficient to contain fish.[20] Columella (*RR*,8,17,2) mentions breeding holes for fish and Pliny (*NH*,IX,78,167) refers to the longevity of fish in Tiberius's Campanian villas, which indicates that probably fish would have been reared there. Such holes have been found in excavations at Sperlonga and elsewhere; these are often referred to as fish refuges and are usually found in the walls of the basin. In the House of Julia Felix at Pompeii, and at Bancroft in Britain, there are square holes lined with stone.[21] In several other instances amphorae are inserted into the walls of the basin so that the neck of the vessel only remains visible.[22] It can then be used as a breeding chamber for fish, or as a refuge from the sun. Environmental evidence is provided at Ivy Chimney, (Essex), where 'certain freshwater fish' remains were found.[23] However, it must be mentioned that not all ponds were used to stock fish.

There are many different types of water basins, yet to date no attempt has been made to classify individual forms. With the exception of a few recent excavation reports,[24] basins when indicated are rarely referred to in the text. Therefore, of necessity, supporting data has been gleaned elsewhere. A summary has proved very difficult, for not all garden areas have been excavated fully, and in many instances dating evidence is imprecise. We are fortunate if a whole century is indicated, or the period of an Emperor's reign. In a number of cases a date for a particular house has been given on an assessment of the style of mosaics present, but this does not necessarily mean that garden features were added or restored at that same time. Water basins have such a variety of forms that I have tried to ascertain a pattern or trend, with the aim of being able to date their types. I had thought that maybe one could see if a particular form became fashionable at a given period. However, one needs to bear in mind that styles perhaps would have been slower to reach the provinces. It also appears that a number of forms were popular throughout the period of study. Evidence for a chronology is slight for there are few cases where excavation has been thoroughly undertaken. But in this area the most unusual are the more informative, and on occasion it has been found that a simple basin was later replaced by a more decorative version.

Given these limitations, I have attempted to provide a system of classification for water features found in gardens, and some indication of their distribution within the Empire.

A suggested typology, following archaeological evidence

A   Simple forms (square, rectangular & circular).

B   Rectangular basin with a semi-circular recess.

C   Rectangular basin, with more than one semi-circular recess, e. g. at either extremity.

D   A basin where the inner outline is shaped, either with semi-circular or rectilinear recesses or both, in a rectangular or subrectangular outer framework.

E   Demi-lune basins.

F   A basin containing water-tight caissons.

G   Complex designs.

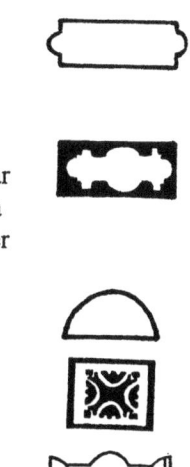

Type A

This form is the most common,[25] and perhaps through the simplicity of its design this type was constructed throughout the Roman periods. It can be found in all the provinces of the Empire. I include in this class elongated forms known as *Euripi* (see below)

Type B

Evidence shows that this form dates at least from the 1st century BC to the 2nd Century AD. If we look at Pompeii, for which we have a useful *terminus ante quem* (of AD79) we may note that at that date there is a predominance of simple basin forms. In the plans shown in Jashemski (1993) many plain rectangular or square types are shown, but I could find only eight in the form of a rectangular basin with recess[26] (type B) indicating that perhaps these were a late feature in Pompeii. Evidence from Vienne, the House of the Ocean Gods, has shown that a simple rectangular basin (Form A) was altered circa 6OAD into one with a semi-circular recess[27] (Form B). At Ostia, in the Schola of Trajan, the type B basin which was dated to the 1st Century BC, was in turn replaced in the Trajanic period by one of type D.[28] (see Pl.17). A particular feature of this type is that a number were placed parallel with a portico, as was the case in the example from Ostia

Type C

This type is shown on maps (from records made by tunnelling) to have existed at the House of the Papyri in Herculaneum, thereby providing an early date of pre AD79.[29] One has been found in Britain, in the partly excavated Governor's Palace at London, however alterations to the basin complicate its dating, which is given as from AD80 to early 2nd century AD.[30] A more typical and complete example is seen in the portico garden of the Library of Hadrian, Athens, which dates to c.AD132.[31] (see fig.14). The form appears to have remained popular at least up to the 4th century AD e.g. at La Malena in Spain.[32]

Type D

The earliest to date is that seen in the House of Meleagro in Pompeii (Pl.18). In Rome this form is associated with the Domitianic phase of the area known as the Adonaea, it also appears in a pair of light wells in the Domus Augustana. An unusually complicated design of brick edging (originally faced with marble) is seen in the large basins found at the Domus Flavia on the Palatine, Rome, which may also be attributable to the work of the architect Rabirius c.AD92[33] (see fig.15). Form D is also seen in later periods, for instance at The House of the Two Olive Presses in North Africa which is dated to after AD238.[34]

Type E

The largest proportion of these basins is found in North Africa,[35] which may reflect chance survival, or that this form originated in this region. They are usually placed close to the peristyle, perhaps to give extra shade to avoid too much evaporation of water in such a hot climate. The basins are often aligned so that they may be seen from important rooms, such as *triclinia* (see fig.16). There appear to be two forms; one completely surrounded with a wide ledge (Pl.12), while the other has marble or stone slabs slotted into position on the straight side of the basin (as in Pl.16). These blocks are often missing presumably lifted by stone robbers in antiquity. However I have found that in a number of cases grooves on the ground and remaining column bases nearby indicate their original position.[36] The type appears to be a later form, for some evidence suggests they were inserted into 3rd/4th century AD houses and villas. Type E is also found in Spain, Germany and Britain.[37]

Type F

This form is typified by those at Conimbriga, here a number of houses contain basins of this sort each with differently shaped caissons. The majority are dated to the 3rd century AD).[38] The water-tight caissons here were filled with garden soil and water surrounded them on all sides making them appear as islands of greenery (Pl.19). The most elaborate is that in the House of the Water Jets[39] (fig.17). In this garden around 400 lead water jets are positioned along the edges of the basin and along the rim of each caisson. Each water outlet was angled to direct, in an arch, a thin jet of water into the basin below. The effect of so many fountains would have been striking, but with such thin jets only a minimal amount of water would have been used (the jets have been restored and the effect can be observed in situ today). Type F is also found in the Domus Augustana at Rome[40] (shown on p.21), in the Leonidaion at Olympia,[41] and at the House of the Cascades, Utica in North Africa.[42] The last two named have been dated to the 2nd century AD, and all available evidence would imply that a basin with features such as caissons, may have been a fashion dating from the time of Hadrian.

Type G

This form includes basins that are multi-lobed, variform, or linked in some manner, such as at Piazza Armerina in Sicily (shown on p.21), or in the Casa de la Exedra at Italica in Spain[43] (fig.18). These flamboyant designs appear to be of a late date, ranging from the 3rd to the 4th century AD, and may have been a development from type F. Multi-lobed basins are seen in a number of late dwellings in North Africa and in the East.[44]

This typology was devised to classify the distinguishing traits between various forms of basins/pools. However the Romans also used water in other garden features, such as in fountains and nymphaea. A large proportion of the gardens at Pompeii had been furnished with a pool or a fountain/nymphaeum, which reveals that they were perhaps a characteristic element to be found in 'Italic houses'. Figures are sporadic elsewhere, but the large grouping of 107 plans of peristyle gardens in North Africa collected by Rebuffat (1969) provide a reasonable starting point for a comparison with those of Campania. He does not provide any dating evidence, however, but it does indicate the range of features present. Out of 107 dwellings, I counted sixty-four that appeared to contain a total of 112 water features.[45]

This information augments my hypothesis that water features were considered an important element in gardens.

The position of water features in a garden

The position of basins can become significant. Often they were placed so that they would be in view from principal rooms, especially from the *triclinium* or *oecus*. The importance of lines of sight from such rooms is demonstrated by the fact that in general a recess in a pool is placed central to that room. More water would then be visible, or alternatively the location where a fountain had room to play, although the remains of fountains rarely survive.

A number of basins of type A and a large proportion of type B had been sited alongside one edge of the peristyle, as at Ostia and Vienne.[46] This may indicate an overlap in forms, or a change of use. This alteration, however, would allow rain water to fall off the roof above into the basin below, thereby eliminating the need to construct a gutter on that side of the garden. I consider that a development (dated to the 2nd century AD) may be seen in France and the Iberian peninsula, where the idea of a gutter basin was extended and made continuous on three sides of the garden. Access was now restricted to the uninterrupted fourth side. The channels here are wide and deep and are a feature in their own right (see Pl.20). These belong in regions with a higher rainfall, therefore it is possible that continuous basins replacing gutters are also more efficient in dealing with a larger flow of rainwater (however, to date this form has not been found in notoriously wet Britain). This scheme exists in a number of houses at Vienne, and is also seen in Frejus in France, Merida in Spain, and in a secondary garden in the House of Cantaber at Conimbriga.[47] This style may have influenced the formation of basins of type F for in the House of the Skeletons at Conimbriga,[48] (also dated to the 2nd c.AD) we see what may be a further development. Here the water channel almost encloses the fourth side, and by increasingly isolating the garden in the middle, it perhaps leads the way towards the introduction of islands in the form of caissons.

Different forms of water feature: *Euripi*

These could really be classified as a type A water basin, for where a rectangular pool appears in an elongated form (more often seen in large gardens) then it is frequently called a *euripus*. These features are first named in works by Cicero,[49] indicating that such artificial water basins or canals recalled famous water channels of antiquity, the *Nile* in Egypt, the *Canopus* canal in Alexandria, or the *Euripus* a narrow tidal channel in Greece. Seneca (*Ep*,XC,15) implies that there were instances where owners of these artificial basins even arranged for a holding tank of water to be discharged further up so that the sudden flow along the basin would recreate a tidal bore. An example of one of these large structures may be seen in the famous *Canopus* at the Villa of Hadrian, where a quantity of Egyptian statuary reaffirms a connection with the Canopus itself.[50] Martial (XII,31,2) in his estate in Spain had a *euripus*, and Seneca (*Ep*,LV,6) mentions how on Vattia's estate there was a euripus-like channel 'running through a grove of plane trees', and adds that it was well stocked with fish. There are other literary references to public gardens with *euripi* in the Campus Martius area of Rome, Pliny (*NH*,XXXVI,24,123) says that Agrippa supplied water to '*euripis*', among other things. Perhaps these were the famous ones remembered with nostalgia by Ovid.[51] The area has been studied archaeologically by Lugli (1938,159) who provides a section drawing (see fig.13). This *euripus* was circa 800m long, 3.35m wide, with a maximum depth of 1.70m, a paved walk ran either side and little bridges were placed where streets traversed its route.[52] In Pompeii the elongated canal-like basins at both the House of Julia Felix & the House of Loreius Tiburtinus were also provided with little bridges (see Pl.21), perhaps to recall the famous one in Rome that was constructed c.19BC.

Caves and grottoes

Originally these were really natural phenomena that were linked into the landscape of the grounds of a Roman villa. Caves were sometimes associated with funerary beliefs such as being the gateway to Hades or the inferno below, but there were other religious aspects. In Greece water was often derived from a hidden spring, and when this occurred in a cave, in the bowels of the earth, it was seen as mystical. Therefore the source was usually linked to a particular divinity, to Pan or in many cases a nymph. Caves were enhanced with the addition of altars and offerings. The mouth of the spring itself was often elaborated upon, so that the spring gushed forth from some form of fountain head, and would be caught by a basin below. Several frescoes depicting landscape scenes include a cave or grotto, where we can see such a spring in its setting (e.g. from Boscoreale[53] (Pl.4).

Caves were sometimes enlarged, and rooms made inside, as in those at Capri detailed by Neuerburg.[54] At Sperlonga, the cave also included large fishponds and a dining area.[55] An indication of the attention given to such features in the grounds of a villa, is highlighted by Suetonius & Tacitus who reveal that the owners of this particular cave named their villa, *speluca*, 'the cavern'.[56] The cave at Sperlonga has been identified as the location of a disaster recorded by Suetonius & Tacitus (Ibid.) for c.AD27 part of the roof collapsed and fell onto diners below, Tiberius who was present on this occasion escaped harm. It is believed that the architects of the Sperlonga grotto, with its Hellenistic Odysseus statuary group, came from Rhodes[57] which reinforces a Greek association with grottoes. Seneca (*Ep*,LV,6) mentions that on Vattia's estate two caves were created, 'one of these does not admit the rays of the sun, while the other keeps them until the sun sets' which would imply that they also contained dining rooms, the former would remain cool for summer use and the latter would be warmed by the sun for the winter months.

Caves could be excavated out of a suitable hillside to make a grotto, but elsewhere they needed to be constructed, either as a recess or a niche. In gardens with a cryptoporticus the essential elements of a grotto would be fairly simple to recreate, for the cryptoporticus of a terrace wall could be made to look like a rock face with an opening in to the bank of a hill (e.g. at the villa of Domitian at Castelgandolfo).[58] Bits of pumice were applied to interior surfaces to create a rustic feel,[59] which mimicked the appearance of natural rock, and that quintessential element, the spring, was piped to the site. The outlet of the 'spring' was often placed in a semi-circular niche. Side walls were often given subsidiary niches usually alternating rectangular with semi-circular. Ancient models of grottoes, such as the one found at Reggio Calabria (fig.19), give an impression of the appearance of these artificially constructed caves.

On level ground these elements were translated into masonry structures that often bore little resemblance to the rocky caves of their origin. Such artificial grottoes tended to be referred to as Nymphaea for they were nevertheless meant to recall the abode of nymphs.

Nymphaea, of basilica form

In large properties these often took the form of a garden room or pavilion. Surviving examples, such as at S.Antonio, the so-called villa of Horace at Tivoli, demonstrate features common to this type of nymphaea[60] (fig.20). The basilica-like structures usually consist of a rectangular room with an apse to the rear. The roof is mostly barrel vaulted, with a half dome over the recess. 'Spring' water issued from a centrally located point in the apse. Side walls are often furnished with niches, with or without further water outlets. In the Auditorium of Maecenas, at Rome, the apse was furnished with a flight of six semi-circular steps. Water issued from a series of points on the uppermost step and tumbled down, like a waterfall, into a basin below (which is no longer there). Some of the original painted wall plaster remains, and the subject depicted in the niches on the upper level of the apse, and those of the main hall, are of a garden, showing birds flying above shrubs and trees, in front of which is either a trellis fence or an urn containing a fountain. Although these buildings are wholly artificial, the decor reinforces links with the elements of nature, and components of this type recreate artificial grottoes and caves. This type of building could really be seen as a large garden pavilion.

Aediculae Nymphaea

Where space was at a premium, such as in small enclosed gardens, the proportions of water features needed to be scaled down to size. We therefore find that the nymphaeum appears in a form similar to *lararia* usually seen in *atria*. These were normally placed against a wall, and like-wise we find these *aedicula*-like nymphaea positioned so that they would enliven a garden wall[61] (Pl.23). For this reason nymphaea are rarely found in a dwelling with a complete peristyle (a portico on all four sides). A nymphaeum placed on a rear wall would serve as a focal point to rooms looking onto this space of greenery, and when placed in an axial position in line with the front entrance of the house, the obvious display would be immediately seen on entry into the *fauces*. The maximum value for money would therefore be obtained.

Aediculae nymphaea were built out from the wall; they frequently had a pitched roof and a porch-like frontage usually with a triangular pediment above. The arched doorway could relate to a cave entrance of a grotto, and the recess inside to the source of a sacred spring.[62] Many nymphaea are encrusted with coloured pieces of mosaic forming a variety of decorative panels, of geometric and figurative designs. Shells were used to frame panels and to emphasize the outlines of the exterior and the archway. Shells although decorative, were also symbolically associated with the watery element of Venus, the goddess of gardens, which gives another dimension to our understanding of this type of nymphaeum.

An inspection of the well preserved examples in Pompeii can show some features in common.[63] Water was fed through a lead pipe at the rear of the recess, either into a fountain statue or a mask (as at the House of the Small Fountain). In six out of the thirteen shown in a survey by Neuerburg[64] I have noted that the water then poured into a basin, whereas, in seven examples[65] water tumbled down a short flight of marble steps before reaching a basin. The sight and sound of water falling in this manner could be seen to recreate the cascading effect of natural spring water. Where statuary would have obscured the decorative scheme the inner surface of the niche was usually simplified, and rustication in the form of applied pumice is found.

Facade nymphaea

This form is also seen against a wall. However in many cases a whole wall is utilized. In the House of the Little Bull (Pompeii,V,i,7)[66] we can see that the *aedicula* form has been enlarged and replicated three times, but water cascading down steps in each niche fell into a communal basin below. A more elaborate example may be seen at the House of Cupid & Psyche at Ostia (Pl.24). Here the garden is decorated with a series of five niches which are separated by columns. In the lower portion there are semi-circular projections, and the recesses of the arched upper section are of an alternating semi-circular and rectangular form. The whole is reminiscent of a theatre facade, and perhaps this type was inspired by the sight of monumental public fountains. Water was introduced into each niche, where presumably it poured from a fountain figure, it fell down a flight of three marble steps (angled in such a way that they form a slope rather than stairs) into a shallow trough. A hole in the side of each trough then directed the water to the projections of the podium, where it would have emerged out of a lion's head or similar outlet. It is believed that a long shallow drainage channel below (now gone) caught the water, as at the House of Fortuna Annonaria, also in Ostia.[67]

This type of nymphaeum is seen in a number of places and in a variety of adapted forms.[68] For instance, a huge curved facade nymphaeum survives in the apse of the domed hall in the Piazza D'Oro of Hadrian's villa at Tivoli (highlighted in fig.10c).

Solitary niches similar to a single recess of the facade type mentioned above, when provided with a water outlet, are

52	Richardson,1992,147.
53	Photographed in the Museum of Boscoreale, this being a copy of one of the frescoes from the Villa of P. Fannius Sinistor (the original is now in New York). Another fresco with a grotto fountain, the 'paysage Barberini' survives only from drawings made soon after its discovery, a copy is kept in the Windsor Royal Library,no.19226 (Lavagne, 1993,748).
54	Neuerberg,1965,115/6,figs.13 & 14. Neuerberg provides a thorough survey of the architecture of nymphaea and grottoes in Ancient Italy. However he includes public street fountains and those found in internal rooms which are less relevant for my purposes, my main concern being to locate material relevant to the garden or garden pavilions. His catalogue was particularly useful to gauge the frequency of forms in existence, but is geographically confined to Italy. I have made some use of his nomenclature e.g. 'facade & *aediculae* nymphaea'.
55	Ricotti,1987,fig.2.
56	Suetonius,*Tib*,39; Tacitus,*Ann*,IV,59 respectively.
57	MacKendrick,1962,175.
58	Neuerburg,1965,156 & fig.34, where there was a series of four grotto-nymphaea in the cryptoporticus wall of the middle terrace. Lanciani (1924?,110) also believed that terrace walls could be 'ornamented with niches, nymphaea and waterfalls'.
59	Pliny (*NH*,XXXVI,42,154) mentions this process in connection with *musaea*, garden structures that were similar (in all but name) to artificial caves or nymphaea. Propertius (*Eleg*,III,3,27/8) describes a green (perhaps moss covered) pumice cave, where instruments of the Muses etc were hung, which implies a recreated abode of nymphs, whereas Statius (*Silvae*,III,1,144) shows the appellation is arbitrary, for he refers to nymphs, rather than muses, in 'pumice caves'.
60	Hallam,1914,figs.8/9. Less well preserved examples can be seen as far afield as Welschbillig in Germany (Wrede,1972,26/7,fig.7); and in the Villa of Cardilius at Torres Novas, Portugal (Alarcão,1988,fig.73). A fresco from Pompeii, Naples National Museum inv.no.8594 (Ling,1991,fig.32) illustrates some features of the interior of a basilica nymphaeum, although only part of the walls are shown. These are however each fitted with five lion head water spouts pouring water into an elongated decorative basin supported by animal-like legs. Above are niches with garden scenes reminiscent of those in the Auditorium of Maecenas.
61	Pompeii,II,ix,6 is an exception (Jashemski,1993,97 & 331).
62	Most recesses are semi-circular, but there are rectangular examples e.g. in the House of the Centenary, Pompeii,IX,viii,3/6 (Neuerburg,1965,fig.116).
63	Aediculae nymphaea are, however, also found outside of Pompeii, e. g. in the House of Augustus on the Palatine (Tomei,1992,921,fig.2) and at Ostia and Tivoli.
64	Neuerburg,1965,figs.115 to 122, 127 to 130.
65	ibid,figs.115,116,121,122,123,127,129.
66	Lauter-Bufe,1975,fig.168.
67	Packer,1967,129.
68	e.g. In the House in the North East Zone at Vienne dated to early 2nd century AD, a possible example mentioned as a 'fontaine quadrilobée' in North Africa (Rebuffat,1969,671, Volubilis 27), and the Villa at Desenzano del Garda, dated to late 4th century AD (Neuerburg,1965,258,fig.165), which all appear in a true garden. Whereas the Neronian facade nymphaeum of the Domus Transitoria on the Palatine (Tomei,1992, figs.4/6), Terrace House no.2 at Ephesus (Vetters,57,fig.60), and The House of the Psalms at Stobi in Macedonia, dated to the 4th century AD (Lauter-Bufe,1975,fig.173), all appear to face onto a paved peristyle courtyard. Both types indicate how widespread they were, and that this type of nymphaeum continued right up to the period of the Late Empire.
69	Multiple niches were also included in large domed structures, such as the Nymphaeum, which served as a pavilion to the Gardens of Sallust (see fig.21).
70	A similar arrangement, but with different shaped basins may be seen in the Casa de los Pajaros at Italica, Spain (Bellido,1960, 85,fig.22), and at the Edifice of the Seasons at Sbeitla, N.Africa. At the House of the Cascades at Utica, N.Africa, fountain basins were placed to the front and back rather than at the sides (Alexander & Ennaïfer,1975, pl.XI.1).
71	Varro,*RR*,III,5,9/17.
72	Varro,*RR*,III,17,6; Martial,*Ep*,X,30,21/4; Luxorius, *Poems*,5, respectively.
73	e.g. Cato sold the fish from his charge's pond for 40,000 sesterces (Varro,*RR*,III,2,17). However Columella raises the figure to 400,000 (VIII,16,5). The figure reaches four million in Pliny (*NH*,IX,80,170). Pliny (*NH*,IX,81,171) also relates that the estate of Gaius Hirrus was sold for four million sesterces on account of its fishponds. This was partly on account of the value of the stock of fish the ponds contained, but also it illustrates the increasing value placed on what was seen as luxury decorative items.
74	Columella,*RR*,VIII,16,6.
75	Wrede,1972,20,fig.4.

CHAPTER SIX: GARDEN ORNAMENTATION

A Roman garden would not be complete without some form of ornamentation. The simplest method was to make garlands by using material grown in the garden or bought for the purpose. Garlands were hung in swags between columns of a portico. On religious days they were hung on altars,[1] and *coronae* or chaplets were placed on statues.[2] These ephemeral items rarely survive.[3] However, literary sources describe their use and components.[4] A large number of frescoes illustrate how garlands decorated architecture. Several garden scenes use them as a framing device, or as a means of linking *oscilla* into the composition for otherwise they would be isolated above (see Pls.37 & 39).

Of a more durable nature are furnishings in stone (especially marble) bronze or terracotta. Evidence for some of these can be found in the numerous frescoes, depicting items in an idealised verdant scene (such as in figs.22 & 23 plus Pls.37 & 39). A number of small examples show sculptural adornments in and on latticework enclosures, see figs. 9 & 27. The large frescoes have a twofold value. They are of especial importance for the identification and use of items shown, and interestingly, if a person could not afford to purchase sculpture, he could have them painted onto his garden wall where, seen from a distance, they would serve as a good substitute.

Contemporary art as a source, although an idealized one, is augmented by evidence supplied by ancient writers who mention sculpture in rustic contexts and public/private gardens.[5] Archaeological evidence has indicated that a proportion of sculpture is found in association with dwellings, as opposed to public monuments, but unfortunately the find spots were until recently rarely recorded, beyond naming the site. Therefore sites subsequently covered by the eruption of Vesuvius are extremely valuable, for items were mostly found in situ, thus enabling us to see the range available in garden ornamentation at that date,[6] and also to determine the significance of the layout (and that of individual pieces in such a collection).

Today old photographs and the few plans that exist need to be consulted, for with the exception of the House of the Vettii, Pompeii, all the sculpture is now in museums or storerooms.[7] However, garden objects taken out of context (unless well documented) lose a great deal of their relevance; for the direction in which an item was facing as well as its location within the garden is of interest.

As an example, fig.24 from the House of the Golden Cupids, Pompeii shows that *oscilla, pinakes*, herms, animal statuary and a sundial have been re-erected in their approximate original positions. As can be seen, in most cases, they appear to have been placed so that they face into the garden, whereas in the collection at the House of Marcus Lucretius (fig.25) they face towards main rooms.[8] This appears to suggest that the outward view from these rooms was of prime importance, and sculpture was used to enhance that view by being placed often in a direct line of sight (This is also noticeable in the location of garden structures such as nymphaea mentioned in ch. five).

The use of sculpture in large gardens can be revealing. Statuary was sometimes placed besides a water basin, where reflections could add to the alluring quality of the scene.[9] The Romans might also feel that the effect of multiple images doubled their value. Another means of display is seen at Oplontis, in Garden A, where a row of herms line a diagonal pathway[10] see fig.5. Presumably the large collections of herms found elsewhere may reveal a similar pattern.[11] In garden B (fig.5) a row of statues on plinths was placed in front of trees lining a path by the large *piscina*. By this method the statues would be shaded and protected by the tree trunk behind, and the dark trees would form a background against which the marble would be seen to advantage. De Caro (1987,129) points out that by setting the line of statues here slightly at an angle, in relation to the pool, they would all be visible from the principal rooms to the north. Again this confirms that sculpture was placed in prominent places where, as status objects, they could reveal the wealth of their owner.

Apart from statues found in gardens at Pompeii and its vicinity, some of which are well recorded, it is difficult to determine if an item found elsewhere ornamented a garden or a building (for as already mentioned their location is rarely given in excavation reports). There are, however, four main features which can be used to aid our identification, these are;

1. Size.   2. Quality.   3. Association.   4. Rusticity.

Firstly, garden statuary is normally of a smaller size; however, their scale depends on the size of the garden (there is an obvious difference between the confines of a Pompeian style peristyle garden and a large public park). Therefore it is understandable that in general the Capitoline triad are rarely represented, for these regal imposing figures (often suitably of Olympian size) were more fitting for public rather than private display.

Secondly, garden statuary is often seen to be of a mass produced kind. Items contained in museums throughout the world show that a number of replicas were made of famous Greek statues, several show minor variations of pose, and some are mirror images. Others show that they were inspired by an original, which in many cases became a standardized form, but there was obviously an allowance for artistic licence, and perhaps for a patrons specific requests. With a large demand for statuary, workshops no doubt produced items of differing workmanship, and the resulting variations in price would therefore suit a range of pockets. Some of the wealthier properties, however, would have contained masterpieces (such as the works of Praxiteles and Scopas displayed in the Gardens of Servilius, Rome, described by Pliny (*NH*,XXXVI,4,23-25).

Thirdly, figures who are linked to a particular divinity associated with gardens, and some of the attributes of these deities, are represented in garden art. Their inclusion serves either to allude to the presence of that divinity, or merely to accompany it. In larger gardens an area could be devoted to a form of theme garden, such as a collection of Egyptian inspired statuary, that could simulate the aura of

Alexandria, Canopus and the Nile delta in general.[12] Alternatively statuary could be site specific, e. g. herms of philosophers in an Academy style garden.[13] However I must add that gardens may have been ornamented by a mixture of pieces acquired over the years, or generations, items that were available at the time as opposed to an exact choice. Sculpture was expensive, so only the rich would have been able to afford to renew a complete collection from afresh. All these factors could mask the original design or program, if there was one.

The fourth element, rusticity, may be compared to our modern taste for garden gnomes. We do not usually place these little ornaments inside the home, for to us they belong in the garden. In antiquity the Romans also did not place the rustic figure of Priapus, for instance, inside a dwelling. Garden statuary was essentially connected to subjects that could be at home in an outdoor context, the countryside or sea, fields or woodland. One can sometimes detect a wish to recreate an Arcadian atmosphere, or a sacred grove, within the garden.

Finally, there is a further feature which identifies a garden statue. If the figure is bored through to take a lead waterpipe, then it may be presumed to have been destined to serve as a fountain figure,[14] and would have been situated close to a water feature of some kind. They may sometimes be destined to pour water into the *impluvium* in the *atrium*, but more often than not they were placed in a garden. The four above criteria would still apply to determine if it graced a public fountain or a domestic one.

To determine the range of items used and the frequency of specific pieces of garden ornamentation, Neudecker's study of the sculptural programmes of seventy-eight Roman villas in Italy was consulted. This detailed study, reviewed by Warden,[15] indicated that Neudecker thought sculpture was primarily site specific. In some cases this may have been so (e.g. Cicero wanted subjects suitable for a palaestra/gymnasium, and an *Amaltheum/ Museion*).

Grimal, however, believes that the Roman love for 'naturalisme' pervaded all, which brought a religious aspect to sculpture, whereas Jashemski sees the sculpture of Pompeii as having the combined functions of religion and ornamentation and, by locating sites of altars in gardens, has proved the worship of particular deities there.

Both Grimal's and Jashemski's approach have much to recommend them. The Romans were a very superstitious people, and would see the presence of their gods in many things. Garden sculptures are essentially ornamental items, and may be accounted for by the fact that many Romans were at the same time sensitive to beauty and form, and could appreciate the decorative aspect of statuary as well as feeling that they have sacred connotations

Today we usually value a statue for its ornamental properties, but in some countries sacred objects are still placed in niches or grottoes, e.g. in a convent garden in Rome, where a statue of the Virgin decorates an ivy covered fountain grotto,[16] which bears many resemblances to ancient Roman nymphaea. The figure is religious yet, by placing it in such a situation, it is highly decorative. Some modern authors (e.g. Grimal) describe works as profane, when used for ornamentation, but this term could hardly be used when referring to the statue of the Virgin Mary in the convent mentioned above. As can be seen, the setting around sculpture is important, revealing its connection (with Bernadette here), but it may also be ambiguous, for one could feel that it was now secular. Some saints, for instance St Francis, who was so in tune with nature, retains a holy yet rustic quality that would make him a very suitable figure for display in a garden. He would become decorative, but would still hold some sanctity for us. I feel that numerous Ancient Roman statues of divinities were seen by the ancients in a similar light. However, not all garden sculpture could be defined as having a religious context, e.g. the rustic figures of mortals and athletes.

The appearance of what I term secular (a word I prefer to use, as opposed to profane) items may be noted in surviving collections. To me these reflect a broader desire for ornamental objects. I believe that this is partly due to the Romans' approach to religion that changed over the centuries. Those of Epicurean or Neo-Platonic persuasion, for instance, would perhaps not be so concerned with statuary depicting deities. Also the syncretism that occurred throughout the Empire no doubt had an effect, with sculpture being tailored to suit tastes.[17] There were many reasons for one's choice of statuary, I will examine the inferences behind specific items later.

To ascertain the range and frequency of items of garden sculpture I studied catalogues compiled by Neudecker, Appelton, Jashemski, Hill, Bieber, Bellido, Kapossy, etc, as well as collections held in museums. From these sources I have found that there are a number of items that may be specific to gardens rather than elsewhere. In Table 1, I have chosen twenty different sites from which there was sufficient documentation of large collections of sculpture. These, although merely a sample of the whole, will I feel contribute to an assessment of the situation

Table I (Pages 30-31)

The first half (ten) are sites from the area covered by Vesuvius, therefore these form a fairly reliable control group. I have chosen a mixture of small and large properties. The second half are from large properties in Italy, for which unfortunately documentation is limited owing to the fact that the ruins were excavated, for the most part before the present century and, largely to acquire saleable commodities. Sculptural finds here, as on most sites elsewhere, need to be regarded as chance survivals after pillage in antiquity and later. Records rarely show if the sculpture originally belonged in a garden, but the sites I will be using contained certain features which could be found within the grounds of large Roman properties. The headings through lack of space indicate only the most recurrent forms of sculpture.

GARDEN ORNAMENTATION

TABLE I: **A SAMPLE OF ANCIENT ROMAN SITES AS AN INDICATION OF THE RANGE AND FREQUENCY OF GARDEN SCULPTURE**

SITE	ALTAR	VENUS	PRIAPUS	CUPID	CHILDREN	ANIMALS	DIANA	APOLLO	MARSYAS	MUSES	HERCULES
Villa of the Papyrii Herculaneum (Neudecker)	-	-	-	-	6	4	-	-	-	-	-
Villa of Poppaea, Oplontis (De Caro)	-	1	-	-	2	1	1	-	-	-	-
House of Camillus, Pompeii (Dwyer)	-	1	-	-	2	5	-	-	-	-	-
House of the Citharist, Pompeii (Dwyer)	1	-	1	-	-	6	-	1	-	-	-
House of Fortuna, Pompeii (Dwyer)	-	-	-	-	2	-	-	-	-	-	-
House of the Golden Cupids, Pompeii (Dwyer)	1	-	-	-	-	3	-	-	-	-	-
House of Marcus Lucretius, Pompeii (Jashemski)	-	-	-	2	-	7	-	-	-	2	-
House of Loreius Tiburtinus, Pompeii (Jashemski)	-	-	-	-	3	3	-	-	-	-	-
House of the Vettii, Pompeii (Appleton +)	-	-	1	-	6	-	-	-	-	-	-
Villa Sora, Torre del Greco (Neudecker)	-	-	-	-	2	1	-	-	-	-	1
Imperial Villa, Anzio (Neudecker)	-	1	-	-	1	1	1	1	-	-	1
Imperial Villa, Castel Gandolfo (Neudecker)	-	-	-	2	-	2	-	-	1	-	1
Monte Cagnolo, Lanuvio (Neudecker)	-	-	-	1	3	9	-	-	-	-	-
Horace's Villa, Licenza (Neudecker)	-	-	-	1	1	6	-	-	-	-	-
Voconius Villa, Marino (Neudecker)	-	-	-	1	1	2	2	2	1	-	1
Villa Maxentius, Rome (Neudecker)	-	3	-	-	-	-	-	-	-	-	-
Villa Quintili, Rome (Neudecker)	-	1	-	1	6	-	2	1	1	5	-
Tiberius's Villa, Sperlonga (Neudecker)	-	-	-	-	6	3	-	-	-	-	-
Villa of Cassius, Tivoli (Neudecker)	-	-	-	-	-	3	-	1	-	9	-
Villa Cynthia, Tivoli (Neudecker)	-	-	-	-	1	-	-	-	-	1	-
TOTALS	2	7	2	8	42	56	6	6	2	17	4

GARDEN ORNAMENTATION

BACCHUS	PAN	SILENUS	SATYR	MAENADS	NYMPHS & RIVER GODS	EPHEBE	HERMS DOUBLE	HERMS SINGLE	OSCILLA	PINAX	SUNDIAL	URNS
-	1	-	2	-	-	3	-	32	-	-	-	-
-	-	-	1	-	-	1	-	7	-	-	1	1
-	-	-	-	-	-	1	-	1	-	-	-	-
-	-	-	-	-	-	-	2	2	12	-	-	1
-	-	1	-	-	-	-	-	2	16	-	-	-
-	-	-	-	-	-	-	3	6	7	4	1	-
-	-	1	2	-	-	-	4	1	6	-	-	-
-	-	-	1	-	1	-	-	-	3	-	-	-
1	-	-	2	-	-	-	2	-	-	-	-	5
-	-	1	4	-	-	-	7	1	-	-	-	-
-	-	-	1	-	-	2	-	4	-	-	-	-
1	-	-	5	-	2	6	-	1	-	-	-	-
1	2	-	-	-	-	-	1	4	-	-	-	2
-	-	-	-	-	-	-	-	2	1	-	-	-
-	-	1	-	-	-	5	1	7	-	-	-	1
-	-	-	-	-	-	-	-	11	-	-	-	-
-	1	3	2	4	1	-	3	19	-	-	-	-
-	-	-	-	-	-	-	-	11	2	-	-	-
1	-	-	3	-	-	-	1	34	1	-	-	-
-	-	-	3	-	-	4	-	8	-	-	-	-
4	4	7	26	4	4	22	24	153	48	4	2	10

The absence of altars on sites in the second group, is perhaps partly due to the preference given to recording statuary which is often of more interest to specialists in Roman portraiture, or monumental art and objects of fine quality. This results in a lower priority being given to publishing the full details of all objects found. Likewise, *pinakes*, were probably omitted because they could appear to be a relief panel (and sundials a block of stone). These entries, therefore, highlight the limitations of catalogues solely aimed at statuary.

As can be seen the few representations of Priapus may reflect the usual practice of installing a wooden statue, which would not have survived, rather than a marble one.

The table indicates the extent of the popularity of statuary depicting children/putti or animals. In a number of cases there were groups of both. Where these occurred I have placed them under the heading for children. The popularity of this combined group is also I feel partly due to the appeal of small creatures in reality, and many are thus small in size.

Under the heading of Satyrs, I have included groups of Bacchic content (e.g. Pan & Satyr); these I have counted as a single item. Satyrs often appear in the plural in mythology and this entry reveals how Romans may have aimed to recreate myth in their gardens.

In table I, I have also placed together under one heading the ephebes and wrestlers. I feel that they are related items in that they both demonstrate an athletic image, and typically show what was considered as the ideal physique of comely, yet manly youth.

The herms are a mixture of types, including Hermes himself. For the full range see under the heading of Herms.

Table II lists garden statuary not included in the first table, partly though lack of space, but also many are less commonly found.

TABLE II

EXAMPLES OF STATUE TYPES LESS FREQUENTLY FOUND IN ROMAN GARDENS

STATUE	PROVENANCE
Amazon	Canopus, Hadrian's Villa at Tivoli.
Athena	Imperial Villa at Anzio (Neudecker,1988,133).
Attis	Pompeii (IX,i,7) (Jashemski,1993,225).
Bes	A terracotta example was found at the House of Loreius Tiburtinus, Pompeii (Jashemski,1993,78). There is also a marble fountain statuette at the Fitzwilliam Museum, Cambridge Inv.no.GR.1.1818.
Endymion	Setti Bassi, now in the B.M. inv.no.1567 (Neudecker,1988,208).
Faun	Pompeii (VI,Viii,5)(Jashemski,1993,133).
Flora	Centocelle (Neudecker,1988,204). Also found at Pompeii (VI,v,5/21) (Jashemski,1993,126).
Fortuna	Villa of Quintilius Varo (Neudecker,1988,235).
Greek archaic & classical style figures	e.g. The 'maidens',Villa of the Papyrii, Herculaneum, now in National Museum Naples, inv.nos.5604/5; 5618/21.
Hermaphrodite	House of Loreius Tiburtinus, Pompeii (Jashemski,1993, fig.91).
Isis	Pompeii (III,iv,2/3) (Jashemski,1993,102).
Mercury	House of Camillus, Pompeii (Dwyer,1982,62).
Negro boy	From Rome, B.M.inv.no.1768 (Hlll,1981,93).
Nereid	Imperial Villa at Pausilypon, now in National Museum Naples, inv.no.6026 (Neudecker,1988,173).
Nike	Villa of Oplontis (Jashemski,1993,300).
Niobids	Gardens of Sallust (Aurigemma,1955,278).
Odysseus	Sperlonga (Neudecker,1988,221).
Omphale	House of the Golden Cupids, Pompeii (Jashemski,1993,166)
Osiris	Villa of Cassius, Tivoli (Neudecker,1988,233).
Paris	House of the Vettii, Pompeii (Jashemski,1993,153).
Pharaoh	House of Loreius Tiburtinus, Pompeii (Jashemski,1993,78).
Pomona	House of the Ephebe Pompeii (I,vii,10/12/19) (Jashemski,1993, fig.38).
Rustic figures, e.g. Shepherds	Villa del Pastore, Stabiae. Now in Stabiae Museum.
Sphinx	House of Sallust, Pompeii (Kapossy,1969,53).
Tritons	Blue Grotto, Capri, (Neudecker,1988,137).

After an inspection of the range and frequency of garden ornaments, and having established a mode of selection for such sculpture, I will now discuss the especial relevance of individual subjects in the following catalogue.

CATALOGUE OF SCULPTURE FOUND IN ROMAN GARDENS

Altars

Perhaps the earliest and simplest item of garden sculpture, they are seen in reliefs and frescoes, often in sacro-idyllic landscape settings which emphasize a rural context. As such they belong to country villa estates as well as temple/shrine enclosures.[18] Of the literary sources, Varro (*RR*,1,5) identifies twelve deities that were considered appropriate to husbandmen, Jupiter & Tellus, Sol & Luna, Ceres & Liber, Robigus & Flora, Minerva & Venus, Lympha & Bonus Eventus. Gardens were essentially areas where plants were grown, and therefore deities connected with agriculture still retained a hold, even on a small plot in town or country. But not all those mentioned above were transferred into the garden environment. Martial (X,92) partly clarifies the situation by providing a list of the deities worshipped at altars on his Nomentean property, the Thunderer (Jupiter), Silvanus, Diana, Mars, Flora, and Priapus. These are closer to what has actually been brought to light, but there were others who may have a particular reason for their inclusion in the garden.

In a domestic setting, such as the garden of a town house, we see altars placed within the peristyle, or in the garden (as in fig.11); sometimes they were painted on a wall, or incorporated into an *aedicula* shrine.[19] Also Pliny (*NH*,XII,2,3) shows that large or beautiful trees were sometimes considered sacred, a belief confirmed by finds of cavities of big roots besides an altar at Pompeii.[20]

Statues of deities were sometimes placed beside an altar;[21] for as previously mentioned religion pervaded all facets of Roman life. However, with the onset of a demand for the acquisition of objects of wealth, statues that were placed in a garden take on a twofold meaning.

Venus

The goddess was the most important divinity in gardens. She was an ancient Roman goddess who was regarded as the protectress of the *hortus* and growing plants.[22] Later she took on the attributes of the Greek Aphrodite, and becomes associated with the fertility of man as well as plants. She also appears to have taken over many of the associations of Flora and Pomona. A statue of Venus is found in numerous Roman gardens, which is testimony to her popularity.[23]

Classic poses of Venus seen in gardens, are of a scantily clad or nude figure of a sinuous sensual form. She may be shown crouching down to pick something (an example of this type is seen in Pl.25), or tying up her hair, placing on a sandal, or as if emerging from the sea (from whence she was born).[24] Her associations with water are referred to by the inclusion in the garden of figures of dolphins or other marine creatures such as fish,[25] and crustaceans.[26] She could be symbolised by a dove, a rose flower, or a sprig of myrtle, all of which were considered sacred to her. The animal used for ritual sacrifices in her honour was the rabbit or hare, whose fertility is well known, and therefore highly suitable. Hares in art are often shown eating grapes, the fruits of a highly prolific plant, and therefore are representative of productivity. They also perhaps provide a second connection, this time with Bacchus the god of wine.[27]

Priapus

Believed to be the son of Aphrodite and Dionysus, this rustic divinity originated in Lampsacus and replaced the old Roman phallic god Mutunus Tutunus.[28] His appearance was sometimes made fun of by Latin authors[29] for he was usually personified by a crudely made wooden statue, with a herm like shaft. Various sacro-idyllic frescoes depict his form (see fig.9c & Pl.35). His well endowed ithyphallic posture, as if by sympathetic magic, would ensure the fertility of the garden, orchard or vineyard where he was usually placed, and was believed to avert the evil eye. In one hand he carried a pruning hook, a reference to pruning and grafting techniques that increased the fertility of fruit trees and vines. This tool was also useful for his other major role, to ward off those intent on plundering the produce of the garden. Priapus' form also served as a kind of scarecrow for birds as well as humans.[30]

Not all were made of wood however. Martial (VI,72) jokes about the risks of owning a marble statue compared to one made of wood, for such a Priapus might be stolen. A large marble example was discovered in the House of the Vettii.[31] Several semi-clad stone statues of him exist; in this type he is often depicted lifting up his robe so that the fruitful produce of the garden might be displayed in the folds of his draperies (while at the same time revealing his symbolic potent ithyphallic character).[32] Little children or Cupids are sometimes shown lifting up his garment (ibid.). The animal often associated with Priapus is the ass.

Cupid

Statuettes of Cupid (Eros) a child of Venus, are often found in gardens.[33] He is shown in a number of ways. e.g. stringing a bow (as in B.M.Inv.no.1673), or as a sleeping child.[34] He is usually distinguished from statues of children by the presence of wings, and a bow and arrows.

Children

The subject of sleeping children probably originated from decorative Greek funerary monuments, but the subject became quite popular, and a number of copies exist. Statues of children are perhaps a development from Cupid models and are often called Erotes, Putti or Amorini (with or without wings). Children are often shown struggling or playing with animals, riding a dolphin,[35] or carrying an urn. Many functioned as fountain pieces, the water outlet being in the mouth of an animal or vessel (see Pls.27 & 28). The children or putti mentioned above are usually plump little toddlers, but slightly older infants, perhaps up to age six or eight years old, are on occasion also found. An example would be the Maid of Anzio (Aurigemma,1955,287), whereas the Spinario,[36] a slave boy extracting a thorn, would really be classed as a rustic figure (for this category see below). Older children that do not appear to have a particular function or distinguishing attributes, I feel may have been included in the garden as a reminder of a child's tender years that pass so quickly, these statues may then be notable in that they might bear some resemblance to a certain member of the household. An image of a plump well fed child held an appeal then, as they often do today. The frequency and wide distribution of statues of young children is indicative of the popularity of this type.

Mars and Amazons

Mars, although associated with war, was also connected to agriculture. Therefore, occasionally he is found in gardens. He is seen as a statue in one of the verdant frescoes at the House of the Marine Venus, Pompeii (Pl.26), but as the consort of Venus he would still have a place in gardens.[37] The mythical Amazons, seem to form a female martial counterpart, and appear together in the colonnade of the Canopus at Hadrian's Villa, Tivoli. A martial theme could also include Athene (who is also associated with the olive) and Diana.

Diana and animals

Her image in the form of a garden statue is recorded in North Africa by Luxorius (*Anth.Lat*,18). She was the goddess of the hunt, and she often appears in frescoes and mosaics depicting rural life. She usually wears a short tunic and carries a bow and quiver of arrows. Grimal (1969,55) believes that a garden could recreate her haunt in the country, for the trees and shrubs would become the woods teeming with animals. A certain type of animal statuary, such as those of the hunt, could therefore be seen as another attribute of Diana. Animals were a very popular art form in gardens, and we find stags/hinds or boars by themselves or with hounds at bay.[38] Appleton (1987,166) however, prefers to transform the garden into a miniature *paradisos*, the aristocratic game park of Hellenistic rulers, where a variety of exotic species were hunted.[39] Alternatively he sees (ibid,146) that the garden could represent provinces where animals were hunted for the amphitheatre. All these theories could have some foundation, for a variety of animals are represented in gardens. The savagery that is portrayed in many is reminiscent of a hunt of sorts, but the exotic species of prey (such as lions and tigers) could not really be said to be associated with the cult of Diana. Another point against this theory is that a number of wild and domesticated animals do appear together. They could have served to decorate the area, or if a message was implied, then animals calmed could collectively be said to recreate a setting where Orpheus charmed the beasts with his music. Domesticated animals, however, could add a certain rusticity to the scene and they might in fact recall a pastoral Arcadia. In this capacity they would then be linked to the rustic god Pan rather than Diana.

Apollo

The brother of Diana, is sometimes found in gardens,[40] perhaps because as Helios-Apollo he was associated with the sun, one of the elements necessary for plant growth. He was also considered the god of poetry and music, especially the lyre. In this capacity we see, in several gardens, figures who are prominent in some of his myths, such as the sculptural re-enactment of part of the musical contest with Marsyas. A gruesome example from the Gardens of Maecenas portrays the punishment of Marsyas: who is tied to a tree then flayed.[41] Companion pieces are a seated Apollo with lyre and a slave whetting his knife.[42] The tree reminds us of the outdoor setting, and the fact that Marsyas was a satyr (a being associated with woodlands), helps to link this contest to a garden environment. Another myth of Apollo, the slaying of Niobe's children also exists as garden sculpture, items of such a group were discovered in the Gardens of Sallust.[43]

Hercules

Hercules appears in the myth of Apollo, for they struggle for possession of the Delphic tripod, but his other labours are more relevant here, such as the apples in the Garden of the Hesperides. The *hortus* could recreate such mythical settings. The popular hero is often portrayed as a well built rustic character, usually nude or carrying his lionskin and club, and more often than not very intoxicated.[44]

Bacchus and his entourage

He was the popular god of wine, and the vine. Otherwise named Dionysus, he merged with Liber an Italic god of fertility. Dionysus was also the god of drama, which was performed at his festivals; therefore, we find representations of theatrical masks and musical instruments in gardens, for these become symbolic of his presence. Another attribute, the vine, could be seen covering pergolas to give shade to summer dining areas in gardens. The consumption of wine at such feasts is reflected by the inclusion in art of a wine cup,[45] urn, or a wineskin. Ivy, often grown in Roman gardens, was also associated with this deity, who was often shown crowned with ivy leaves and flowers, and sometimes bunches of grapes. Ivy was also used to make the head of the thyrsus carried by Bacchus, his revellers, or members of his *thiasos*. In fact all of the figures associated with his myth appear to be at home in a Roman garden, either singly or small groups.[46] We see Ariadne his consort,[47] Sileni,[48] Satyrs,[49] Fauns,[50] Pan,[51] Centaurs,[52] Maenads,[53] Bacchantes,[54] Nymphs and at a later date Silvanus[55] and Priapus, all of whom are creatures or beings associated with nature, woods or countryside. Animals linked to Bacchus are, dolphins (who represent the pirates who tried to abduct him), and a panther associated with the god's triumphs in India.

In statuary many of the male figures of his entourage are shown in various stages of inebriation. Satyrs and Sileni are often shown staggering and leaning on or carrying a wineskin, which is sometimes used as a fountain outlet. The water in this case would appear to represent wine.[56] Some examples from the large variety of forms in this group are illustrated in Pls.29 & 30. Many have been given a rocky base which gives them a rustic touch that matches their outdoor setting.

An assorted collection from this group, forming a Dionyisiac theme garden, seemed to be quite popular. This kind of statuary appears pleasant and is often humorous, perhaps even slightly irreverent, but is in keeping with the carefree attitudes of Bacchus himself. Gardens were places for recreation, or relaxation, where one could commune with nature growing all around; therefore a Bacchic theme could be highly suitable.

Muses

Are sometimes seen in gardens and further aspects of contemplation and inspiration,[57] they are also linked with Apollo. Varro (*RR*,111,5,10) possessed a Museion, a dwelling place of Muses, situated besides a stream, these structures however are connected to nymphaea.

Nymphs and River Gods

Nymphs, three of whom were entrusted to nurse the infant Dionysus, are associated with caves and clear spring water. Therefore they were ideally suited to be fountain figures. They are usually semi-clothed, and appear either standing or reclining. In the former they hold either an urn, or a scallop shell or bowl, from which pours water, here symbolic of a sacred spring[58] (as in fig.22). In the latter the urn, used as a fountain outlet, is at their side (see Pl.31). Reclining nymphs appear similar to personifications of rivers, such as the Nile or Tiber[59] but these are large rivers, and were more suited to public or imperial display. Whereas the nymph, being associated with naturally small sources of water, a mere trickle in some instances, is more suited for inclusion in a residential *hortus*, where a corner or wall could be utilized to form a cave-like niche or nymphaeum. Nevertheless, some of these structures contained other dionyisiac statuary.[60] Masks of fluvial deities or attendants, however, could be large or small and were therefore appropriate in private or public spheres.

Rustic genre (mortals)

In this group are peasants who are portrayed with a realism that enhances their rusticity. Examples are shepherds carrying young animals to market on their shoulders,[61] and men fishing,[62] or in the act of selling their catch (as in Pl.32). Small statue groups also exist, such as the fishing scene that once graced the courtyard of the Garden Houses at Ostia.[63] Also sculptural relief panels placed in gardens (see under *pinax*) often depict rustic or sacro-idyllic subjects. Rustic statuary could be seen as a desire to people an idealized landscape[64] or they could symbolize the 'fruits of their husbandry',[65] perhaps referring to sources of family income, through the land or sea.

These figures appear to be primarily ornamental, but because they do not refer specifically to a god some Romans, who may have needed to mask their religious beliefs (because of the threat of persecution), may have seen them as less pagan and therefore more acceptable for display in such households. A number of pagan iconographic details had infiltrated into Christian imagery and perhaps some of the pastoral statues, such as fish, sheep, or a shepherd could also be seen to represent Christ in the role of the Good Shepherd[66] (or alternatively Orpheus, to the Orphites), while fishermen could appear as fishers of men (the Apostles).

Ephebes, athletes, wrestlers etc

These are figures seen in association with bath buildings or land nearby, but when placed in the garden with philosopher herms (or statues) they create a theme where the garden could resemble the Athenian Academy, gymnasium, palaestra, or hippodrome,[67] where philosophers could commune with young men resting from their exercise training.[68] Large estates could contain several gardens, and afford areas of garden so termed, as well as specific statues to enhance a particular concept.[69]

Herms

Originally representing the Greek god Hermes, these were a very popular art-form in Roman gardens, as can be seen by the number present in Table. I. They consist of a bust of the god on a pillar-like shaft, some with feet at the base.[70] Many retain male organs which were customary on Greek herms. The shaft might incorporate a cross beam at the shoulder, originally to hold a cloak, but several Roman herms were carved already wearing some form of drapery (as in Pl.33). The type was adapted by the Romans into a means of displaying a portrait bust. Therefore we find famous and illustrious men portrayed, ranging from Greek philosophers,[71] historians, heroes, Hellenistic rulers or Roman Emperors and their wives, to idealized portraits of men or women.

Numerous deities were also represented in the form of a herm, e.g. Athene or Mars. The most popular of this group are Bacchic subjects. Members of his *thiasos* were shown singular or paired. Therefore we find double or janiform herms, where two busts facing outwards share the one shaft (see Pl.34 & fig.24). They often comprise a young and old Dionysus, or Bacchus and Ariadne. Others might show a Satyr paired with a Maenad, or a young Satyr paired with a Silenus. Like Janus, the two faces can present different aspects, here age or sex.

The large number of herms from Welschbillig (Wrede,1972) has enabled us to determine, in part, the range in existence in the 4th century AD and if they complete a particular sequence. The busts comprised those already cited, plus ones with provincial features, such as Africans, Asiatics with Phrygian caps, or Germans with long hair and a torque. In a number of instances a herm type was repeated elsewhere, in many cases as a mirror image. However, the presumed location of each herm has not revealed a pattern; they appear to have been placed around the pool in a random manner (see fig.26b).

Where herms were utilized as part of a decorative low wall, the shaft became the upright baluster, and the Herm head the finial (see fig.26a & Pl.7). We can see examples in frescoes, and reliefs.[72] Bronze versions survive from Lake Nemi (fig.26a). These were janiform, draped, with a bust of Silenus paired with a Satyr or Maenad. Several stone examples may be seen in museums, and are distinguished from normal Herms by beam slots for the wall on the shaft.[73]

Herms remained popular throughout, perhaps because of their versatility. They were a convenient way of displaying an illustrious image, partly because the bust was mounted on a simple shaft (decorated or plain) making it more cost effective than sculpture in the round. Also, if a statue fell and was unrepairable, all would not be lost, for the head could be mounted onto a shaft and would then continue service as a herm.

Oscilla

There are three types of *oscilla*, the circular form, small rectangular, peltae shaped and those in the form of a mask (see fig.27 & Pls.35 & 37). Most examples are of marble.[74] With the exception of mask like *oscilla*, they usually had a plain border around their rim, and are carved in low relief on both sides.[75] The subject matter depicted on *oscilla* is mostly confined to figures and motifs of the Bacchic *thiasos*.[76] However, we also see attributes of Venus.[77]

Oscilla are thought to have originated from the Greek practise of hanging trophies in a stoa, or on a tree[78] beside a shrine (these are seen in a number of ancient reliefs). On the other hand the pelta form being derived from a mythical shield carried by Amazons was a motif that was often used for decorative purposes, and so continues the mystic or mythical associations seen in many collections of garden sculpture. The peltae *oscilla* seem to have griffon head terminals on either side of the shield, and at the apex we usually find a palmette design from which the shield was suspended. The mask type are lightweight in that they are concave in form, have an open mouth, and holes drilled for the eyes.[79] *Oscilla* have been found in a number of provinces in the Empire.[80]

As can be seen in several frescoes, *oscilla* were usually suspended in some manner so that they could, as their name suggests, oscillate in a breeze (see fig.27 & Pl.37). They were generally positioned within the intercolumnations of a garden peristyle (as in fig.24) or an atrium.[81] Many *oscilla* were presumably broken on falling to the ground; for reconstructed examples often show a break radiating from the point where the iron hook for suspension had been drilled into the upper rim (as in Pl.35). Cords or wire attachments as far as I know have not survived, but in frescoes they show as either a straight white line (which I feel could be a cord or rod of metal) or as a decorative white attachment (perhaps a linked chain or again a metal rod fashioned into a bead and reel like design).

Rectangular *oscilla* appear very similar to *pinakes* and our evidence depends on whether there were fixtures for suspension or provision for mounting onto a post[82] (as is the case with a *pinax*). Both are depicted in frescoes (e.g.fig.27a & Pl.37) and basically the size determines its function, for if a relief panel was too large it would be too heavy to suspend above one's head.

Pinakes

Like the *oscilla* these were usually of marble and carved in low relief on both sides. They were mounted on top of a marble post that was often decorated with carvings, mostly of foliage such as trailing vine (see fig.28 & Pl.37). *Pinax* is a Greek word for a wooden board and stone examples do bear some resemblance, for they usually retain a rather thick outer frame. This is seen in frescoes and stone reliefs, where we may also note that *pinakes* are depicted in two ways.[83] One can see the normal *pinax* with its post embedded into the garden soil, and others placed higher, on top of a light portico-like framework or on a wall.[84]

Sundials

These need to be placed in an open sunny position to be able to read the time, and so the ideal place was in a garden or court. A simple method was to scratch a dial on a column of the peristyle.[85] Several free-standing examples have been discovered by excavation (eg.no.14 in fig.24). They are usually of stone, and have a dial inscribed on the concave semicircular surface. Some retain the triangular metal gnomon or pointer (see fig.29). Vitruvius (*De Arch*,IX,8,4) credits the invention of this type of sundial to Berosus the Chaldaean; Vitruvius then continues to name other forms, including the water clock invented by Ctesibius which he describes in detail. Varro (*RR*,III,5,17) describes a water clock functioning in his elaborate aviary/dining room, within the garden. Here the prevailing winds as well as the hours of day and night were shown. This he informs us is like the one in Athens.

Urns & Bowls

These ornamental objects are seen in numerous garden frescoes, where they are often used as the central focal point in a symmetrical composition (see figs.22-23 & Pls.37 & 39). Often birds are shown perched on the rim to drink water contained inside the bowl. This scene re-enacts a theme of doves representing souls drinking the water of everlasting life. The model was perhaps a Hellenistic one, made in mosaic by Sosus of Pergamon, which was widely acclaimed.[86] Several frescoes also depict water bubbling up from the centre of a bowl, indicating that many functioned as a fountain basin. Pliny (*Ep*,V,6,20) had a marble fountain basin in a courtyard garden, at Tusculum. However, he did not describe its appearance. In surviving examples such as inv.no.26 in the Gall Horti Lamiani, at the Conservatori Museum, Rome, I noted a central hole in the bowl to take plumbing.

The forms of garden urn are diverse. There are huge versions like the Warwick Vase, found at Tivoli, and small scale ones seen perched on top of walls or fences in frescoes. The stems and handles also vary greatly, from a tall, fine, twisted stem (in the fresco at the House of Neptune and Amphitrite at Herculaneum) to others which splay outwards at the base.

In the Auditorium of Maecenas the frescoes in the apse are of alternate designs, one showing a tall narrow urn, the other a wide brimmed shallow bowl (see fig.23). The variety seen in frescoes is reflected in life, confirming the usefulness of frescoes for comparative purposes. In a number of frescoes we can see that a sculptural figure is used as a support for the bowl above (e.g. centaurs or sphinxes, see fig.27a). In museums the range widens.[87]

Occasionally we see fountain bowls in the form of a rectangular table, with a shallow water basin on top (as in Pl.28).

Water Stairs

These are usually seen only in museums. A typical example is Pl.36. They are really an elaboration of the single waterstairs often seen in association with nymphaea. These decorative versions, however, are free-standing and therefore not confined to a niche positioned against a wall. Today one can be seen in situ, under a pergola, in the lower garden of the House of Loreius Tiburtinus, Pompeii. This type of ornament was also thought suitable to adorn and enliven a small area such as a lightwell in a house, for one is recorded (but today covered by soil) in the House of Apollo, Pompeii.[88]

The upper portion of these fountains contain a shallow water trough. Presumably a small fountain figure or fitting was placed over the central aperture, to give a jet of water or bubble effect above. Water pooling in the trough was then (as in Pl.36) directed, through holes at the sides, into scallop shells, from which it poured down a steep flight of steps.[89] The water then collected into another basin below. Most of the examples I have seen now have this part missing, like that in Pl.36.[90] Generally these fountains have a number of waterstair panels (Pl.36 has four) alternating with panels of relief sculpture.

Fountain outlets

Cicero (*Ad Frat*,III,2,3) mentions that his brother's fishpond had '*jets d'eau*', but unfortunately he does not specify which type. Many water outlet points would have been simple bronze nozzles, with no additional adornment, as at the House of the Water Jets at Conimbriga.[91] Sidonius Apollinaris (*Epist*,II,2,8) however, refers to a pool furnished with six water jets in the form of lion's heads. Water would have poured out of the open mouth of the lion. These were perhaps the most popular type, and examples have been discovered at Darenth in Britain[92] and elsewhere. A lioness or panther's head are also found. Another form, that of a dolphin, was widely used and are recorded at Ephesus and Pompeii.[93] Multiple jets could be obtained by perforating a bronze or stone item, such as a pine cone, with numerous holes. An example is B.M.inv.no.2579. Because of the transference of religious connotations pine cone fountains continued into use during the Christian era and may be seen in numerous Early Christian & Byzantine mosaics.[94] As previously mentioned lead pipework could be inserted into a fountain figure (either of stone or bronze) and water could be made to appear as if escaping from a vessel, or a creature's mouth.

Automata

Evidence for these is unfortunately confined to literary sources, such as Vitruvius, Athenaeus and Hero of Alexandria. Vitruvius (*De Arch*,X,7,4) confirms their existence, but as he views them to be frivolous, he advises us to consult the works of Ctesibius. Athenaeus (*Deipn*,V,198,f) describes a statue of Nysa in Ptolemy's carnival-like procession, that bore all the features of automata described in the *Pneumatics* of Hero of Alexandria (who was a pupil of Ctesibius). The statue of Nysa was said to rise automatically, then after a libation was given it would sit down. The addition of liquid would trigger the operation of a siphon which would force compressed air to activate the figure. In other experiments a number of siphons caused birds to sing a song, or figures to blow trumpets.[95]

As several of the inventions contained in this book require running water[96] I feel that many would have been placed in open areas, such as gardens. Experiment No.47 specifically requires the 'action of the sun's rays' to function, and further evidence which confirms my belief is found in the description of experiment no.14. Here Hero explains an ideal situation for such a contrivance, 'The figures of several different birds are arranged near a fountain, or in a cave, or in any place where there is running water'. As many of these figures were dependent on movable parts, such as an owl that turned, it is likely that they were made of bronze rather than stone. Once removed from its connecting pipework, siphons, and system of levers, its function would be less clear, and it would subsequently resemble an ordinary fountain outlet rather than an automaton, which might be the reason why none have been recorded. Morton (1970,24) mentions that a working copy of Hero's owl fountain[97] (see fig.30) was installed in the Renaissance gardens of the Villa d'Este at Rome,[98] proving that such artifices were feasible.

NOTES TO CHAPTER SIX

1. Cato (*De Agri*.143,2) mentions that the Matrona was responsible for growing and placing flowers on altars.
2. Pliny,*NH*,21,8.
3. However, the dry conditions in Egypt is conducive to good preservation, as can be seen in B.M.inv.no. GR.1890.5-19.7, which was made with everlasting flowers, *Helichrysum Stoechas (L.)*, for funerary purposes in this case.
4. Cicero (*Ad. Fratrem*,III,1,5) has living ivy swags decorating colonnade and statues. Athenaeus (*Deipn*,XV,674f) and Pliny (*NH*,21f) detail different types of garland or chaplets and the plants used to make them.
5. Virgil (*Eclog*,VII,30&34) and Tibullus (I,11/18) provide examples of rustic shrines, while Martial (III,19,1) informs us that effigies of wild beasts (including a bear) adorned a plane grove in a public park at Rome. A statue of a bear, but perhaps not the same one, may be seen in the Getty Museum inv.no.72AA-125 (Vermeule,1981, no.121).
6. The area serves as a model; for it also appears fairly representative of other periods. Many pieces seem to remain popular throughout, and are the result of centuries of iconographic development. However, owing to the limits of this present study, aspects of art history

	must be neglected. I am here more concerned with how certain items are relevant to gardens.
7	This is to safeguard them from theft, but unfortunately they are mostly out of sight, for the museum at Pompeii is not open to the public, including myself.
8	Appleton,1987,172,fig.58.
9	e.g. at the Canopus of Hadrian's Villa at Tivoli.
10	De Caro,1987,94. Fig.5 is based on De Caro's fig.2, which locates sculpture found at Oplontis, and reveals their relationship between principal rooms and gardens. Evidence of plant material was supplied by Jashemski, (1993,plan.131).
11	Neudecker (1988,234) notes that there may have been a 'Hermgalerie' in a garden at the Villa of Cassius, Tivoli. These herms may also have been used to line pathways.
12	This is believed to have been the case in the Canopus area at Hadrian's Villa, Tivoli (Aurigemma,1971,31).
13	e.g. Cicero specified that he desired subjects suitable for a gymnasium and *xystus* (*Ad.Att*,I,8), plus an Academy (ibid,I,9), for which Muses were thought more suitable than Baccantes (*Ad. Fam*,VII,23).
14	Kapossy (1969) provides a catalogue of fountain figures (including monumental) which shows the diversity of subjects and how widespread they are throughout the Empire.
15	*JRA*,Vol.4,1991,259.
16	This recreated the cave at Lourdes, where the Virgin Mary appeared to St Bernadette, as at the convent of the Sisters of the Ascension in Rome.
17	Flora and Pomona appear to merge into the Venus figure, and therefore are under-represented in gardens. However, with the introduction of eastern cults we see the inclusion of figures or the attributes of Isis, Osiris, and Bes, also Attis and Orpheus are sometimes encountered.
18	Perhaps the earliest known inscription naming altars within a sacred enclosure is that of the Agnone tablet of circa 250BC (now in the B.M., inv.no.Br.888,1873.8-20.119) which names several divinities connected with agriculture, including Ceres, Proserpina, Rain, Nymphs, Hercules, Genita, Flora and possibly Venus (Bonfante,1990,57).
19	The *S.H.A.* (*Marcus Ant*.VI,9) mentions a shrine of Apollo in the garden belonging to the mother of Marcus. In the House of the Golden Cupids, Pompeii, there were two altars/shrines; a lararium on one side of the peristyle, and a painting on the eastern corner wall of the peristyle showing an altar between two large snakes (which were believed to ward off evil).
20	Jashemski,1979,134.
21	Several have been found in Pompeii, e.g. (Pompeii,VI,ix,6) and (Pompeii,I,xi,12), respectively Jashemski,1993,139 & 52.
22	As shown by an inscription on a vase from Pompeii (Jashemski,1979,124). Varro (*RR*,I,6), and Pliny (*NH*,IXX,50) also mention that Venus protected the garden, a role that continued even with the introduction of pleasure gardens.
23	Pliny (*NH*,XXXVI,4,16) mentions a statue of Venus at Rome known as 'Aphrodite of the gardens'.
24	Because of her associations with water, Hill (1981,93,fig.16) believes that the half figure of the Venus of Benghazi was placed to appear rising out of a pool. This type, plus the crouching Venus, would look very effective with their image reflected in water. Hill (ibid.fig.17/18) shows that this statue was a fountain figure, and the mouth of an accompanying dolphin served as the water spout.
25	A large fish, serving as a fountain outlet, has recently come to light at Tockenham in Britain (Harding & Lewis, forthcomming,fig.5).
26	A scallop shell in particular, for Venus is often depicted emerging from such a shell. Larger creatures such as Nereids, Tritons, Hippocamps, etc, are usually seen in association with large water features e.g. the Nereids of Formia in Naples National Museum (Maiuri,1959,25).
27	Bacchus was one of the deities named in the Vigil of Venus as accompanying Ceres, Nymphs, Eros, Diana, Apollo and the Graces (*Per.Ven*.28). All have links to Venus through myth; therefore their inclusion in a garden could form a theme.
28	Daremberg & Saglio,1900,645.
29	e.g. Martial,*Ep*,VI,73.
30	Horace,*Sat*,VIII,6/7.
31	Where his member served as a fountain outlet (Clarke,1991,210/211).
32	e.g. from Barcelona (Bellido,1949,fig.101). There is also a large example in Sousse Museum from Ain Jelloula.
33	Luxorius (*Anth.Lat*.61) mentions a fountain statue of Cupid in a late Roman garden in North Africa. In poem 46 he is shown to be at home in the garden with Diana, Nymphs, Venus and the Muses. This grouping of deities is similar to that in the Virgil of Venus mentioned above, and their presence helps to confirm their suitability for a sculptural metamorphosis.
34	e.g. B.M.inv.no.1673 where he is stringing a bow, and inv.no.1678, from Tarsus, which shows him sleeping. The latter was also a fountain figure. the outlet being in an overturned urn. In a similar example from Nea Paphos, Cyprus, a shell appears to serve as a water outlet; however, Hunt (1990,111) does not mention the statue's function.
35	e.g. Bardo Museum inv.no.C58, from Uthina.
36	In the Conservatori Museum Rome.
37	A second association is formed through Cupid who was one of their children. Martial (X,92) mentions the existence of Mars at Nomentum, although the god may have been present on this occasion because he was also the patron of Martial's birth month.
38	As in the Boar & Hounds from the House of the Citharist (Pompeii,I,iv,5/25) now in Naples Mus.inv.nos.4899/4901.
39	A number of wall paintings depict *paradisoi* hunt scenes, with boar hunting as well as more exotic species such as lions etc. Varro (*RR*,III,12;&13,2) mentions friends (such as Hortensius) who owned a game enclosure in their domain.
40	Virgil (*Eclog*.III,62) refers to the god's presence 'my garden is Apollo's seat', and Pliny (*NH*,XXVI,4,36) mentions the existence of a statue of Apollo in the Gardens of Servillius at Rome (although the latter example was probably an exceptionally fine one that was worth noting).
41	This is now in the Conservatori Museum, Rome. It has been particularly well executed; for the sculptor utilized marble with red veins which appears to portray raw flesh after having been flayed.
42	A slave from such a grouping was found in the *Horti Luculliani*, and is now in Florence Museum (Lanciani,1897,421). The scene is recounted by

43 Philostratus the younger (*Imagines*,2) and is seen in a relief on a Christian sarcophagus from Szekzard (Lengyel & Radan,1980,pl.cxl). Such scenes could have inspired similar sculptural groupings.
43 e.g. Therme Museum inv.no.72274, which was found in the Gardens of Sallust, Rome.
44 As in the House of the Stags, Herculaneum,inv.no.525.
45 A rhyton was also used, a large example was found in the Horti Maecenas, Rome, now in the Conservatori Museum.
46 Including symplegmata, of Satyrs and Maenades or Hermophrodite (e.g. Liverpool Museum,inv.no.Ince.75).
47 An example exists in the Vatican, Galleria delle statue (Amelung,1912,fig.3). Ariadne is usually shown recumbent, and is differentiated from reclining nymphs by holding her right arm over her head, so that she appears to be awakening. This statue re-enacts the myth of her abandonment and subsequent encounter with Dionysus.
48 Virgil (*Eclogues*,VI,14f) mentions a rather drunken Silenus, still holding his wine cup, reclining in a grotto-like cave. This image was partially recreated in garden frescoes such as at the House of Romulus and Remus (fig.22).
49 Pliny (*NH*,XIX,19,50) informs us that 'Only in gardens and the Forum do we see statues of Satyrs dedicated as a charm against the sorcery of the envious', which partly explains their popularity as suitable subjects for gardens. Propertius (*Eleg*,II,32,14) recalls that in Pompey's portico garden, at Rome, there was a reclining fountain figure of a Satyr called Maro.
50 A mirror image pair, with wineskins forming fountains, were found at the Villa Quintili, Rome, and are now in the Vatican, Museum Braccio Nuovo,inv.no.2277.
51 This bestial, pastoral god originated in Arcadia, and became symbolic of the Roman view of this place as a Utopia. He was known for playing tricks, and is often seen in the company of Satyrs or Nymphs. This popular god, strongly associated with nature, could be symbolized by a set of pan pipes.
52 Creatures (half horse, half man) who are often shown pulling the triumphant chariot of Bacchus. They are seen in frescoes and sculptural form at Oplontis (Jashemski,1979.figs.466 & 470).
53 They are often depicted in reliefs, e.g. on the reverse of an *oscilla* in the Vatican, Cortille Oct.inv.no.1019. In statuary form a seated Maenad exists in Brussels Museum,inv.no.A 1142. She was part of a group (with a satyr) known as 'the invitation to the dance'.
54 Maenads and Baccantes are usually shown with wild flowing hair and swirling draperies, as if in a dance. Baccantes, more often found in reliefs, are mostly shown carrying parts of dismembered animals as a reminder of their role in Dionyisiac excesses.
55 Silvanus was the ancient Roman god of woodlands. Later he appears to join the Greek woodland throng of Satyrs. His presence in gardens also indicates that he retained some influences in areas of garden covered by trees.
56 Kapossy (1969,74) draws our attention to the symbolic meaning of water pouring from different types of fountains.
57 Two were found at the House of Loreius Tiburtinus, Pompeii (Jashemski,1993,81).
58 As in the example from Crete, now in Istanbul Museum, inv.no.7T (height approx.1.10m).
59 Both of the River gods are represented at Hadrian's Villa, Tivoli, where they had been positioned in front of the Canopus.
60 e.g. in the House of M.Lucretius (see fig.25 statue no.1).
61 e.g. The old peasant with a lamb, found in the Horti Lamiani, Rome, now in the Conservatori Museum, Gall. Horti Lamiani, inv.no.8.
62 A small bronze fisherman is shown in Pl.23.
63 Ostia Museum,inv.no.1110.
64 As in the famous paintings of *topia* by Studius described by Pliny (*NH*,XXXV,37,116/7).
65 As described in paintings seen by Philostratus the Elder (*Imagines*,II,17).
66 A small shepherd (0.69m) from the Villa del Pastore, now in Stabiae Museum dates to pre AD79. The type remained popular and at a later date is found at Ostia in the Aula Bon Pastore (Appelton,1987,fig.29).
67 Cicero,*Ad.Att*.I,9; & 1,10.
68 Cicero's friends exclaim how part of a garden at Tusculum was suggestive of the shady haunt of Socrates (*De Oratore*,I,7,28).
69 An example of this category is the mirror image pair of bronze wrestlers from the Villa of the Papyri, Herculaneum, now in Naples National Museum, inv.nos.5625 & 5627.
70 As in examples found at the Villa of Cassius, Rome (Neudecker,1988,Taf.16) which are now in the Vatican Museum.
71 These were particularly admired by Cicero who negotiated for herms of bronze (*Ad. Att*.I,8).
72 e.g. A fresco from Nis (Borsch-Supan,1967,fig.82), and a relief in the Hippodrome at Istanbul.
73 Slots appear on either side of the shaft, or one side only perhaps indicating that this herm was placed beside an entrance passage. Alternatively slots may have been cut into the side and front part of the shaft revealing that this particular herm shaft occupied a corner position in the wall, and that the wall changed direction (e.g. Therme Museum, Rome, inv.no.13-V20; or Vatican, Chiaramonti Museum, inv.no.19 which portrayed a Satyr with a lionskin draped over his shoulder).
74 However, at New Paphos in Cyprus, a pair of terracotta masks have been found in the House of Dionysos (Karageorghis,98, 1974,892/3.fig.78). I believe that these may have been *oscilla*.
75 However, one face is sometimes carved in high relief and the reverse in low relief (e.g. B.M.inv.no.2456).
76 Such as Silenus, Faunus, Pan, a Satyr or Maenad, an altar, theatre masks, a *tympanum, pedum*, etc.
77 e.g. Dolphins, sea monsters, or hares/rabbits.
78 The hanging of Bacchic objects in trees is mentioned by Virgil (*Georgics*,II,388/389).
79 The suspension point is usually at the top of the head. They are shown hanging between columns in fig.24. Theatre masks are fairly common, but there are masks of maenads or satyrs.
80 Circular & rectangular *oscilla* were recorded by (Pailler,1969,figs.4/lO) in France. Bellido (1949, figs.436; 440/1) lists circular & *peltae* shaped examples in Spain. A circular oscilla was found at a villa at Ramla Bay in Gozo (Ashby,1915,74). They were also present in North Africa (Baradez,1952,41&90). This shows that their use was widespread.

81	As in the House of the Relief of Telephus at Herculaneum where they are still in situ.
82	A circular *oscillum* from Bolsena was found to have evidence for both but, as Pailler (1969,632) suggests, after it fell it was perhaps reused by inserting it into a horizontal surface, presumably a post in the manner of a *pinax*. Alternatively *oscilla* could have been placed on a wall, but most show no traces of mortar used to secure them into such a position.
83	Respectively at the House of the Fruit Orchard (Pompeii,I,ix,5) (Jashemski,1993,fig.363); and in the relief panel of Bacchus visiting the house of a mortal (B.M.inv.no.2190).
84	Decorative reliefs for insertion into a wall were among the requests made by Cicero (*Ad Att*,6,3-4). Examples of this type have been discovered in the peristyle of the House of the Golden Cupids, Pompeii (Jashemski,1993,163).
85	As at Pompeii,VII,iv,57 (Jashemski,1979,112).
86	Pliny,*NH*.XXVI,184.
87	e. g. Vatican Museum, Gall.Candelabri, inv.no.2495 which has four Sileni (each carrying wineskins) holding up a large shallow dished bowl.
88	Pompeii,VI,vii,23 (Richardson,1988,334). A larger pyramidal example, comprising waterstairs on the four corners and mosaic panels of fishing scenes between, survives at Herssonisos, Crete. It was found in a courtyard 'of a building of unknown function' (Sanders,1982,146), the size of which has not been given, presumably this courtyard may have been planned as a form of garden, either domestic or public.
89	An example from Tarracena uses bivalve shells (Bellido,1949, fig.432).
90	Two exceptions are the example from Tarracena (*op.cit.*), and the dog fountain in the B.M.inv.no.2536 which both appear to sit in a much wider shallow square basin, which was provided with an overflow outlet at one corner.
91	Alarcão & Etienne,1981,fig.15.
92	Zeepvat,1988,18.
93	Erdemgil,1989,fig.116; and Jashemski,1993,45 respectively. Another bronze dolphin from Constantinople is now in the B.M.inv.no.1922. A stone dolphin, although believed part of a statue group, was used in the *natatio* of the Baths at Caerleon (Knight,1994,21). Other forms include a raven found at Stabiae (Jashemski,1979,fig.531), and a recent find from Tockenham, Britain, of a stone outlet in the form of a moray eel, (Harding & Lewis, forthcomming, fig.5).
94	An example depicted in a floor mosaic comes from Bordeaux in France and has been dated to the 5th-6th century AD (Balmelle,1994,fig.5). The pine cone outlet is also seen in the mosaic Annunciation scene on the wall of the Byzantine church of the Dormition at Daphni (Underwood,1975,fig.7).
95	Hero,*Pneumatics*,44 & 49.
96	Ibid.28.
97	Hero,*Pneumatics*,15.
98	Prior to AD1580, when Montaigne observed it functioning.

CHAPTER SEVEN: FLORA & FAUNA IN GARDENS

If we wished to recreate a Roman garden we would need to stock the area with plants that would have been available at that time. There was not such a wide range of species and hybrids as there is today; for instance, we have in our gardens plants from the New World, the Antipodes, and Japan; lands which were unknown to the Romans. Plants represented in Roman gardens were, therefore, mainly those originating from provinces bordering the Mediterranean Sea. Plant selection and hybridization was beginning to take place but was in some ways still in its infancy. In general we find that species were only one step removed from wild varieties.

Ancient authors did not have a Linnaean system of botanical nomenclature, and therefore some terms are slightly ambiguous, and this renders a modern identification of a number of ancient Roman plants somewhat difficult. However, Pliny the Elder in his *Natural History* (which often included information compiled by Theophrastus and others) identifies and describes a wide range of plants. His descriptions help to clarify which variety or species is referred to, and they reveal that plants were mostly identified by the colour and shape of a flower, rather than by the structure of the whole plant and its seeds. This can be seen in the varieties listed under rose. Pliny includes a flower that 'springs from a stem like that of the mallow' (*N.H*.XXI,10,19). This was not the Hollyhock (*Althaea rosea(L.)*) for this is named elsewhere, so I feel that perhaps it may be a form of Lavatera or Oleander. The single flowered peony, or alternatively the rock-rose, may also have been considered a rose, for non-scented varieties are mentioned by Pliny.[1] We therefore find that a number of species are sometimes included under one given name; e.g. laurel[2] which appears to include the Bay (*Laurus nobilis L.*), the *Viburnum tinus L.*, Butcher's Broom (*Ruscus aculeatus L.*), a 'gelded laurel' which could tolerate considerable shade (this may be the cherry laurel (*Prunus laurocerasus L.*), and a crinkly black leaved variety from Cyprus, which so far remains unidentified.

The modern system of classification devised by Linnaeus in AD1737 solved the obstacle of each country having a different word for almost every plant; by using Latin the Linnaean nomenclature would become universal. Wherever possible he used the existing Ancient Roman Latin names,[3] which in itself is a testament of the ongoing dissemination of species that Roman horticulturists had set in motion. In the case of the Viburnum mentioned above, which Pliny (*N.H*,XV,39,128) records as perhaps being a 'separate kind of tree' because of its blue berries, its other name (*tinus*) was retained by Linnaeus. However, some ancient plant names, such as the *Rhododendron* (*N.H.*,XVI,33,79), are not as we imagine; for this example is commonly believed to have been the Oleander (at other times it is called a 'rose-laurel' by the translator).[4]

Flowers are not generally mentioned in the context of early forms of Roman gardens, for as previously mentioned, the plants represented would have been ones associated with an orchard and/or a vegetable plot. One of the exceptions is that of the poppy, the seeds of which were used in bread making. A reference in Pliny (*N.H*.XIX,53,168/9) shows that these flowers were grown in gardens at least as early as the 6th century BC when Tarquinius who was armed with a cane 'knocked off the heads of the tallest poppies in his garden'. For other plants Pliny the Elder, and the agriculturalists, mention the species grown and give advice on their culture. Cato (*De Agri*,CLVI) says that the cabbage 'surpasses all other vegetables' and he shows that over a dozen ailments could be cured by means of ingestion, infusion or application.[5] Apart from the cabbage the only other vegetable he mentions is asparagus.[6] Pliny (*N.H*,XIX,19,58) informs us that garden produce was mainly of the salad variety, for these required little cooking, thereby saving fuel, and because they could be grown throughout the year (if well watered) would remain fresh when needed. Species grown would include herbs used for seasoning, e.g. the berries of myrtle were used as a form of pepper before eastern spices were generally available.[7] To establish which culinary vegetables and fruits were available during the Roman period, and which were grown in Roman *horti* I have taken data from Pliny the Elder (this remains our most comprehensive source) and compiled a table in Appendix III. A list of plants which he mentions were grown in Kitchen gardens appears under the heading of their usage: e.g. Culinary. This list includes species used for their seed, root or leaves.

The Romans of the Republican era and early Empire were essentially of a practical nature and therefore plants grown in a *hortus*, other than culinary ones, were usually those which served a particular purpose. Some species were used in the preparation of medicines. Ailments and homeopathic cures are detailed by Pliny in book XX. Many show that by either internal or external application a cure could be effected. An example is Mustard, which Pliny (ibid,XX,87) shows was used to cure snake bite, mushroom poisoning, tooth-ache, stomach ailments, eased asthmatics and epileptics, and soothed bruises and sprains.

Other plants were utilized to make cordials or wines;[8] many recipes contain a number of ingredients. Pliny, and others, also include a section on species planted specially to provide nectar, food for bees. The production of honey was highly regarded by the Romans, who used it as a sweetener (sugar was not yet available), and because of its value Varro (*RR*,III,16,12/15) advises placing hives near the villa for protection. He adds that 'some people place the apiary actually in the portico of the villa'.[9] Palladius (I,144) mentions that the *hortus*, should be placed in such a position that flying chaff and straw from a threshing ground would not blow onto plants; for flowers, buds, and tree blossom could be ruined. These were vital to provide nectar for bees to make honey, and also the bees would ensure a good rate of pollination for the production of fruit and seed, for consumption this year and to provide seeds for next years vegetable and herb harvest.

In the area where bees are kept Palladius (I,147) advises his readers to 'plant trees on the north side and bushes all about'. The trees would protect the bees from strong winds, which they disliked, and bushes such as thyme (that all authors claim is the best for bees) would ensure a ready food supply for them. Columella (*RR*,IX,6) shows that to ensure the good health of bees it is wise to include nearby species which they could use as a form of medicine, such as the trefoil; he also included rosemary. The latter herb is not mentioned as a garden plant by Pliny,[10] which is unusual, but also highlights that the list in appendix III may not be exhaustive, for this plant is also known to have an ornamental value.[11]

Scented foliage and flowers, from trees and herbaceous plants, were highly esteemed. At first they were used as a means of freshening the air indoors, and later with the advent of luxury goods for the making of perfumes and scented oils. Fragrant parts of plants were boiled down and then mixed with oil obtained from a number of sources, e.g. either olives, myrtle, cypress, or terebinth-resin. Salt and gum was added to preserve the mixture and to stop evaporation.[12] Scented oils were possibly made on a domestic basis, but the majority of perfumes would have been manufactured from commercially grown plants.

Many plants, however, owe their inclusion into a garden to the fact that they were necessary for making garlands, wreaths, and later for chaplets. Varieties used for this purpose are listed in appendix III. In chapter six we saw that it was the duty of the matrona to grow flowers for garlands to hang by places of worship.[13] In frescoes and reliefs swags of garlands can be seen decorating walls and spaces between columns of a peristyle, and may have originally only been used on festive occasions (including birthdays). See fig.34a & in the upper zone of Pl.37.

The components of these long garlands would perhaps have been the plentiful long tendrils of ivy or the vine, interwoven with seasonal foliage and flowering plants. Some illustrations include fruits in garlands. These perhaps may represent offerings at an altar, or belong to a funerary context, but would not really be suitable for suspending above a walkway!

Shorter garland/wreaths and chaplets for wearing on feast days and at banquets were, on the other hand, more inclined to contain scented plants, and otherwise more delicate species. At first *coronari* (crowns or chaplets) were honorific, and were composed of myrtle or the laurel we call bay; these shrubs have scented foliage and therefore they must have also been pleasant to wear. In the earlier days, Pliny (*NH*,XXI,6,8,) says at least up to the 2nd Punic War, one of the laws of the Twelve Tables controlled the wearing of *coronari*, but later this rule was relaxed and decorative chaplets were more frequently worn. Sources indicate that chaplets and garlands could be formed by linking chains of flowers; or by stitching, coiling, plaiting or weaving[14] together several stems of plants or young pliant branches of shrubs. Theophrastus (V,6,2) informs us that there was a framework or 'hoop' of flexible wood (he mentions mulberry or fig), and this would have prevented an untimely disintegration of a garland or chaplet. Athenaeus (*Deipn*,XV,677f) mentions a number of named types of floral crown.[15] He also says that for a banquet one made of ivy would soothe a sore head, whereas one of gillyflowers[16] (perhaps meaning stocks, carnation/pink or wallflower) would be too strongly scented and would oppress the senses. Decorative flowers and foliage were united together. When the seasons were unfavourable for the production of flowers garlands were made with dried flowers, or dyed flakes of horn.[17]

Horace (*Odes*,II,7,24) refers to the earlier practice of having myrtle or pliant parsley garlands.[18] However those made with violets or roses came to be the most popular of all.[19] Several mosaics depict garlands made of roses. One from Thuburbo-Maius[20] has patterns made with sprays of roses, and garlands are used to frame the figurative panels. In mosaics depicting the seasons, spring is often shown beside a scene of rose gatherers;[21] and at the Piazza Armerina a mosaic shows young girls both gathering roses and making the garlands[22] (see fig.31). The *coronariae* tie one end of the garland to a branch of a tree, and while seated on a basket they fix on the flower heads.[23] Large rose coloured terminal flowers were placed at either end of the line of roses, with loose ribbon beyond to tie the garland round the neck. Pliny (*N.H.*XXI,10,18) confirms the image we see in frescoes and mosaic, when he says that a *centifolia* a 'cabbage' type of double rose, is placed at either end.

Pliny also refers to plant species used in gardens for decorative purposes, *opus topiarium*. Several plants in this category (listed in appendix III) do not have any special benefit to man, other than a pleasing appearance, but were nevertheless considered worthwhile. An example is the date palm which was able to grow in Italy, but was usually stunted and would not fruit.[24] Acanthus has a statuesque appearance and was highly valued. The Romans appear to have preferred to plant the 'smooth' leaved form.[25] As with periwinkle it was used as a ground covering plant on banks, borders, or in the case of the latter where 'other flowers fail'.[26] Perhaps this means in dry shady conditions found under trees. In general many of the species grown in decorative Roman gardens were evergreen, and the seasonal flowering forms would have relieved the scene. Contrasting foliage and grey leaved varieties such as southernwood[27] were also used, however. Pliny mentions a silver-leaved shrub called 'Jupiter's Beard' that was clipped into a round bushy shape,[28] this I have taken to be *Anthyllis barba-Jovis L.* which also has attractive clusters of yellow pea-like flowers. The evergreen bay-laurel and myrtle were particularly favoured, for they had scented foliage and could be clipped to make chaplets when needed. It is recorded that on some estates large areas were converted into groves of these shrubs.[29] Box has an pungent smell but was hardy, and could stand the constant trimming required in topiary work.

Of the decorative trees, we hear of the pitch-pine and cypress which were also clipped into various shapes.[30] The yew, however, was not utilized for it was highly poisonous. References indicate that people liked to sit beneath the shade of a tree; in the case of the yew it was thought this could be fatal.[31] Trees described as having 'an exuberance of spreading shady branches',[32] 'often leaping across to the neighbouring mansions',[33] were particularly useful. The plane was highly esteemed for this capacity, and also provided illusions of the plane groves in the Greek Academy at Athens. It was brought to Rome by way of Sicily and Regium, and its widespread use was censured by some[34] as a worthless unproductive tree as opposed to useful species providing nuts/fruit. In contrast the prized lotus or nettle tree (*Celtis australis* L.), six of which grew in the Palatine garden of Crassus,[35] furnished small edible fruits (somewhat like cherries). These graceful deciduous trees belong to the Elm family. Pliny, referring to these remarks that although 'no shady foliage is more short-lived,...No trees have bark that is more agreeable or attractive to look at.'[36] Other species that were described as being a 'particularly good decoration for terraces'[37] were introductions to Rome (c.AD23); the tuber-apple from Syria, and the jujube from Africa, which produces small edible berry-like fruits. The Pontic cherry was brought to Rome by Lucullus c.60BC and was widely acclaimed, so much so that it was introduced to other provinces; varieties were grown in Germany and Belgium, and are recorded as being established in Britain by AD46.[38]

Plants were sought from far and wide to extend the flowering or fruiting seasons, especially for the rose.[39] Pliny (*N.H.*XXI,10,16/7) mentions that there are roses, with five, twelve, or a hundred petals; some with a fiery colour, others less so, or white. Pl.37 shows that a *versicolor* form may have existed.[40] In fact a variety of red, and pink forms of rose appear in Roman paintings.

Frescoes used as confirmation of plant species

Literary evidence of species grown in gardens is complemented by their contemporary depiction in frescoes. Some frescoes were painted in a primitive manner and details of plants are simplified,[41] others like those in Pls.37 & 38 show such meticulous draughtsmanship that in many cases positive identification and analysis is possible. Unfortunately many are now quite faded or lost altogether; therefore drawings were also consulted. However, caution is needed for art work is not always such an authentic witness, e.g. the two paintings, executed by different artists, of a fresco now lost at the House of Orpheus, Pompeii, appear to differ on a number of points.[42]

It is difficult to say if the verdant scenes represent a window whereby we can look into an actual Roman garden, or if these were an idealized vision of a sacro-idyllic scene. The fact that plant species are shown flowering and fruiting at the same time makes one suspect that an idyllic garden to recall that of Alcinous may be implied. However, statuary added to these scenes returns one to reality, and because of the position of these paintings, which are mostly on walls behind an actual *viridarium*, I feel that they do imply some elements of a true Roman garden.[43] The addition of fences in the foreground, which often form a border in such depictions, allows us to visualise the garden continuing beyond (in the manner of trompe l'oeil works of art).

Small plants are shown to the fore, and shrubs/trees fill the background, often with a blue sky beyond. Some bushes are treated in a more distinguishable manner, with individual leaves and flowers highlighting a selective number of plants; others are less clearly defined, and a green haze between indicates, generally, a continuance of the shrubberies. The most common shrubs depicted are: laurel, myrtle, oleander and viburnum. Laurel and myrtle look fairly similar, but can be identified by their characteristic leaf pattern; laurel being alternate, and myrtle opposite. The former also has red berries, whereas the latter has black. Box would appear as a compact version of myrtle, whereas Oleander is shown with a closer leaf density, slender willow-like leaves and pink flowers.

Of the trees, the most common appears to be pine or cypress. In many fresco panels a large, or particularly fine tree was sited in a central position, as can be seen in fig.23 & Pl.38 where the pine tree is flanked by laurels. In the larger fresco from the House of Livia, at Primaporta, Rome (Pl.38) the central tree is highlighted by a recess in the decorative wall, and fruit trees were the main accompaniment. Fruit trees were less common in frescoes, but a variety are shown in one house in Pompeii, thus providing its name (the House of the Fruit Orchard). Species depicted were: apple, cherry, fig, lemon, pear, yellow and blue plums, and a peach or pomegranate.[44] In the now quite faded fresco at the House of Adonis, Pompeii the relatively darker pigment used to paint pomegranate fruits helps to locate the position of the tree.

Towards the centre of this composition you can only just discern a madonna lily. The lily was considered next in favour after the rose,[45] and was highly acclaimed for the purity of its white flower and for its perfume. Another variety, the red martagon lily also appears in some paintings. a possible example may be seen at Oplontis, Pl.40.

At the House of the Marine Venus (see Pl.39) the plants are not so accurately drawn, but in the large garden painting on the right of the rear wall there are narrow elongated bushes of myrtle and oleander in flower, roses, and a grey-green bush with feathery foliage, which may be southernwood (although this does not appear in Jashemski's table of plants represented in Pompeian frescoes (1993,Append.III,405).

Plants in the foreground were mostly low growing varieties, as can be seen in Pls.37 & 38. They include plants with daisy-like flowers, ivy, lily, poppy, and rose. Unfortunately the violet, which was much admired by the Romans, is not normally found, perhaps because their ground hugging form would be difficult to reproduce successfully amongst larger herbaceous plants. In addition, sources suggest that there may have been a habit of having separate beds for these plants,[46] and therefore they would belong elsewhere. Large garden scenes appear in the so-called third Pompeian style, sometimes covering the whole wall, or confined to the middle zone. A painted fence could form the dado, but at other times there is a clearly delineated dado zone. In many third style frescoes this dado was often decorated by low growing plants. Low garden walls (*plutei*) were treated in a similar manner and species were usually positioned in individual groups composed mostly of clumps of grasses or herbaceous varieties. An example is Pl.41 which depicts an

Acanthus mollis L. and hart's-tongue fern. Several plants appear to be indistinguishable, having grass-like leaves with tall stems of daisy-like flowers, and may well be the product of the artist's imagination rather than a life-like study. However, some could represent a form of plantain, or perhaps the cynoglossum (a member of the borage family) which is recorded as a garden plant by Pliny.[47]

Ivy and smilax often appear in art.[48] The latter has a similar leaf shape, but has many small thorns and corkscrew tendrils. Ivy is well recorded as a plant used for decorative purposes in gardens, to grow up trees and in the manner of garlands link tree to tree.[49] Others were, as Cicero describes, carefully arranged to drape over statues.[50] Pliny (*N.H*,XVI,62,149) shows that there were a number of different forms of ivy; green, white,[51] and one with a variegated leaf called Thracian ivy. He also mentions that some 'differ in the arrangement of their markings.' A variegated form is depicted in the foreground of Pl.37; this type is less commonly painted than ivy which has been trained to grow around a supporting cane, thus forming a mound. Ivy mounds depicted in frescoes are usually found in the dado zone, and can be seen at the House of Ceii, or the House of the Vettii, Pompeii. Ivy has actually been planted, and trained in this manner in a number of recreated gardens at Pompeii, although many are now quite overgrown (e. g. House of the Golden Cupids, Ancora Nera, and Julia Felix).

Some species in gardens were considered as harmful,[52] e.g. the oleander and the strawberry tree (*Arbutus*). Their inclusion into the garden therefore indicates their decorative value was considered higher than their utilitarian properties although the latter was noted as providing fruits that were good food for birds.

Birds of all kinds are shown in frescoes. This was not just a device to enliven the painting, but it appears that birds were encouraged to enter gardens. Romans enjoyed the pleasant sight and sound of these multi-hued creatures; some, especially singing or talking birds, were turned into pets.[53] The peacock features in many frescoes, partly for their ornamental value and partly because they were regarded as an exotic introduction to Rome. Varro (*RR*,III,6,6) informs us that Q.Hortensius had created a precedent by serving peacock meat at a banquet, and thereafter they were considered a delicacy. Likewise small birds were also thought food to eat. Therefore cages or aviaries (*ornithones*) could be both decorative and profitable, and would be found in some part of the garden or grounds of an estate. A bird cage is depicted sitting atop of the low wall in one of the frescoes at the House of Livia;[54] they are also shown in some mosaics.[55]

Unfortunately these birdcages do not survive archaeologically, for they were usually made of wood, and or, wicker work.[56] However, there is more evidence for aviaries. A circular one is believed to have existed at Pompeii (VII,vii,16),[57] and perches in the form of brackets fixed to walls or columns may indicate that part of a peristyle could be utilized as an aviary. The netting which would have been of hemp, would not survive, but perches might, as at the House of the Dioscuri, Pompeii.[58]

Pigeons and doves are also depicted in garden scenes in frescoes, and dovecotes or pigeon lofts were recorded as originally being in the roof space of house or farm.[59] Later turrets (*columbaria*) painted white, were constructed[60] to maximise the availability of fresh meat and eggs, but also to aid the gathering of their guano, which the agriculturalists reckoned to be the best form of fertilizer for gardens.[61] It was stressed that these structures needed to be kept clean for the birds,[62] and as the dung would always have been cleared away for use elsewhere, this would render the building difficult to identify archaeologically. So far I have not been able to trace any.

Archaeological evidence of plant species grown in gardens

The largest proportion of our evidence comes from Campania, where housing, and the ground surface, was covered by a thick layer of volcanic ash or debris thereby sealing and preserving the archaeological layers. The original soil contours of AD79 were revealed on excavation, showing in some areas rows or plots of garden cultivation. In some cases plant material was carbonised; fragments of tree branches, seeds, and nuts of fruiting trees survived in places.[63] As some ancient Roman plants/trees decayed through lack of light and air, the ash/lapilli that covered them infiltrated the spaces they left behind. Excavators had used plaster as a means of producing a cast of some of the voids they came across, these revealed the shape of humans and animals who had been overcome by the catastrophe. Jashemski pioneered the use of this method to reveal plant roots in Roman gardens. Here the lapilli were carefully removed from below ground level, and the resulting voids were filled with concrete. After setting the cast was cleared of soil and the shape of the roots were studied in comparison with those of today, thus enabling their identification. An example is fig.5 which shows the patterns of find spots of tree roots in each garden area at the Villa of Poppaea, Oplontis. In Garden A, a row (running from north to south) of very large roots, identified as plane trees,[64] indicate that these trees would have provided shade for the *ambulationes* beneath, and the adjacent portico (see Pl.42).

An analysis of soil samples can reveal grains of ancient pollen, spores of fern or fungi, and remains of insects found in gardens. Some pollen, however, from wind blown varieties may have come into the garden from elsewhere. Another factor which needs to be taken into account, is that a number of plant species do not seed freely, and in some cases flower/seed heads are cut off prematurely (or before flowering, as is the case with clipped box), thereby reducing the ratio of their presence in any pollen count. Jashemski (1993, Appendix III) has identified 56 genera from pollen found within the Vesuvian area. From information discovered at the House of the Chaste Lovers, Pompeii, Ciarallo (1993,113) has drawn a grid plan of the garden showing root cavities (see fig.32). When compared with two tables (one detailing the microscopic analysis of carbonised wood, the other a pollen spectra) they provide what must be the best indication of the appearance and distribution of plants in a Roman garden. Along rows C & F macrofossils show that juniper alternated with roses in a symmetrical manner, while pollen analysis indicated that some so-called ornamentals were found to be present. Plants were mainly those that flower in August when the eruption occurred. These include southernwood, myrtle, members of the aster family, pink family, mallow, *campanula, fabaceae, lychnis, cerastium* (the grey leaved 'snow in summer'), ferns and plantains. Interestingly *brassicaceae* were also present, besides a low percentage of genera considered as weeds, perhaps showing that some food plants (or wallflowers which are of the same family) may also have been included in this garden.[65]

Many of the gardens at Pompeii were excavated without the scientific methods used today, but in a few cases the presence of soil contours or a large carbonised tree root were briefly noted, but their significance was not at that time recognised. Jashemski has found that in gardens excavated more recently (within the last thirty years) a large tree, often fruit or nut bearing, was placed in the centre and/or one at each corner of the peristyle.[66] These would shade the garden and portico, and trees and drought resistant shrubs once mature would require little watering thus not being too much of a drain on water stored in cisterns. With the advent of a greater supply of water piped to houses from an aqueduct, a more diverse planting scheme becomes possible, and we find that lower growing shrubs and herbaceous plants are then more numerous. A number of gardens were laid out formally, whereas others appear informal;[67] there was evidently a mixture of tastes then as there is today.

Outside of Campania, the archaeological evidence for ancient plant material is considerably more limited.[68] Most sites have many periods of occupation, and self-seeding weeds and trees would confuse the original surviving planting schemes. In some cases pits corresponding to the dimensions of tree roots could mark the position of an alignment or random planting of trees, but unless dating material is included in the hole these trees could have been planted at any time. In Britain, we have evidence from Frocester Court, where stake holes thought to provide support for young trees were discovered in a number of planting pits.[69] The rough nature of the original ground surface in the front (south) garden has indicated that part could be interpreted as an orchard. At Fishbourne a row of posts alongside a portico in the large garden is believed to have supported a line of cordon fruit trees or vines.[70] However, similar alignments of posts close to three porticoes at Piddington have been interpreted by the excavator as fences enclosing vegetable plots.[71]

At some sites plant beds are identifiable by the long term practice of enriching the natural top soil with compost or manure, or even the importation of better soil. These areas can therefore be traced by differential soil colouration, the darker soil normally being that of cultivation.[72] This is more marked on otherwise poor land. At Frocester, the land was fairly fertile, but areas of enriched soil besides gravel paths (or cut into the gravel, as in the north, rear, garden) suggested the location of plant beds. Spade cuts into the sub soil in these regions further suggest deep digging in cultivated areas.[73] At Fishbourne, where the top soil was thin and poor, the silhouette of plant beds was clearly visible by their darker colouration. Their highly decorative sinuous shape, in a typically classical rectilinear and curvilinear design, was suggestive of hedging (see fig.33). Cunliffe believes that the width and depth of the trenches would have been suitable for box[74] which, if trimmed, would retain the overall pattern. This assumption is supported by the number of clippings from box found at several other sites in Britain (e.g. Frocester, Silchester, Winterton, and Farmoor).[75] Ancient authors, like Pliny (*Ep*,V,6,16ff), attest to the practice of topiary using box. He reveals that it could be trimmed into tiers, obelisks, figures of 'innumerable shapes', or letters spelling out names.[76] At his house at Laurentum rosemary was an alternative, and was used to fill in gaps in the box hedge where the underlying soil was too dry.[77] In countries with shallow soil overlying rock, such as at Malta,[78] trenches were excavated into the bedrock to allow sufficient depth for root growth.

The identification of Roman garden plants in Britain, and other parts of the Roman world, is mostly dependent on the work of environmental archaeologists specialising in paleobotany. The preservation of seeds and pollen is crucially linked to sites which have waterlogged conditions, such as wells, ditches or pits, where preservation occurs because the soil becomes anaerobic. However, Murphy and Scaife show that preservation can only take place if the soil also has a fairly high Ph. Unfortunately fertile garden soil is more likely to be the opposite, for lime and manure,[79] added to ensure a healthy fine tilth, is not so conducive to preservation. Also a friable soil necessary for cultivation will let in air, and the constant turning of earth causes oxidization which destroys pollen and inhibits the survival of macrofossils. The species that are likely to be present in a soil analysis would therefore tend to consist of those that prefer an acid soil, and cultivars that were wind blown as opposed to insect pollinated varieties which do not produce as much pollen. Considering these limitations it is surprising that a range of garden plants can be identified.

A list of plants known to the Romano-British, and attested by archaeobotanical means, is at present being undertaken by staff at Fishbourne Museum.[80] Murphy & Scaife (1991,88,tbl.8.2) produce a table of 'garden and orchard crops identified from macrofossils at Roman sites in Britain' listing thirty-two species (however they exclude ornamentals such as box, columbine, and some 'exotics'). Cunliffe (1981,98/99) lists twenty-nine of the more significant Roman introductions to Britain, which are of fruit/nut/vegetables or culinary herbs. Some examples have come to light from an analysis of waterlogged material from wells at Chew Park and Low Ham.[81] At Bancroft a pit within an enclosure close to the villa's farm buildings, and what may be an artificial lake, has revealed species that could be associated with a *hortus*, or vegetable garden;[82] but unfortunately soil found in the ornamental fish pond close to the villa was not waterlogged, and therefore cannot inform us of plants that may have grown in the presumed flower bed nearby.[83] However, at Farmoor Robinson discovered rose, oxe-eye daisy and flax,[84] and at Roman Alcester Moffett (1988,76) records charred seeds of columbine (*Aquilegia vulgans L.*) which may not have been native to that area and may indicate the presence of ornamental garden plants. Appendix IV is a compilation of archaeologically attested Romano-British and Gallo-Roman flora in comparison with that found in the area covered by Vesuvius.[85]

Fauna in gardens

Open spaces and porticoes were home to a variety of creatures, the abundant bird population can be seen from frescoes and has already been discussed (p.44). The bones of numerous species of bird are also found on excavation in Britain and elsewhere, although many may have been brought to site as a potential food source rather than having lived all their life in the garden. However, birds would have been sold live, and would still need to be housed prior to cooking. Birds, scavengers and insects[86] would have helped to clean up scraps and debris thrown out onto the garden after meals.[87]

Cats who could have reduced the rodent population could equally kill the birds loved by Romans, therefore it is not surprising that little evidence for their presence in gardens is found. One has been found at the villa of Montmaurin in Gaul,[88] and a couple of mosaics depict a cat devouring in one case a bird,[89] the other a mouse.[90] A few cats may have been considered pets, for one is depicted in the arms of a young girl in a stele from Bordeaux.[91]

There is, however, much more evidence for dogs as pets, for instance Martial (I,109) mentions a lap dog belonging to Publius. There are also numerous representations in art of dogs either as companions, hunting-dogs, or as guard-dogs for flocks or home. Bones of dogs have been found in gardens at Pompeii, and a cast was made of one of the unfortunate victims of the eruption; they provide evidence that the dogs would have resembled those seen in Pompeian *cave canum* mosaics.[92] Many would have been watchdogs guarding the premises and valuable garden produce from thieves. Evidence for the provision of a kennel was found in the Garden of Hercules Pompeii (II,viii,6)[93] where a half dolium cut lengthwise had been placed on bricks. Columella (*RR*,VII,12,1/9) advises on the qualities thought desirable for a guard-dog. He adds that if the dog is tied up during the day (when staff are about) then when let loose at night it would be more alert and on the prowl; and if the dog is black in colour he would appear more fierce and would not be so easily detected by thieves, until it was too late.

Already mentioned are fish (ch.5,p.21) that swam in fishponds in Roman gardens (and lakes on more spacious country properties); and bees in hives positioned within large gardens, or under the protection of a portico.[94]

Dormice which were considered a delicacy, were also perhaps kept in peristyles; for Varro (*RR*,III,15,2) records that many were fattened in *dolia*, in villas. He continues with a description of these specially designed receptacles that match the terracotta jars seen at the Boscoreale Museum.[95] Wooden hutches would not have been used for these creatures eat wood. A dormouse enclosure, *Glirarium*, was considered a profitable sideline on an estate. So too was a *locus Cochleariis*, a moated enclosure used for breeding edible snails. Descriptions of both are provided,[96] but they would leave little trace archaeologically. For larger animals the *Leporaria*, originally an enclosed hare warren, later accommodated a range of wild or semi-wild animals.[97] The animals were fed and watered, when summoned, or drinking holes/pools were created.[98] Some estates incorporated large preserves.[99] They provided enjoyment for owners who liked to hunt on their own land, and were an extra source of food.[100] Varro (*RR*,III,13,2/3) reports that Hortensius would entertain guests in his game preserve, providing music which charmed and attracted the beasts as Orpheus did.

Frescoes depicting gardens occasionally include Orpheus and the animals, or scenes of hunting either from a *leporarium* or its more exotic form, an eastern style *paradeisos*.[101] A more conventional tableau of landscape or plants is usually found beneath or beside these scenes, giving an impression that they are part of a large country garden. Thus the painting is linked to the actual garden below.

Basically, the Romans were in tune with nature, wild or domesticated, and pleasure gardens large or small were very much a living part of the *Domus* or *Villa*. The Romans seem to have had a need to include in their life some of the rich flora and fauna native to their region or imported from further afield.

NOTES TO CHAPTER SEVEN

1   *N.H.*XXI,16/8. The Peony and rock-rose are considered as endemiic in some areas, such as Rhodes, which was named after the rose said to have abounded there. An image of this enigmatic flower was struck onto the island's coins, but to me it resembles a rock-rose rather than a true rose. The rock-rose, however, was known as *ledon* by Pliny (*N.H.*XXVI,30,47).

2   Pliny,*N.H.*XV,39.

3   Some were latinized Greek names.

4   Pliny (*N.H.*XXIV,53,90) says that this was a Greek name, and that it was also called *rhododaphne* or *nerium*.

5   Lawson (1950,98) says that 87 remedies using cabbage are recorded by Pliny the Elder.

6   Cato,*De Agri*,CLXI.

7   Pliny,*N.H.*XV,35,118.

8   These are to be found in Pliny,*N.H.*XIV,19.

9   Varro (*RR*,III,16,15) also lists several different types of hives; there was one made 'of fennel stalks, building them square', or there were 'round hives of withes... others of wood and bark, others of a hollow tree, others build of earthenware'. The last form was condemned by Columella (*R.R.*IX,6,2) for it would be too hot in summer and in winter it was not frostproof.

10   Rosemary, however, appears in a medicinal capacity (Pliny,*N.H.*XXIV,59,99/100), but is included with wild species, perhaps indicating that it may not have been so widely cultivated at that time. Pliny (*NH*,XVI,221,98) shows that it was propagated by layering, therefore it was definitely cultivated, so I have decided to include rosemary in Appendix III. Pliny (*N.H.*XIX,62,187) mentions its scent was like frankincense and that it was alternatively known as *libanotis*; or *conyza* (ibid,XXI, 32,58). Under these two names it appears that it was in fact used in chaplets; for bees; and as a medicinal kitchen herb.

11   For instance it was used in hedges at Laurentum (Pliny,*Ep*,II,17,14)

12   Pliny,*N.H*,XIII,2,7/8.

13   Cato,*De Agri*,CXLIII,2.

14   Pliny (N.H.XXI,1,2). Rose stitched chaplets are mentioned by Martial (IX,40,6) and Pliny (N.H.XXI, 8,11).

15   An example is one called *cosmosandala*, made with narcissus, roses, lilies and larkspur (*Deipn*,XV,681).

16   A Greek λευκόϊνον.

17   Pliny,*N.H.*XXI,3,5.

18   A simple garland/chaplet is also mentioned in (*Odes*,IV,11):
      'in my garden, Phyllis, is parsley for weaving garlands; there is a goodly store of ivy, which, binding back thy hair, sets off thy beauty'.

19   Pliny,*N.H.*XXI,10,14. The most highly regarded and most widely grown chaplet flowers were the rose, violet and lily. The twice blooming rose of Paestum was extremely desirable; and the strongest scented was that from Cyrene (ibid,XXI,10,19).

20   Bardo Museum inv.no.1400. 3rd century AD.

21   Carthage Museum inv.no.9. From the House of Tellus.

22   This is in the room of the Child Hunters. In the room of the Actors is a mosaic showing chaplets being made.

23   The garland was probably made by piercing through the centre of the flower. This style and concept of garland adornment (for the person or sacred object) can be seen in India today.

24   Pliny,*N.H.*XIII,6,26.

25   Ibid,XXII,34,76. This was *Acanthus mollis L.*, which is native to Italy.

26   Ibid,XXI,39,68.

27   Ibid,XXI,34,60.

28   Ibid,XVI,31,76.

29   Martial,III,58,2 & XII,50,1; and Horace,*Odes*,II,15,5/6.

30   Pliny *N.H.*18,40, & XVI,60,140 respectively. Pines were: '*in domos recepta tonsili facilitate.*'

31   Ibid,XVI,20,50,1.

32   Ibid,XVII,1,5.

33   Ibid,XVI,53,124.

34   Horace,*Odes*,II,15.

35   Pliny,*N.H.*XVI,1,2f.

36   See note 32.

37   Pliny,*N.H.*XV,14,47.

38   Ibid,XV,30,102/3.

39   e.g. Horace (*Odes*,I,38): 'A truce to searching out the haunts where lingers late the rose!'.

40   Franchi (1992,237). He also provides the identification of species depicted in Pl.37. His term, *versicolor*, was used because the rose appears to be two tone; the outer petals being red and the inner pink. However I feel the artist painted these two colours simply to clarify the double row of petals. The species of rose cultivated in Roman times are believed to be: *Rosa gallica L., R.Phoenicea, R.centifolia L., R.damascena, R.Canina L.,* and possibly *R.alba L.*

41   e.g. at Pompeii,I,vi,13 (Jashemski,1993,fig.357); & as seen at the House of the Carbonised Furniture, Herculaneum,V,5.

42   One was painted by Niccolini, the other by Presuhn (Jashemski, 1993,figs.399 & 400 respectively).

43   Jashemski (1979,87) is also of this opinion. She argues that Pompeian frescoes could not be Greek or Alexandrian. For instance, items found within show plants etc that were common to the area, such as oleander, which does not grow in Alexandria.

44   Jashemski,1993,318/22.

45   Pliny,*N.H.*XXI,12,25.

46   *Violaria*, violet beds are specifically mentioned by Columella (*R.R.*X,259), and in (id, *De Arboribus*, XXX,1) violets were planted in 'little trenches a foot deep'.

47   Pliny,*N.H.*XXV,41,82: '*topiariis operibus gratissima*'.

48   Ivy is also associated with Bacchus, and its inclusion could partly allude to a Bacchic atmosphere.

49   Pliny,*Ep*,V,6,32.

50   *Ad Fratrem*,III,1,5.

51   I believe that this form is called elsewhere 'pale ivy', as in Virgil,*Georgics*,IV,118.

52   Pliny,*N.H.*XXIII,79,151.

53   Ibid,X,59,120. We also hear that Stella had a pet dove (Martial,*Ep*,I,7,1); and Catullus' friend a sparrow (II & III).

54   Daremberg & Saglio,Vol.3,1900,fig.3900.

55   e.g. from Carthage, now in the Bardo Museum (Fradier,1994,96).

56   Some birdcages, however, may have been made with metal, e.g. Statius (*Silv*,II,4) refers to Melior's parrot that was housed in a cage of silver and ivory.

57   Jashemski,1993,188.

58   Jashemski,1979,108 & 348,n.88. This form is confirmed by a passage in Varro (*R.R.*III,5,8) which informs us that M.L.Strabo at Brundisium, 'was the first to keep birds penned up in a recess in his peristyle, feeding them through a net covering'. The position and arrangement of perches is mentioned by Varro when he describes his own aviary at Casinum (*R.R.*III,5,10/14).

59   Varro,*R.R.*III,7,2.

60   Perhaps similar to that shown in the Palestrina mosaic (Whitehouse,1976,fig.17a). This circular building has a conical roof pierced with rows of nesting holes. Varro (*RR*,III,7,3 & III,8,1/2) provides a description of such structures.

61   Cato, *De Agri*,XXXVI; Varro,*R.R.*III,7,5; Columella,*R.R.* II,15,1.

62   'You see how the doves come to a white dwelling how an unclean tower harbours no birds' Ovid (*Trista*,I,9).

63   However, some items may have been brought to the site, and were being stored in the vicinity.

64   Jashemski,1993,295.

65   Wallflowers are now believed to have been the yellow violets that were admired for their scent by Romans. Pliny (*N.H.*XXI,14,27) describes three forms of scented violet, the purple, yellow and white. These are now thought to be different species; the *Viola odorata L., Cheiranthus cheiri L.* (wallflower), and *Matthiola incana (L.)* (stocks), (Jashemski & Ricotti,1992,

594,n.36).
66 Pliny (*Ep*,V,6,20) mentions that at his Tuscan villa he had 'a small court shaded by four plane trees'. Archaeological examples are found at Oplontis (in garden F) where three trees out of the four were planted, for the fourth would have blocked the entrance into that garden. However other houses show that a number of trees could shade the garden. At Oplontis, in garden D, a large chestnut tree is thought to have been centrally placed in the rustic garden-court, evidenced by a huge root cavity, and carbonized nuts found at roof height (Jashemski,1993,293/4).
67 Jashemski,1981,37/9. Many of the gardens at Pompeii have been replanted (although a number of those kept locked are now quite overgrown). Many of these reconstructions appear formal and symmetrical in design following ideas prevalent at the time of excavation rather than as a result of evidence through archaeology An example is that of the House of the Labyrinth, which incorporated a maze design (Ciarallo,1992,2).
68 At Thuburbo Maius, Tunisia, Jashemski (1995,563) has discovered that where wind blown soil has covered and sealed an abandoned site, ancient tree roots can be identified when soil of a different colour or texture has formed by the decaying process of woody material. This is similarly observed in former post pits elsewhere.
69 Unpublished. Information supplied by the excavator, E.Price at the C.I.A. Conference 23/7/1994.
70 On the east side of the formal garden (Cunliffe,1971, 138) see fig.33.
71 Two rows are illustrated in a reconstruction drawing and site plan in Friendship-Taylor,1994,fasc.2, being an Interim report on work during 1989-1993. However, in August 1993 a third row of post holes was discovered (seen at the site open day, and during the summer excavation the following year). I feel that these may have supported a decorative yet functional screen/trellis of fruit trees or vines as is believed to be the case at Fishbourne.
72 A black earth theory is currently being used to reveal former Roman cultivation sites by comparison with field names incorporating the word 'black' (Richardson, 1992,b,439).
73 See note 69.
74 Cunliffe,1981,104-105.
75 Respectively, Bond & Iles,1991,36; Boon,1974,198; and Murphy & Scaife,1991,88.
76 Pliny,*Ep*,V,6,16-17; ibid,V,6,35-36
77 Ibid,II,17,14. Cypress was also used in topiary work (Pliny,*N.H.*XVI,60,140.
78 Ashby,1915,56.
79 Wood ash was also an effective fertilizer mixed into garden soil. Charred remains of wood from the Vigna Barberini, Rome (the presumed site of the *Horti Adonaea*) have been studied by Arnould & Thebert (1993,438-439). The identification of species present indicates that the trees could not have grown there originally, for the charcoal originated from woodland trees (non resinous) from mountainous regions. They further showed that they had been specifically brought to site from charcoal burners, rather than as green faggots. After use as fuel, the residue with ash, would have been added as fertilizer onto plant beds. Such evidence could equally apply elsewhere.
80 Unpublished information received from C.Ryley,1995.
Jashemski (1987,34) notes that in 1978 Riccardi identified 475 plants known to the Romans in the 1st century BC.
81 Bond & Iles,1991,36.
82 Williams & Zeepvat,Vol.I,1994,154 & 209.
83 Ibid,565.
84 Murphy & Scaife,1991,88.
85 I have used data from both the south and north of Gaul, for the former is likely to show some Mediterranean flora, whereas the latter, I believe, would be climatically closer to that of Britain. However, difficulties arose when I tried to correlate various plant lists, for two different criteria are used today. Columns V (from the area covered by Vesuvius) & L (from Lescar) are examples of one form, where pollen analysis had been used to reveal plant species. Here it is customary to give the botanical family name of a plant, for in many cases the pollen grain of plant genera and species within a particular family cannot be separately identified (genera are included where identification was possible). The second method, of which columns N (from Neuss) & B (from sites in Britain) were compiled, is taken from evidence of macrofossils (e.g. preserved plant tissues and charred material, including seeds and nuts). In this form individual species within a genera are more easily identified, and plant lists consist of either common names (French and English here) or Latin botanical names. An example of the system used by palynologists, is the family of rose, *Rosaceae*. This would include the rose, briars, blackberry, salad burnet, hawthorn, fire thorn, medlar, almond, cherry, plum, apricot, peach. I have therefore, where possible, expanded the name of some plants in Appendix IV to include the wider spectra of that plant family. I have also thought it would be beneficial to include into column V the two macrofossils found by Ciarallo (juniper & rose) *op.cit*.
86 Murphy & Scaife (1993,93) discuss the usefulness of faunal remains found in gardens, as 'indicators of features of the habitat'. Wild fauna (molluscs, insects, beetles, small mammals, amphibians and reptiles) may throw light on species of plant grown in the garden. e.g. some insects feed only on one plant and therefore would be indicative of the presence of that plant whereas remains of fish, birds, and mammals could reveal the manner in which the garden was stocked.
87 Jashemski (1979,96) has found evidence for this practise at Pompeii (I,xiv,2).
88 Ferdière,1988,152; cat bones are also reported as rare in Britain, e.g. at Silchester (Boon,1957,172/3).
89 From the House of the Faun, Pompeii, now in Naples Museum (Maiuri,1959,124).
90 From Orange in Gaul (Ferdière,1988,151).
91 Ibid,153.
92 Jashemski,1979,103.
93 Ibid & 279,fig.422.
94 See note 9.
95 This complete example with lid, in terracotta, is approximately 60/70mm high. Breathing holes were made on the exterior while the clay was still wet. A strategically placed mirror showed that the interior was furnished with a spiralling ledge, where the dormice would be housed. Nuts would have been placed in the central void. Ciarallo said that three dormice pots have been discovered in gardens at Pompeii. They do not, however, appear in works by Jashemski. (Information

FLORA & FAUNA IN GARDENS

	was obtained during the discussions after Ciarallo's lecture on 'The Gardens of Pompeii' during the Discovering Pompeii Exhibition London,1992).
96	Respectively Varro,*R.R.*III,15,1 & ibid,III,14,1. Pliny (*N.H.*IX,9,82,173) records that F.Lippinus, prior to 49BC, was the first to construct ponds for keeping snails.
97	Varro,*R.R.*III,3,2. He states that there were three divisions of villa-husbandry, which could 'afford him both profit and pleasure'. These were '*ornithones, leporaria, piscinae.*'
98	By the blowing of a horn (Varro,*R.R.*III,13,1). Columella (*R.R.*IX,1,2) refers to the provisioning of water in such places.
99	Varro (*R.R.*III,12,2) mentions one in Gaul that enclosed circa 4 sq.miles. At Welschbillig, near Trier, the '*Langmauer*' encircles an area of approx. 220km². The area has been interpreted by Grenier (1931,484) as an imperial game preserve.
100	Columella,*R.R.*IX,1,1.
101	For Orpheus see note 42. An example of a *paradeisos* seen in conjunction with various garden scenes, is to be found on the rear wall of the House of Ceii, Pompeii.

CHAPTER EIGHT: ROMAN HORTICULTURE

Garden technicians

In the early days, prior to and during the Early Republican era, Romans do not seem to have had decorative gardens, and therefore those who practised horticulture were farmers, working in the *hortus* (the potager) on the family's smallholding. However during the Late Republic the increasingly affluent society enabled property owners to possess or hire servants/slaves to perform various tasks on their estates, including gardens. Inscriptions indicate that on large properties such as the *Horti Antoniani* in Rome, the grounds would be administered by a *villicus*, and *subvillicus*.[1] Staff under their control were generally named after the role they performed; therefore one who tended vegetables was called an *olitor*;[2] an *arborator*[3] looked after trees (mostly orchards), and a *vinitor*[4] vines. An *aquarius*[5] watered plants; such a person is immortalised in a mosaic in the Vatican Museum[6] (see Pl.43). There does not appear to have been an all-embracing term for a gardener, although there are some references to a *hortulanus*,[7] but these are thought to be late (2nd century AD) and may refer to workers in non-decorative as opposed to ornamental gardens.

A *topiarius* was originally employed to clip hedges, (*nemora tonsilia*), and would therefore be engaged to maintain pleasure gardens, as distinct from orchards and vegetable plots. This term also appears when referring to a landscape gardener, one who created *opus topiarium*. Pliny (*N.H.*XII.6,13) provides a date for such work when he ascribes the introduction of the art of topiary to Gaius Matius during the reign of Augustus. *Topiarii* seem to have been held in some regard; revealing comments are found in Cicero (*Ad Fratrem*,III,I,5), who praises his brother's workman for creating a rustic atmosphere by draping ivy over statues and porticoes, so much so 'that I declare the Greek statues seem to be advertising their ivy', while Pliny (*Ep.*V,6,35) shows that it was permissible for gardeners to clip their own names alongside that of their master's in box hedges. Surviving tombstones of *topiarii*, some of whom may have been freedmen, give their names and on a number of occasions their place of work.[8] One was appropriately named Florus; another records the existence of a principal gardener.[9]

Contemporary depictions of the above mentioned technicians can be found in genre or rural scenes showing work (albeit agricultural) in the form of a rustic calendar. Some of these, however, show scenes that could equally pertain to horticulture. Examples are shown in figs.9c & 34: sowing seed in a *hortus*, hoeing, transporting manure to the garden/fields, pruning trees, gathering fruit. Those that could be more specific to a pleasure garden show staff picking flowers, or tending potted plants, e.g. fig.35 a mosaic from Carthage incorporating a scene of a man Ennaifer (1973,cover ill.) refers to as 'the lily grower'.

Gardening tools and equipment

Cato (*De Agri*,X) includes agricultural tools, *ferramenta*, some of which could equally have been used within the *hortus*, such as: *falces silvaticas* (tree hooks), *arborarias* (pruning hooks), *falculas viniaticas* (grape knives),[10] *ferreas* (forks), *palas* (spades), *palas ligneas* (wooden spades), *rastros quadridentes* (four-toothed rakes), *crates stercorias* (manure hurdle), *sirpiam stercorias* (manure-basket), *quala sataria vel alveos* (planting baskets or troughs), *situlum aquarium* (a watering bucket), *nassiternam* (a watering pot). Varro (*R.R.*I,22,3) adds a *sarculum* (that worked like a dutch hoe or mattock) which has either a pointed or straight edged blade. Different types of tools for weeding and loosening the soil are mentioned, including the *bidens*, which had two tines;[11] and the *ascia-rastrum* that incorporated two heads (a *sarculum* & a *bidens*) see fig.36. Literary sources do not mention the tool used by *topiarii* to clip hedges, but hand held shears of the same type as those used to clip sheep's wool may have also served that purpose.[12] As can be seen in fig.36 many implements believed to have been used in gardens appear similar to those of recent times (before mechanization), demonstrating the effectiveness of their design.

A number of these tools have been found on Roman sites, in Britain and Gaul, but few have specifically been noted in garden contexts,[13] however at Frocester an iron shoe belonging to a wooden spade was found in one of the plant beds.[14] Depictions of these spades, or the more expensive type with a solid metal blade, show that they had a straight shaft and were not provided with a handle (appearing similar to ones used in parts of Europe today. e.g. France & Italy).

The form of planting troughs and baskets for gathering fruit/flowers may be gleaned from numerous depictions in frescoes and mosaics (e.g. fig.31). However, they do not survive archaeologically, in contrast to terracotta flowerpots. One pot and one base were discovered at Fishbourne,[15] and ten from Eccles.[16] Several have been excavated from within ancient gardens in Campania, and show a range of sizes, and number of pierced holes for drainage.[17] At Oplontis, Hadrian's Villa at Tivoli,[18] and the *Horti Adonaea* in Rome,[19] the excavators also found broken amphorae which had been utilized as flower pots. The amphorae had been cut in half, and turned upside down, with the open neck serving as a drain hole. The use of both types of flower pot date at least from the classical period in Greece.[20] Theophrastus refers to the use of pots for plants,[21] and Roman agriculturalists describe how the pots were utilized to make layered cuttings of bushes.[22] Flower pots (presumably large ones) were also used to grow shrubs/trees, for according to Palladius (VII,12) they would make pomegranate trees more fruitful. Presumably the roots became pot-bound and this promoted flowering/fruiting.

Horticultural techniques

The greatest proportion of our evidence in this field has been gleaned from literary sources. They say that plants were increased in various ways. Seeds were saved to sow the following year, or cuttings could be taken.[23] Slips with a heel from the mother plant were planted in special nursery beds where extra care could be lavished on them.[24] The Romans noted that it was wise to plant cuttings in soil similar to that of its mother.[25] When the cutting had grown sufficiently notches were cut into the bark marking points of the compass,[26] so that when planted out the slips would still face in the same direction as accustomed, and would then not be set back by winds from a different direction.

Romans practised layering by burying the tip of a shoot, by air layering, or a more specialised way where branches were bent down and fed into or through a flower pot.[27] Soil was packed around the shoot and the pot was then buried. After two years the layered cutting would have made sufficient root and was severed from its mother. The plant, still in its pot, was then planted into its new position. Excavators have often found that the pot was broken, this may have been done beforehand so as not to retard root growth, or the roots actually grew and broke the pot themselves. The latter is believed to have been the case at Oplontis, in garden B, which Jashemski (1992,583,fig.6) identified as a result of air-layering. The former method was used in garden C, where two rows of citron/lemon trees were planted each in line with columns of the portico.[28]

The citron was a new introduction that took time to acclimatize in Italy. If protected by being against a portico as at Oplontis, netting and reeds could protect the trees, enabling them to withstand the winter.[29] Early crops could be protected in the same manner.[30] *Specularia*, were used to force flowers such as lilies, or cucumbers to fruit early.[31] These miniature greenhouses made out of transparent stone, are described as having wheels so that they could follow the course of the sun, and therefore ripen produce early. The same machine could equally be used to retard a crop by keeping them in constant shade. It was also noted that grey-leaved plants 'were chilly' and that they needed to be placed in the sun,[32] which is current practice today, for these are usually classed as being more tender than green varieties.

Stocks were improved by pruning out unwanted or less productive branches, and strains of good fruiting trees were grafted onto others. Descriptions of the methods used are given, and also the techniques of budding.[33] We learn of experiments in producing different flavours when grafting plums onto apples or almonds onto plums etc.[34] As these all belong to the *Rosaceae* family a successful graft might be possible. References also speak of apples grafted onto plane trees;[35] these, however, were noted as producing a pink fruit but with impaired flavour. Trees with several different fruiting branches were invented;[36] some would have held a novelty value, as today, for if space is limited we can resort to a so-called 'Family tree' (often having three varieties in one).

Romans searched far and wide to find new or better varieties, and a programme of acclimatization was undertaken.[37] Also new improved strains were being bred locally. We hear of new varieties of apple or pear that were named by the owner of a particular estate where it was produced, such as the Scaudian apple or Dolabellian pear.[38] Pliny (*N.H.*XV,15,50) reveals that such a service was not only confined to the aristocracy, for he makes a point of mentioning that freedmen were also involved in the search for new strains. A glance at several names of prominent Romans indicates the extent of their families' involvement in horticulture/agriculture in the past, for the Romans themselves changed several of their names; e.g. Stolon whose ancestor had invented a new process of pruning (*stolon*, if the interpretation is correct, being the name for an unwanted shoot or sucker, the removal of which would promote better growth).[39]

Root pruning was performed, and is recorded as an operation undertaken by *topiarii* to keep plane trees dwarfed.[40] Also the flowering of roses is reported as benefiting from regular pruning and 'burning'.[41] Some techniques appear somewhat brutal, for instance unproductive fruit trees were forced into fruiting by driving a stake into their roots.[42] This sounds more like inflicting a punishment on the trees concerned, but could have had the effect of root pruning which would in fact promote flowering.

Evidence indicates that Romans espalier-trained some fruit trees to grow against a garden wall.[43] Otherwise plantations, orchards, and vineyards were planted in a *quincunx*, rather than the straight rows of the Greeks.[44] Descriptions of this formation indicate a diagonal view could be achieved, and therefore each row was staggered. This would ensure more root space per plant, and make better use of the land.

Varro (*R.R.*I,23,5) says that a 'sunny ground should be chosen for planting violets and laying out gardens as these flourish in the sun.' However shady positions were thought suitable for asparagus beds. Roman plant beds are described by Pliny (*N.H.*XIX,20,60) as having raised borders. The agriculturalists imply that flower beds were treated in a similar manner to those containing vegetables. Columella advises to make these:

> '10 feet wide and 50 feet long, to allow water to be supplied by way of the footpaths and to provide a means of access on both sides for the weeders.' (*RR*.II,10,26)

This would ensure that weeds could be reached without treading on plants. The depth of soil varied per plant bed, 4ft was recommended for trees, 3ft for roses, and 1ft for violets.[45] Individual plants, not in a bed, were often encircled by a ring of raised soil, again to ensure that precious water would be directed straight to the plant and not be wasted elsewhere.[46] These forms of planting are still in use in dry climates around the Mediterranean[47] (see Pl.44).

Soil was improved in a number of ways, by the application of manures, fertilizers, and kitchen waste, incorporating bramble leaves and straw,[48] or by applying clay to gravelly ground or vice versa.[49] Also better drainage could be achieved by planting a layer of potsherds or round stones at the bottom of planting holes.[50] Archaeological evidence of plant beds, and irrigation channels have been found at Pompeii. In the Garden of Hercules, which Jashemski (1979,286) believes was a commercial flower and/or vegetable garden, an elaborate system was devised to make the maximum use of additional water that had to be brought to site. Channels were laid to reach each bed in turn. The natural gradient of the land was used to advantage, and submerged dolia at each turn would slow the pace and facilitate a change of direction for the life-giving supply. Remaining water passed through a hole in the wall to the next garden, lower down.

Recent excavations have also revealed that an ingenious system of irrigation was built into the design of the garden in the Piazza D'Oro at Hadrian's Villa at Tivoli.[51] This garden had a thin covering of soil, so a network of planting holes and trenches had been excavated into the underlying rock. Water from the nearby nymphaea was fed into irrigation ducts, and by the operation of sluice gates allowed to flow into the trenches, where by capillary action plants could be watered. Remarkably the water then passed through a series of tubes under the *euripus* water feature in the centre of the garden and continued to irrigate the other side. This watering system is believed to have been labour saving, and also as evenings are the traditional time to water a garden,[52] the reduction in staff would save distracting the emperor and his guests when dining, in what was one of the prime banqueting areas of the villa.

Frescoes show that gardeners used reeds as a stake, to protect/support, or train a plant.[53] Palladius (VI,32) records that a split reed could keep a rose stem straight and the flower fresh. Vines and gourds were allowed to grow over trellis work to make arbours. Even the cucumber was allowed to climb and give shade.[54] The flowers of this plant are recorded as being placed into a shaped sheath or binding, to produce fruit 'in the shape of man or beast'.[55] Apparently those shaped like a snake were the most popular.[56] Artifice and novelty are usually the most noteworthy, but indirectly such references do demonstrate the advances in technological skills made by Roman horticulturalists.

Due care and attention was given to the well-being of plants, and it is interesting to note that olive or wine lees were considered a tonic for ailing trees.[57] The flamboyant lifestyle of some aristocrats like Hortensius, however, led to many criticisms. One example decried his conduct in leaving the senate early in order to give his plane trees their customary tipple. Such extravagances were naturally censured as an affectation that was turning 'even trees to be wine bibbers!'[58]

Controlling garden pests and diseases (without modern chemicals) was, however, a problem and a number of 'organic' remedies are discussed. Compounds or liquids containing the unsalted lees of olives, or soot, and/or the juice of horehound or houseleek were used.[59] The latter appears to have been the most effective method of killing or deterring pests. Seeds could also be pre-soaked in this juice to thwart rodents from eating them once planted. At certain times infestations of caterpillars, or 'ground fleas' (perhaps thrips or aphids), and ground worms (possibly eelworm or carrot fly larvae) occurred. Therefore if all else failed it appears that ancient rustic rites were resorted to.[60] A skull of a female horse, or the shell of a land crab was fixed on a post in the garden.[61] More improbable was the recourse involving a menstruating young girl who was requested to walk barefoot (and with hair loose) three times around plant beds and garden hedges.[62]

In the case of mildew and rust, these were prevented by sacrifice to *Robigio* (goddess of rust).[63] During the festival of the *Robigalia* the rites demand the sacrifice of a rust coloured dog.[64] The presumed outcome was probably that like would cure like. A blight. such as rust or mildew, has the potential to threaten seriously or devastate the year's harvest, and taken in this light it would seem necessary to propitiate the god concerned. Rust can be avoided by crop rotations, which is recommended by the agriculturalists,[65] or by leaving land fallow for a time. This is, however, more difficult to do in gardens where every part is utilized.

A month by month calendar of work was provided by Columella and others, detailing such things as the times to dig beds, sow seed, take cuttings, graft, or replant. Most of the work was aimed to coincide with the change in weather at the spring or autumn equinoxes that are a feature of the Mediterranean climate.[66] However, he also includes advice for colder climates in upland regions, where various tasks sometimes needed to be delayed a month. The manuals were essentially practical, and reflect the mixture of accumulated wisdom or science of horticulture that had developed under the Roman aegis, but also at times they reveal the underlying ancient lore of superstitious magic that was still prevalent at that time. However, the following quotation by Columella remains valid and to me could also apply to Roman horticulturalists:

> 'Surely these examples remind us that Italy is most responsive to care bestowed by mankind, in that she has learned to produce the fruits of almost the entire world when her husbandmen have applied themselves to the task.' (R.R.III,8,5)

NOTES TO CHAPTER EIGHT

1 Daremberg & Saglio,1900,276. C.I.L.VI,2,9990/1. Also C.I.L.VI,2,9005 records a *vilicus* at the *Horti Sallustiani*.

2 Pliny(*N.H.*XIX,23,64); Columella(*R.R.*X,177 & 229). Three inscriptions C.I.L.VI,2,9457/9 record the names and occupation of *holitoris*, an alternative spelling of *olitoris*. Their names being Ariarathes, Horatius and Sergius respectively.

3 Columella (*R.R.*XI,1,12).

4 Ibid,*RR*,IV,24,1.

5 Daremberg & Saglio,1900,276.

6 This mosaic had no number, but is located on the floor, in the entranceway of the Rotunda Gallery.

7 C.I.L.VI,2,9473 is believed to relate to an [H]*ortulanus*, and would therefore confirm that this was a recognised occupation.

8 Some came from Columbaria for ex staff, e.g. *ex familia Augusta*, or may have been members of a funerary college e.g. C.I.L.VI,2,8639.

9 Respectively C.I.L.VI,2,9945 & C.I.L.VI,2,9947. Among the named stones of *topiarii* there are: Fortunati (CIL,V,2,5316), Claudius Tauriscus (CIL,VI,4360), Dorio (CIL,VI,4361), Cerdone (CIL,VI,5353), Sasa

(CIL,VI,6370), Alexandri from Spain (CIL.VI,2,9943), Lucrio (CIL.VI,2,9946), Apolonis (CIL.VI,2,9948), Lucrio (CIL.X,1,1744). Others bear a simple message such as CIL.VI.6369 which reads *'Felix Topiarius'*.

10   Sharp knives would also have been used when making cuttings, grafts, or budding eyes.

11   I believe this may be another name for the *'bicorni'* mentioned by Columella (*R.R.*X,148) & Palladius (I,166,1161). However, White (1967,107/10) shows that the fork, a larger tool, could also be two (or three) pronged.

12   White (1967,119) discusses the *forfex* (sheep-shears); however he only refers to their pastoral use. His work is primarily concerned with agricultural tools and he rarely refers to their usage in a garden.

13   In Campania, however, a number of tools have been found in gardens, e.g. a *sarculum* in the Garden of Hercules (Pompeii,II,viii,6) (Jashemski,1979,280, fig.423). Also in garden D at Oplontis Jashemski (1979,290) found 'a pointed hoe, a six-pronged rake, and a pruning hook'.

14   Gracie & Price,1979,31,fig.13.4.

15   Information received from C.Ryley, Education officer at Fishbourne Palace,1995. c.f. Down (*Ant.J*,1989,308-309).

16   Detsicas,1974,305,fig.8. At that time they had been wrongly identified as candle holders. See fig.36k.

17   Jashemski,1981,34,n.8/11. The pots range from 12cm to 18cm high, have three or four holes in the side and one below. The holes are usually round and appear to have been made while the clay was still wet.

18   Jashemski & Ricotti,1992,582/3.figs.5 & 6.

19   These are illustrated in Tomei (1992,942,fig.18). Morel (1993,431) shows that the 'normal' type of flower pots were here used in the Julio-Claudian phase, whereas in the Flavian/Severan period reused amphorae were employed. I believe that this practice would help in some way to diminish the growing pile of empty vessels if they could not be reused for food/liquid storage purposes.

20   Adonis gardens planted in broken amphorae were pictured in the Karlsruhre Greek vase painting, and true pots containing shrubs were planted around the Hephaistion in Athens. These however had no side holes (Thompson,1963,figs,50 & 12/3).

21   Enquiry into Plants,VI,7,3.

22   See note 27.

23   Pliny (*N.H.*XIX,36,121) mentions that cuttings could be taken from some perennial herbs such as rue, marjoram and basil. He later adds that violets are also planted from cuttings (XXI,14,27).

24   *'Pomarium Seminarium ad eundem modumatque oleagineum facito.'* (Cato,*De Agri*,XLVIII). In (*De Agri*..XLVI, and *De Arboribus*,XXV,2) he describes the appearance of these nursery beds, and their culture.

25   Virgil,*Georgics*,II,266.

26   Ibid,II,269. Columella (*De Arboribus*, XX,2) recommends marking slips with 'ochre or anything else you please'.

27   The agronomists say that a basket could also be used to layer plants in the ground. Cato (*De Agri*,CXXXIII) and Pliny (*N.H.*XVII,21,97) describe all three processes. When air layering, however, the pot was left suspended on the tree until it had taken root.

28   Jashemski,1979,293/5. Citrons are also referred to by Pliny (*N.H.*XII,7,15) as a Median apple. These were valued for their medicinal properties, and may have been the prized golden apples of the Hesperides. They are thought to be the precursor of lemons. Citrons are larger than a lemon, less acid, but have a thick uneven rind.

29   Palladius (IV,64,445). Pliny (*N.H.*XII,7,16) speaks of the difficulties in acclimatizing the citron in Italy. Friedlander (vol.II,1968,169) mentions that Florentinus (circa AD200) records them growing under protection, and by the 4th century Palladius (IV,67/69) reports that it was established in Campania and Sardinia. The medieval English translation of Palladius that was available to me, however, has wrongly translated citrons as oranges. As this fruit was believed to be an Arab introduction and no Latin text is shown, I have accepted Friedlander's version.

30   Columella (*R.R.*XI,3,63) describes this method; 'low trellis are constructed with reeds, and rods are thrown in and straw on top of the rods, and thus the plants are protected from frosts'.

31   Columella (*R.R.*XI,3,52/3). He records that they were used to provide early cucumbers for the Emperor Tiberius. Seneca (*Ep*,CXXII,8) mentions their use for lilies, and from Martial (VIII,14) we hear that they protected tender fruiting trees from Cilicia. Another method to bring forward flowering/fruiting was to pour hot water into a trench around the plant (Pliny, *N.H*,XXI,10,21).

32   Pliny (*N.H.*XXI,34,60) mentions this when referring to the grey-leaved southernwood.

33   Cato (*De Agri*,XL). Also Columella (*De Arboribus*, XX,2) says that:
>   'a tree which is engrafted is more fruitful than one which is not'.

In *De Arboribus*, XXVI he describes the techniques used in both methods, mentioning that 'Any kind of scion can be grafted on any tree if it is not dissimilar in respect of bark'.

34   Pliny (*N.H.*XV,9,35 & XV,12,42). Calpurnius Siculus (*Eclog*,II,40/3) claims that crosses were made between pears and apples, and peaches and plums.

35   Pliny (*N.H.*XVI,26,121). Palladius (XII,24,166) refers to how peaches turn red if grafted onto a plane tree.

36   Pliny (*N.H.*XVII,26,120) mentions a famous one at Tivoli which had 'nuts on one branch, berries on another, while in other places hung grapes, pears, figs, pomegranates and various sorts of apples'. With so many grafts it is quite understandable that 'the tree did not live long'.

37   Pliny (*N.H.*XV,39,132) records the introduction of laurel to Corsica.

38   Respectively Pliny (*N.H.*XV,15,49 & XV,16,54). Columella lists both amongst other sought-after fruit trees to plant in gardens.

39   Pliny (*N.H.*XVII,1,7). In (*N.H.*XVIII,3,10) Pliny lists Piso, Fabius, Lentulus, and Cicero whose names derived from the cultivation of respectively: pea, bean, lentil, chick pea.

40   Ibid,XII,6,13.

41   Ibid,XXI,10,21. No method of burning is given however.

42   Palladius (III,108,750f & XII,20,134f). A similar method was said to produce cherries without stones (ibid,XI,34,232f).

43   As at the House of C. Julius Polybius (Pompeii,IX,xiii,1-3) (Jashemski,1993,249).

44   Pliny,*N.H.*.XVII,15,78.

45 Pliny (*N.H.*XVII,16,81) recommends planting at a depth of 4ft on damp ground, so that brushwood (which would help to drain and lighten the soil) was placed at the bottom of the pit, adjusting the depth to about 3'4". For gardens Pliny (*N.H.*XIX,20,60) mentions a depth of 3ft. Columella (*De Arbor*,XXX) gives 1ft for violets.

46 See note 45. From Pliny (*N.H.*XVII,4,42) we also learn that in dry climates plants could obtain moisture from dew collecting overnight in the trench encircling the plant.

47 Such planting methods were seen in modern Campania, Tunisia and Istanbul.

48 The merits of manure from different animals are discussed by Columella (*R.R.*II,14,50). Fertilizers such as ash and cinders, or the use of a crop of lupines or vetch as a 'green manure' are also mentioned. Columella (ibid,II,14,6) refers to the use of leaves.

49 Ibid,II,15,4.

50 Pliny,*N.H.*XVII,16,82.

51 Jashemski & Ricotti,1992,588/93,figs.9/12.

52 Pliny,*N.H.*XIX,60,183.

53 A reed supports a rose in the fresco on the south wall of the garden *diaeta* at the House of the Wedding of Alexander Pompeii (Jashemski,1993, figs.418/9). At the House of the Vettii, Pompeii, a dado on the peristyle wall depicts a reed used to train an ivy plant to grow into the shape of a mound (Jashemski,1993,fig.402).

54 Pliny (*N.H.*XIX,23,64) & Columella (*R.R.*X,395).

55 The practice is also attested by Palladius (IV,30.204/8) and Pliny (*N.H.*XIX,24,70). The latter informs us that for both gourds and cucumbers sheaths were made of plaited wicker.

56 Pliny (*N.H.*XIX,24,70). Columella (*R.R.*X,390) says those in the form of a snake were made by wrapping the fruit in knotted grass.

57 Columella (*R.R.*II,14,3) for olive lees as a remedy, and Palladius (XII,16,111/2) for wine dregs to cure sick peach trees. The minerals that these substances contain would in fact be beneficial to plants.

58 Pliny (*N.H.*XII,3,8); Macrobius (*Sat.*3,13,3).

59 Columella (*R.R.*X,352); Palladius (I,122/3,848). Columella (*R.R.*XI,3,60/1) speaks in favour of the houseleek:

> '*eodemque remedio adversus bestiolas uti: quod verum esse nos experimentia docuit.*'

Pliny (*N.H.*XIX,58) also recommends the use of heliotrope if plants are attacked by ants.

60 Columella (*R.R.*X,341); Palladius (I,120,835).

61 Pliny (*N.H.*XIX,58,180); Palladius (I,124,862).

62 Columella (*R.R.*XI,3,64 & X,358); Palladius (I,123,860).

63 Columella,*R.R.*X,342.

64 The festival was held on 25th April. Ovid (*Fasti*,IV,906-942) describes the rites. The colour of the dog is mentioned by Seyffert (1894,548).

65 Virgil,*Georgics*,I,94-98. This practice was also used to improve the fertility of the soil.

66 e.g. Pliny (*N.H.*XVII,65,242) says that the kitchen garden and rose-beds needed attention at the time of the spring equinox.

CHAPTER NINE: CONCLUSIONS

As can be seen the Roman garden could be one of many things, for our term garden and the Latin term *hortus* are both all-embracing. Therefore, the actual appearance of an individual Roman garden is difficult to specify, for the term *hortus* could be used in a domestic sense, to imply a small or large town garden, but could also apply to any contained within the domain of a country villa. *Hortus* could equally refer to what we would consider a market garden, or a rustic vegetable plot and orchard, green funerary enclosures, or an urban park. Gardens also appeared in certain inns and corporate buildings, and were often incorporated into temple complexes or other public structures. Therefore a garden could equally have a public usage. The type of garden may be varied, but research shows that many of these green areas share elements in common, helping us to visualize the appearance of various Roman gardens.

In this study my first objective was to ascertain if the gardens seen at Pompeii were representative of those throughout the Empire. From all the evidence at my disposal, I believe that gardens in the provinces were basically similar to those in Italy (but in the east this may be less so for it appears that in many town houses Greek tendencies for paved courts may have continued). The gardens visited, and plans consulted, show that in general Roman housing (like other forms of buildings) in the provinces tends to follow the fairly standardized patterns set by Rome. Therefore, it is not surprising to find that gardens within these dwellings also bear some similarities with those of Italy, and in particular Pompeii.

My second objective, on the effects of climate, is difficult to answer because little archaeological evidence exists. However, in regions with a drier atmosphere (such as in parts of North Africa) certain measures were taken, such as the provision of large cisterns. I also found that in general smaller water basins were installed which used less water. Some gardens were at a lower level to conserve moisture, and plant holes were shaped to funnel precious water close to roots, and not be wasted elsewhere. In dwellings belonging to a more northerly latitude, however, there may be some differences, if only because frost limited the introduction of 'exotic' species of plants, and could damage exposed pipework and fine statuary. One notable concession, to protect owners from cold winds, is that a number of houses have less open colonnades bordering gardens as opposed to those in the south.

My third and fourth objectives will be considered together, for several factors need to be taken into account when determining the characteristic elements of a Roman garden. One aspect is that garden details vary with time, for the Roman period extends over many centuries.[1] Gardens of the Late Republican Era, for instance, differ from the humble *horti* preceding it, and from those of the late Empire. Also great differences are apparent between gardens that are fed by water drawn from a cistern against those having piped water from an aqueduct. This crucial element, water, could effect the range of plants that could be grown, and the way that they were planted. For in general informal gardens seem to exist in gardens with limited water resources, and formal plantations and bedding patterns often require low growing plant species which tend to need more watering. Insufficient water would also restrict the installation of fountains and water basins. Each has great implications for the overall form of the *hortus*. The most influential element, however, is that of an individual's taste and aspirations. As can be seen today, some people carefully tend and furnish gardens, while others merely mow the lawn or neglect theirs. Such is human nature, and to some extent a garden is an expression of the owner. As can be seen in Pompeii the shape and appearance of gardens are varied.

When comparing plans of housing and public gardens, with the occasional archaeological reference made in reports, many garden areas show a significant number of features of a similar nature, so much so that I feel that these may represent some of the characteristics that could be regarded as typical in a Roman Garden. I had hoped that a perusal of the reports could reveal a pattern of trends within the long time-scale of the Roman period, such as appears in comparisons of different types of water features. However, the picture is too incomplete, for so few gardens have been adequately recorded. With fuller reportage today, however, this may in time be resolved.

In most Roman gardens that are found to have had an adequate supply of water the area contained some structures. A number show that water features held a special place as a focal point and a means to decorate the garden. However, in some cases only paths survive. Sculpture was spread out, amongst the greenery, in such a way that it ornamented the garden and could enhance particular views. Owners made use of architecture and landscape to enhance the vista of the house and garden (both within and looking outwards).

The Roman love of nature and growing things is shown in the many areas that were given over to greenery in Pompeii and elsewhere. Evidence shows that gardens were not only the preserve of the wealthy, for even small homes were able to include a corner of greenery, or a few plants in containers or a window box, which could give joy and would relieve the tedium of cramped conditions in cities. The possession of a garden, no matter how small, would give some release from the pressures of an urban existence. Also a sense of space could be created if a verdant painted backdrop was provided. A tromp l'oeil work could extend a garden, or if employed behind just a strip of plants, an illusion of a garden could be created.

Why did the Romans have a Garden? There are many reasons in answer to this question. Firstly the nurturing of living green plants fills a basic instinct for a closeness to nature, often associated with the idea of a wholesome country life. Many were required to live in cities, therefore, the garden could play an important role in providing a little *rus in urbe*. Another benefit was that plants grown in gardens were often scented forms so that the area would be fragrant and could freshen any stale odours in the house nearby. Gardens in internal courtyards would also allow more light and air to rooms facing onto it, and the surrounding porticoes of a garden made an ideal extra living space or workplace that was used to advantage. Evidence of loomweights at Pompeii[2] suggest that the womenfolk spun and wove where there was good light but shelter from rain or the fierce sun of summer. Garlands could be made there and vegetables prepared for meals. Fish for later consumption could be kept fresh in a fishpond in the garden, and likewise birds for the table could be housed in an aviary. Plants were grown for effect, and yet provided food and medicines. Bees were welcomed into gardens to pollinate food plants and to convert nectar into honey, while flowers and foliage provided materials for making garlands to decorate the building, shrines, or the person. The garden was in fact an additional living area for man and the birds and bees. As the garden was an area that required frequent attention it was a place of work for some, and therefore it was necessary to provide for those occupied in its maintenance; this fact was a valid consideration when Pliny the Younger considered buying a nearby villa.[3]

Archaeological discoveries confirm textual evidence that a garden was an ideal location for parties and feasting, especially in summertime when most use would be made of *al fresco* dining areas. A place within the garden, perhaps a *diaeta, pergula,* or other shady location, would also have been allocated for study or relaxation, contemplation and inspiration. Numerous references include time spent relaxing on the grass or a seat under the shade of a tree. Cicero (*De Leg,*II,2,1) found peace in a little glade on an island in a river on his property, and there are several occasions when he goes for a walk with friends to have a discussion in the garden.[4] Ovid, the younger Pliny, and Maecenas each drew inspiration from their garden,[5] so gardens could be seen to have health giving properties and could revive the spirits.

A peaceful existence in the country beckoned to some, especially in dangerous times under tyrannical emperors,[6] and could in fact be a reality for those who could afford to retire from city life. Pliny recommended retirement,[7] and even the Emperor Diocletian expressed his desire to retire to his palace at Split so that he could grow cabbages;[8] which perhaps suggests that retirement was considered respectable, if time would be spent in one's *hortus*.

With an increasingly wealthy society the nouveaux riches of the middle classes and freedmen aspired to own larger properties or *villae urbanae* which had previously been the preserve of the landed gentry, who in turn vied to own larger estates than their rivals. References indicate that many former properties in Italy were turned into vast pleasure gardens and this indirectly threatened the economy of Rome,[9] so much so that a significant proportion of provisions then needed to be imported. The decline of agriculture in many areas may have contributed to the eventual fall of Rome.

During the late Empire, which was a period of general unrest, there was a tendency to construct walls and fortify country villas.[10] Unprotected gardens now being vulnerable to attack, may have shrunk in size, and to some extent this fact seems to have been compensated for by a concentration or elaboration of architectural designs in courtyard gardens.

Large pleasure gardens became less practicable and many would have shared a comparable fate to those at the Villa on Via Gabina, where the once decorative terraced gardens overlooking Rome returned to agriculture.[11] Also Ellis shows that from the fourth century there was a great influx of poor from the countryside into the town, with these people setting up squatter type accommodation in public buildings and large houses of the former middle classes. From evidence available it seems that gardens if kept would have been shared, and now would have only really existed in the large *domus* of local magnates, who basically ruled from their homes. So as the quality of urban life decayed many gardens in town houses (other than those of the ruling class) may have been converted to the provision of food or were abandoned altogether.

Survivals of the Roman garden

A simple peristyle form of garden survived in the atrium of Early Christian Churches. In the Byzantine and Medieval periods these cloister gardens were often called a 'paradise' or a Garden of Eden.[12] Some elements of a Roman garden were even taken over into Christian iconography, such as a well or fountain as a font of life, and birds in the garden (especially doves and peacocks) as symbols of peace or eternity, which indicates that these items at least were considered wholesome (unlike idolatrous statuary such as Pan). Monastic establishments continued the tradition of a cloister garden and the Medieval *Hortus Conclusus* may owe some of its design to the gardens within fortified Roman Villas. The only other surviving remnant, however, can be found in the enclosed watergardens of the Arab invaders of the Byzantine Empire. These people kept the tradition of elaborate water features and continued to value a knowledge of horticulture which was re-introduced into Spain following their conquest there.

In most of Europe horticulture was almost non-existent during the Dark Ages until in the Medieval period surviving ancient texts were examined anew. Cato, Varro, and Palladius were especially read at this time and a recent article by Ellis-Rees discusses the effect this had on Petrarch and the Age of Humanism. During the Renaissance ancient sculpture was increasingly collected and studied.[13] The ancient myths gave the figures a new meaning, and consequently they were no longer profane images to be broken up. Instead, gardens were created in which these *objets vertus* could be seen and admired.[14] Works of art such as the Bacchus by Michelangelo were commissioned by Jacopo Galli (c.AD1497) to act as a focal point in a linked Bacchic theme.[15] Gardens were constructed on terraces, and in the 16th century elaborate nymphaea, grottoes, and water features were added. In gardens such as the Villa D' Este their architect P.Ligorio (c.AD1568), who was also an antiquarian and excavator, modelled his work on archaeological remnants found at Hadrian's Villa and at Rome.[16] His knowledge of classical texts was combined with an adaptation of the spectacular examples that had survived from antiquity. From the list of plants chosen to decorate this garden it appears that he actively sought to further the atmosphere of a Roman pleasure garden by including species previously mentioned by ancient authors.[17] Plantings in Italianate villas tend to favour clipped evergreen bushes or trees, so much so that these gardens and their furnishings could well resemble the splendid grounds of an Ancient Roman *Villa Urbana*.

In Britain Castell in 1728 published a volume on Ancient Roman Villas based on the literary references of Varro and Pliny the Younger. Here he attempted to reconstruct the plans of whole estates, including garden structures, into a rather fanciful landscaped setting. His interpretations are believed to have contributed to a new style of horticulture, where large country parks were landscaped and dotted with classical ruins and pavilions. This tradition was brought one step further at Port Lympne in Kent, where the owner (circa 1919) specifically decided to recreate a garden in the Roman style, where tiers of topiary recalled descriptions by Pliny the younger.[18] Here the Italianate gardens with terraces of topiary overlook Romney Marsh and the sea beyond, in the spirit of a *Villa Maritima* or *Littorale*.

Interpretative Archaeology and Roman Gardens

Today there is interest in recreating the past and in some areas reconstructions of Roman buildings are undertaken. These would appear more complete if the associated open areas or gardens were also reinstated following the same principles. If we wished to recreate a Roman garden today, we must first determine the characteristic elements that were suitable for the period. This task has been achieved in Pompeii, although to a great extent only the modern reconstructions are archaeologically accurate (and in these cases sculpture is usually omitted for security reasons). However, this is not such a problem inside the controlled environment of a museum. The Paul Getty Museum in California was modelled on the Villa of the Papyri at Herculaneum and in the comparably warm climate garden furnishings were included. The pristine state of the building and its collection enables you to visualize the whole as it would have appeared in antiquity. However, the large peristyle garden here contains a number of items that belonged to other Pompeian gardens,[19] so the area is really an accumulation of elements found in a typical Roman garden.

In Britain the cooler climate would mean some adaptations are necessary. The Museum at Cirencester, which has a small irregular shaped courtyard, has opted for a style similar to that found in Campania, and the result is somewhat crowded but successful. On the other hand the newly inaugurated Roman garden at the Birmingham Botanical Gardens is misleading on several points, e.g. the use of yew. They wished to show a Romano-British garden of the 3rd Century AD, but they acknowledge the lack of evidence on which they could draw, and therefore settled for an adapted Pompeian style,[20] but to me the result is not successful. One needs to take into account the practices of the relevant period. One example is the treatment of pathways, at Vienne they have been restored in sand as Vitruvius recommends, whereas at the Archeodrome a pebble surface is used. As this, gravel, or broken stone is common on archaeological sites; it is a pity that Birmingham opted for York paving.

To conclude, Roman gardens are an important source of information on the Roman way of life, and numerous facets of their civilization can be found within the confines of the hortus itself.[21] In order to gain an understanding of how the garden was used I was necessarily brought into contact with many areas of study, such as the role that religion played in gardens. My research shows that religion pervaded the area, in the form of altars, shrines and statues of deities. Ritual was observed and superstitious precautions taken to avert the evil eye away from growing plants, or the family in general.

A study of the ancient sources reveals that gardens and gardening appear as a subject worthy of mention, and in examples such as Pliny's[22] the garden was as important to him as his house, and evidently a feature that he wished to bring to the attention of his friends.

The provision of a garden, and its growing importance, could also be said to have influenced the architecture of the Roman *domus* and certain public buildings. Some gardens contained pavilions or nymphaea bringing architecture into the garden, and features which had been originally designed for inclusion in a *hortus* such as nymphaea in turn infiltrate decorative schemes inside rooms.

Art in gardens is displayed in the form of decorative frescoes that adorned architectural elements within the garden, *plutei,* and walls of the peristyle, while mosaic was used to ornament nymphaea and some water basins. In many cases the subjects chosen were taken from themes associated with gardens, such as the verdant scenes of flora and fauna, attributes of deities of the *hortus*, or elements in some way connected to water, which was such an important feature in gardens. In the case of sculpture it appears that the garden was an ideal place to display items; this is confirmed by comments made by Pliny the Younger.[23] Evidence for the mass production of specific forms depicting rustic qualities shows that a large proportion of sculpture had been made specifically for a garden; and together with other garden furniture they would have complemented the scene as a whole. All of these items would form components of a typical Roman garden.

Literary references can put the flesh on the bones found through archaeological means, and both are important sources of information leading to an understanding of an artefact or feature, its mode of employment, and the context in which it appears. Each field needs to be studied thoroughly, and new inroads are being made by the use of modern scientific methods of archaeology. Techniques used in the study of the environment have now been applied to the previously neglected area of the Roman garden, and the relatively new field of Garden Archaeology holds great scope for the further understanding and interpretation of this area and aspect of the past.

CONCLUSIONS

NOTES TO CHAPTER NINE

1. Unfortunately few gardens have a stratigraphic record showing different phases within the Roman period.
2. Jashemski,1979,102.
3. *Epistles*,III,19,3.
4. Ibid.; cf. *Acad*,II.3,9; *De Oratore*,I,7,28.
5. Ovid (*Tristia*,I,11,37); Pliny (*Ep*,IX,36); and the *Eleg.Maec* (I,35/6) which reminisces on how Maecenas was fond of:
   'Honouring the Muses and Apollo in luxurious gardens, he reclined babbling verse among the tuneful birds.'
6. Seneca,*Ep*,LV,3.
7. Epistles,I,3.
8. *Epit.Caes*.39,6 (cited by Littlewood,1987,27,note 174).
9. Pliny (*N.H*.XVIII,7,35) 'large estates have been the ruin of Italy'. Horace (*Odes*,II,15) continues this theme:
   'A short time and our princely piles will leave but few acres to the plough; on all sides will be seen our fish-ponds spreading wider than the Lucrine Lake, and the lonely plane-tree will drive out the elm; then will beds of violets and copses of myrtle and the whole company of sweet perfumes scatter their fragrance amid olive groves that once bore increase to their former owner'.
10. Percival,1976,176.
11. Wildrig,1987,259. Here a large barn was constructed in the garden and the area was then believed to have been given over to the production of grain and olive oil.
12. Gothein,1966,172. The 5th century AD account of the life and miracles of St.Thecla are mainly set in garden areas or an atrium attached to the church (at Meriamlik). In the atrium an assortment of birds were reared; doves, pheasants, swans, geese, cranes, and perhaps ibis from Egypt (Miracle 24). In Miracle 26 we find that there were numerous trees and flowers, a flower bedecked lawn, with water playing in the background. The whole is likened to a *paradise* (Dagron,1978,69).
13. Petrarch 'paved the way' (Lee,1981,171).
14. Coffin,1991,17f.
15. Lee,1981,224.
16. Heydenreich & Lotz,1974,266/7.
17. Coffin,1991,195.
18. Ottewill,1989,190/3.
19. J.Paul Getty Museum,1992,52 & 53. One example is the nymphaeum constructed in the East Garden, this does not appear on maps of the Villa of the Papyri at Herculaneum, but is a replica of that in the House of the Great Fountain at Pompeii.
20. Birmingham Botanical Gardens,1994. Outside the garden, but at the end of the pathway linking the three period gardens (the others being Medieval & Tudor), there was a statue of Proserpina. This figure was meant to be Roman but her attire was inappropriate for the period, it had a terracotta finish which is not normally found in sculpture of the third century AD, and I cannot find an example where a statue of Proserpina has been found in a Roman garden. The aim was obviously that the garden areas would be viewed from the front, but the lack of a suitable focal point within this Roman garden detracts from its supposed authenticity.
21. Grimal (1969,437) notes that:

    Religion, litterature, architecture domestique et urbanisme, arts plastiques, il n'est presque aucun domaine de la civilisation latine qui n'ait apporte sa contribution à notre etude: le jardin a mis sur tous son empreinte. et tous ont agi sur lui

    His quote still applies. However, in the intervening sixty years since this was first published a great deal of work has taken place, by people such as W.F.Jashemski, and new scientific methods of archaeology have provided valuable new information which enables one to expand further on the aspects which touch onto gardens. Both Grimal and Jashemski helped to make people aware of the possibilities that research into garden archaeology was a valid discipline and avenue of study.
22. *Epistles*,V,6,32.
23. He mentions that his acquaintance
    'on the very day he bought a large garden he was able to beautify it with quantities of antique statues...' (Ep,VIII,18)

    This perhaps indicates that a garden would obviously appear incomplete without statuary.

APPENDICES

APPENDIX I

MUSEUMS AND ARCHAEOLOGICAL SITES VISITED TO COLLECT MATERIAL FOR THIS STUDY.

Where there is no accompanying reference to any literature in the text, this indicates that my judgement on the matter under discussion was made through personal observation in situ.

In Britain
The British Museum.
The Museum of London.
The Ashmolean Museum.
The Fitzwilliam Museum.
The Liverpool County Museum.
The Corinium Museum at Cirencester.
The Museum of Transport and Archaeology at Hull (which displays mosaics & frescoes from Rudston Villa).
Rediscovering Pompeii Exhibition at the Accademia Italiana London (Here I inspected the frescoes and mosaic fountain from the House of the Wedding of Alexander, Pompeii, but no photographic record was allowed).
Birmingham Botanical Gardens.
Garden areas in villas at:
Bignor,
Chedworth,
Fishbourne
Frocester Court,
North Leigh,
Piddington,
Wortley,
The Mansio at Wall.
France
The Louvre in Paris.
The Archaeological Museum at Nimes.
The Archeodrome (which has a reconstruction of a Roman garden).
Roman housing and gardens at:
Glanum (which included a paved Hellenistic peristyle court),
Saint-Romain-en-Gal,
Vaison-la-Romaine (including the Portico of Pompeius).
Belgium
The Royal Museums of Art and History, Brussels.
Villa at La Malagne nr. Rochefort.
Luxembourg
Musee National d'Histoire et d'Art.
Germany
Rheinisches Landesmuseum Trier.
Malta & Gozo
The Roman House and Museum at Rabat, Malta (This house has an interesting mosaic covered courtyard. I was unable to see the villa mentioned in this text).
The Archaeology Museum at Victoria, Gozo.
The Roman gallery in the Archaeological Museum at Valetta was closed during my visit.
Greece
The Agora and the Hepheistion.
The Kerameikos funerary area.
Istanbul
Archaeological Museum.
The carved obelisk base in the Hippodrome (which depicts decorative walling with herms utilized as balusters).
Sicily
Villa at Piazza Armerina.
Tunisia
The Bardo Museum.
Museums at Carthage, Sousse, El-Jem, Sbeitla, Nabeul.
Roman housing with gardens at:
Carthage,
Dougga,
Sbeitla,
El-Jem,
Thuburbo Maius (including the Portico of the Petronii).
Punic housing at Carthage and Kerkouna.
Turkey
Side
Italy
Museum at Ostia.
Roman housing and gardens at Ostia.
Hadrian's Villa at Tivoli.

Rome
The Vatican Museums.
The Conservatori & Capitoline Museums.
The Therme Museum (The garden frescoes from the House of Livia were at that time under restoration and could not be viewed).
The House of the Vestal Virgins in the Forum.
Imperial gardens on the Palatine.
The Auditorium of Maecenas.
The Mausoleum of Augustus.
The so-called temple of Minerva Medica.
Part of the Horti Sallusti.
The *Muro Torto*, and the site of the *Collis Hortulorum*.
Campania
The National Museum at Naples.
The Archaeological Museums at Stabiae and Boscoreale.
Villa Jovis on Capri.
The Villa of Poppaea, Oplontis.
A terraced garden associated with the Baths at Baiae.
Housing and gardens at Herculaneum and Pompeii.

For Pompeii I include two lists for the houses I have personally inspected because so few are now open to the public. On my second study tour in 1992, I was able to obtain a student's permit to study a number of gardens that are normally locked.
Gardens for which there was open access (Sept.1991&Sept1992)
Public gardens associated with the Triangular Forum;
The portico garden in the so-called Palaestra by the Amphitheatre.
House of the Faun (Pompeii,VI,xii,2).
House of the Hunt (Pompeii,VII,iv,48)
House of the Little Fountain (Pompeii,VI,viii,23).
House of Sallust (Pompeii,VI,ii,4).
House of Ceii (Pompeii,I,vi,15).
House of Loreius Tiburtinus (Pompeii,II,ii,2).
House of the Vettii (Pompeii,V,xv,1/2).
Hortus of the Shop/House (Pompeii,I,xx,5).
Hortus of the Fugitives (Pompeii,I,xxi,2).
Villa of the Mysteries (nr. Pompeii).
Gardens for which a permit was obtained
House of Adonis (Pompeii,VI,vii,18).
House of Apollo (Pompeii,VI,vii,23).
House of Ancora Nera (Pompeii,VI,x,7).
House of the Dioscuri (Pompeii,VI,ix,6).
House of the Epigrams (Pompeii,V,i,18).
House of M.L.Fronto (Pompeii,V,iv,A).
House of the Golden Cupids (Pompeii,VI,xvi,7/38).
House of the Great Fountain (Pompeii,VI,viii,22).
House of Julia Felix (Pompeii,II,iv,2/3).
House of Marine Venus (Pompeii,II,iii,3).
House of Meleagro (Pompeii,VI,ix,2).
House of Obellio Firmo (Pompeii,IX,xiv,A&C).
House of the Silver Wedding (Pompeii,V,ii,J).

A limited view of some gardens was made through locked doors or windows, including:
House of the Bear (Pompeii,VII,ii,45).
House of the Coloured Capitals (Pompeii,VII,iv,31/51).
House of the Tragic Poet (Pompeii,VI,viii,5).

APPENDIX II: PLINY'S *HIPPODROMUS* GARDEN

This extract forms the most descriptive account of a Roman Garden (of those belonging to a Villa Urbana). Pliny here is describing, to a friend, his Tusci Villa (*Epistles*, V,6,32ff).

' The design and beauty of the buildings are greatly surpassed by the riding-ground (*hippodromus*). The centre is quite open so that the whole extent of the course can be seen as one enters. It is planted round with ivy-clad plane trees, green with their own leaves above, and below with the ivy which climbs over trunk and branch and links tree to tree as it spreads across them. Box shrubs grow between the plane trees, and outside there is a ring of laurel bushes which add their shade to that of the planes. Here the straight part of the course ends, curves round in a semicircle, and changes its appearance, becoming darker and more densely shaded by the cypress trees planted round to shelter it, whereas the inner circuits-for there are several-are in open sunshine; roses grow there and the cool shadow alternates with the pleasant warmth of the sun. At the end of the winding alleys of the rounded end of the course you return to the straight path, or rather paths, for there are several separated by intervening box hedges. Between the grass lawns here and there are box shrubs clipped into innumerable shapes, some being letters which spell the gardener's name or his master's; small obelisks of box alternate with fruit trees, and then suddenly in the midst of this ornamental scene is what looks like a piece of rural country planted there. The open space in the middle is set off by low plane trees planted on each side; farther off are acanthuses with their flexible glossy leaves, then more box figures and names.

At the upper end of the course is a curved dining seat of white marble, shaded by a vine trained over four slender pillars of Carystian marble. Water gushes out through pipes from under the seat as if pressed out by the weight of people sitting there, is caught in a stone cistern and then held in a finely-worked marble basin which is regulated by a hidden device so as to remain full without overflowing. The preliminaries and main dishes for dinner are placed on the edge of the basin, while the lighter ones float about in vessels shaped like birds or little boats. A fountain opposite plays and catches its water, throwing it high in the air so that it falls back into the basin, where it is played again at once through a jet connected with the inlet. Facing the seat is a bedroom which contributes as much beauty to the scene as it gains from its position. It is built of shining white marble, extended by folding doors which open straight out into greenery; its upper and lower windows all look out into more greenery above and below. A small alcove which is part of the room but separated from it contains a bed, and although it has windows in all its walls, the light inside is dimmed by the dense shade of a flourishing vine which climbs over the whole building up to the roof. There you can lie and imagine you are in a wood, but without the risk of rain. Here too a fountain rises and disappears underground, while here and there are marble chairs which anyone tired with walking appreciates as much as the building itself. By every chair is a tiny fountain, and throughout the riding-ground can be heard the sound of the streams directed into it, the flow of which can be controlled by hand to water one part of the garden or another or sometimes the whole at once ....'.

APPENDIX III: GARDEN PLANTS MENTIONED BY PLINY IN HIS *NATURAL HISTORY*

NAMES OF PLANTS	ORNAMENTAL	CHAPLET	WINE	BEES	MEDICINAL	CULINARY
Acanthus	x	-	-	-	x	-
Adonis	-	x	-	-	-	-
Amaranth (Immortales)	-	x	-	-	-	-
Anemone	-	x	-	-	x	-
Anise	-	-	-	-	x	x
Anthyllis (barba-jovis)	x	-	-	-	-	-
Apiastrum	-	x	-	x	x	-
Asparagus	-	-	x	-	x	x
Basil	-	-	-	-	x	x
Beans	-	-	-	x	x	x
Beet	-	-	-	-	x	x
Blite	-	-	-	-	x	x
Box	x	-	-	-	-	-
Brussels Sprout	-	-	-	-	x	x
Cabbage	-	-	-	-	x	x
Caper	-	-	-	-	x	x
Cardoon	-	-	-	-	x	x
Carraway	-	-	-	-	-	x
Carrot	-	-	x	-	-	-
Casia	-	x	-	x	-	-
Catmint	-	-	x	-	x	x
Cedar	-	-	x	-	-	-
Cerintha	-	-	-	x	-	-
Chervil	-	-	-	-	x	x
Chicory	-	-	-	-	x	-
Chives	-	-	-	-	-	x
Chrysanthemum (parthenium)	-	x	-	-	-	-
Citron	x	-	-	-	x	-
Convolvulus	-	x	-	-	-	-
Coriander	-	-	-	-	x	x
Cornflower (Cyanus)	-	-	x	-	-	-
Cress	-	-	-	-	x	x
Crocus	-	-	-	-	x	x
Cucumber	x	-	-	-	x	x
Cumin	-	-	-	-	x	-
Cunila	-	-	-	x	x	-
Cyclamen	-	x	-	-	-	-
Cynoglosum	x	-	-	-	-	-
Cypress	x	-	x	-	x	-
Dill	-	-	-	-	x	x
Dittany	-	-	x	-	-	-
Elecampane	-	-	-	-	x	x
Endive	-	-	-	-	x	x
Fennel	-	x	-	-	x	x
Gallic nard/Valerian	-	-	x	-	x	-
Garlic	-	-	-	-	x	x
Gentian	-	-	x	-	-	-
Germander	-	-	x	-	-	-
Gourd	-	-	-	-	x	x
Ground pine/ pine	x	-	x	-	-	-
Heliotrope	-	-	-	-	x	x
Hemp	-	-	-	-	-	x
Holly	x	-	-	-	x	-
Horehound	-	-	x	-	x	-
Hyacinth	-	x	-	-	x	-
Hyssop	-	-	x	-	x	-
Jujube tree	x	x	-	-	-	-
Juniper	-	-	x	-	-	-
Iris	-	x	-	-	x	-
Ivy	x	x	-	-	-	-
Laurel	x	-	x	-	x	-
Lavender	-	-	x	-	-	-
Leek	-	-	-	-	x	x

NAMES OF PLANTS	ORNAMENTAL	CHAPLET	WINE	BEES	MEDICINAL	CULINARY
Lettuce	-	-	-	-	x	x
Lily	x	x	-	x	x	-
Linseed	-	-	-	-	x	-
Lovage	-	-	-	-	x	x
Lychnis	x	-	-	-	x	-
Maidenhair (Adiatum)	x	-	-	-	x	-
Mallow	-	-	-	-	x	x
Mandragora	-	-	x	-	-	-
Marjoram	-	x	x	-	x	x
Mastic tree	-	-	x	-	-	-
Melilot	-	x	-	x	x	-
Melissophyllum (balm)	-	-	-	x	x	-
Mint	x	x	x	-	x	x
Moss	x	-	-	-	-	-
Mustard	-	-	-	x	x	x
Myrtle	x	-	-	-	x	-
Narcissus	-	x	-	-	x	-
Nettle tree	x	-	-	-	x	-
Oleander	x	x	-	-	x	-
Onion	-	-	-	-	x	x
Orache	-	-	-	-	x	-
Orage	-	-	-	-	-	x
Date Palm	x	-	-	-	x	-
Parsnip	-	-	-	-	x	-
Parsley	-	-	x	-	x	x
Partridge plant	-	-	-	-	-	x
Pennyroyal	-	-	-	-	x	x
Pepperwort	-	-	-	-	x	x
Periwinckle	x	x	-	-	x	-
Plane tree	x	-	-	-	x	-
Poppy	-	-	-	x	x	x
Purslain	-	-	-	-	x	x
Radish	-	-	-	-	x	x
Rape	-	-	-	-	-	x
Rocket	-	-	-	-	x	x
Rose	x	x	x	x	x	-
Rosemary (*libanotis/conyza*)	-	x	-	x	x	-
Rue	-	-	x	-	x	x
Saffron	-	x	-	-	x	x
Sage	-	-	x	-	-	-
Smilax	x	x	-	-	-	-
Sorrel	-	-	-	-	x	x
Southernwood	-	x	x	-	x	x
Spalax	-	-	-	-	x	-
Squill	-	-	-	-	x	x
Strawberry tree	x	-	-	-	-	-
Summer beet	-	-	-	-	x	-
Sweet rush	-	-	x	-	x	-
Terebinth	-	-	x	-	-	-
Thapsia	-	-	-	-	x	-
Thyme	-	x	x	x	x	x
Tree medick	-	-	-	x	-	-
Tuber apple	x	-	-	-	-	-
Turnip	-	-	x	-	x	x
Vetch	-	-	-	x	-	-
Vine	x	x	x	-	x	-
Violet	x	x	-	x	x	-

References (from Loeb editions)
Plants that ornamented gardens: Volumes IV; V; VI.
Garden plants used to make chaplets: Book XXI.
Garden plants used in making wines/cordials: Book XIV.
Garden plants for bees, to make honey: Book XXI,41,70.
Garden plants with medicinal properties: Book XX.
Culinary garden plants: Book XIX.

APPENDIX IV: ARCHAEOLOGICAL EVIDENCE OF ROMAN GARDEN FLORA

COMMON NAME	BOTANICAL NAME	V	L	N	B
Anise	(*Pimpinella anisum*)	-	-	-	x
Apple	(*Malus*)	-	-	x	x*
Asparagus	(*Asparagus officinalis*)	-	-	-	x
Beans	(*Leguminosae*)	-	x	-	x
Beet	(*Beta vulgaris*)	-	-	-	x
Bellflower	(*Campanula*)	xc	-	-	-
Blackberry	(*Rubus fruticosus*)	-	-	x	x*
Borage family	(*Boraginnaceae*)	-	x	-	-
Box	(*Buxus*)	-	x	-	x
Buttercup family	(*Ranunculus*)	x	-	-	-
Cabbage etc	(*Brassiceae*)	xc	-	-	x*
Campion	(*Lychnis*)	xc	-	-	-
Caper	(*Euphorbia lathyrus*)	-	-	-	x
Carrot	(*Daucus carota*)	x	-	-	x*
Celery	(*Apium graveolens*)	xc	-	x	x*
Chamomile	(*Anthemis*)	-	x	-	-
Cherry	(*Prunus avium*)	-	-	x	x*
Cherry laurel	(*Prunus laurocerasus*)	-	-	-	xs
Chestnut	(*Castanea sativa*)	x	-	-	x*
Chervil	(*Anthriscus*)	-	-	-	xs
Cinquefoil family	(*Potentilla*)	x	-	-	-
Chicory	(*Cichorioideae*)	xc	-	-	-
Columbine	(*Aquilegia*)	-	-	-	x
Coriander	(*Coriandrum sativum*)	-	-	x	x*
Cornflower	(*Centaurea*)	-	x	x	-
Cucumber	(*Cucumis sativus*)	-	-	-	x*
Cypress	(*Cupressaceae*)	x	-	-	-
Daisy/Aster family	(*Compositae*)	-	x	-	-
Dill	(*Anethum graveolens*)	-	-	-	x*
Elder	(*Sambucus*)	-	-	-	xs
Fennel	(*Foeniculum vulgare*)	-	-	x	x*
Ferns	(*Dryopteris & Polypodiaceae*)	x	-	-	-
Fig	(*Ficus carica*)	-	-	-	x*
Flax	(*Linum*)	-	-	-	x
Geranium family	(*Geraniaceae*)	x	-	-	-
Grasses	(*Gramineae*)	x	x	-	xb
Hawthorn	(*Crataegus*)	-	-	-	xs
Hazelnut	(*Corylus avellana*)	x	x	x	xs
Holly	(*Ilex aquifoliaceae*)	-	-	-	xs
Juniper	(*Juniperus*)	xc	x	-	-
Ivy	(*Hedra*)	-	x	-	-
Lily	(*Liliaceae*)	x	x	-	-
Lotus	(*Lotus edulis*)	-	x	-	-
Mallow	(*Malvaceae*)	x	x	-	xs
Medlar	(*Mespilus germanica*)	-	-	-	x*r
Mulberry	(*Morus nigra*)	-	-	-	x*
Mustard family		x	x	x	x*
Myrtle	(*Myrtus*)	x	-	-	-
Nettles	(*Urticaceae*)	x	-	-	xb
Oak family	(*Quercus*)	x	x	-	-
Oleander	(*Nerium Oleander*)	xj	-	-	-
Parsnip	(*Pastinaca sativa*)	-	-	-	xs
Parsley	(*Petroselinum sativum*)	-	-	-	x*s
Pea	(*Pisum sativum*)	-	-	-	x*
Peach	(*Prunus persica*)	-	-	-	x
Pear	(*Pyrus communis*)	-	-	x	x*
Pine	(*Pinaceae*)	x	x	-	x*
Pink	(*Caryophyllaceae*)	x	x	-	-
Plantain	(*Plantaginaceae*)	x	x	-	-

COMMON NAME	BOTANICAL NAME	V	L	N	B
Plum/damson/bullace	(*Prunus domestica*)	-	-	x	x*
Poppy	(*Papaver somniferum*)	-	-	-	x*
Radish	(*Raphanus sativus*)	-	-	-	x*s
Raspberry	(*Rubus idaeus*)	-	-	-	x*
Rose	(*Rosaceae*)	x	x	-	x
St.John's Wort	(*Hypericum*)	-	-	x	xs
Scabious	(*Scabiosa*)	-	x	-	-
Snow in summer	(*Cerastium*)	xc	-	-	-
Southernwood/Wormwood	(*Artemisia*)	x	x	-	-
Strawberry	(*Fragaria vesca*)	-	-	-	x*
Strawberry tree	(*Arbutus unedo*)	x	-	-	-
Summer Savory	(*Satureja hortensis*)	-	-	-	xb
Thyme	(*Thymus. Labiatae*)	-	x	x	-
Vervain	(*Verbena officinalis*)	-	-	x	-
Vine	(*Vitis*)	x	-	-	x*
Violet	(*viola*)	-	-	-	xs
Walnut	(*Juglans*)	x	x	x	x*

KEY

V = Sites covered by Vesuvius.
L = Lescar, a southern Gallo-Roman site (Atlantic Pyrennes).
N = Neuss, a northern Gallo-Roman site (near Cologne).
B = Sites in Britain.
B*= Introductions to Britain.

SOURCES

V : Jashemski,1993, Appendix III.
Vj : Jashemski,1993,p.299.
Vc: Ciarallo,1993,113,tables 1 & 2.
L : Ferdière,1988,124.
N : Ferdière,1988,108 & 118.
B : Murphy & Scaife,1991,88,table 8.2.
Bb : Williams & Zeepvat,Vol,II,1994,568f,tables 66 &68.
Bs : Boon,1957,171; ibid,1974,249/50.
B*: Cunliffe,1981,98/9.
B*r: Ryley,1995.

LIST OF ABBREVIATIONS

AJA	*American Journal of Archaeology*
Ant. J	*Antiquaries Journal*
BAR	*British Archaeological Reports*
BCH	*Bulletin de Correspondance Hellenique*
CBA	*Council for British Archaeology*
CIL	*Corpus Inscriptionum Latinarum*
JHS	*Journal of Hellenic Studies*
JRA	*Journal of Roman Archaeology*
JRS	*Journal of Roman Studies*
L	C.Linnaeus (1707-1778)
MEFRA	*Melanges de l'Ecole francaise de Rome, Antiquite*
NSc	*Notizie degli scavi di Antichità*
PBSR	*Papers of the British School at Rome*
RA	*Revue Archéologique*
RICA	*Researches in Campanian Archaeology*
RM	*Römische Mitteilungen des Deutschen Archäologischen Instituts*
SHA	*Scriptores Historiae Augustae*

BIBLIOGRAPHY

AKSIT I.	(1994) *Ancient Ephesus*, Antalya.
ALARCÃO J.	(1988) *Roman Portugal*, Warminster.
ALARCÃO J & R. ETIENNE	(1981) 'Les Jardins à Conimbriga (Portugal), in *Ancient Roman Gardens*, Washington, pp.69-80.
ALEXANDER M. & N. ENNAÏFER	(1975) 'Quelques Precisions À Propos de la Chronologie des Mosaiques D'Utique', in *La Mosaïque Gréco-Romaine II,* ed.H.Stern & M.LeGlay, Paris, pp.31-39.
————	(1980) *Corpus des Mosaiques de Tunisie, Thuburbo Majus,2.1*, Tunis.
AMELUNG W.	(1912) *The Museums and Ruins of Rome*,I, London.
APPLETON G.	(1987) *Animal Sculpture from Roman Gardens*, PHD thesis, University of Newcastle-Upon-Tyne.
ARISTOTLE	(1961) *The Athenian Constitution*, trans. J.Warrington, London.
ARNOULD P. & Y. THÉBERT	(1993) 'Secteur D: note sur des charbons de bois provennant de la fouille 1992', in 'Chronique, Rome: le Palatin (Vigna Barberini)', *MEFRA*,105.1, pp.419-492.
ARRIAN	(1949) *Anabasis of Alexander*, trans. E.I.Robson, Loeb.
ART ANTIQUE	(1972) *Collections Privées de Suisse Romande*, Geneva.
ASHBY T.	(1906) 'Classical Topography of the Roman Campagna-II', *PBSR*,3, pp.3-197.
————	(1915) 'Roman Malta', *JRS*,5,1, pp.23-80.
ATHENAEUS	(1957) *The Deipnosophists*, trans.C.B.Gulick, Loeb.
AURIGEMMA S.	(1955) *The Baths of Diocletian and the Museo Nazionale Romano*, 3rd edn. Rome.
————	(1971) *Villa Adriana (Hadrian's Villa) Near Tivoli*, 8th edn.Tivoli.
BALLU A.	(1910) *Guide Illustré de Timgad*, Paris.
BALMELLE C.	(1994) 'Les représentations d'Arbres fruitiers sur les mosaiques tardives d'Aquitaine', in *Fifth International Colloquim on Ancient Mosaics, JRA*, supplementary series no.9, Ann Arbor, pp .261-272.
BALTY J.C.	(1981) *Guide d'Apamée*, Bruxelles.
BARADEZ et al	(1952) *Tipasa, Cherchel, Tebessa*, Algiers.
BIEBER M.	(1955) *The Sculpture of the Hellenistic Age*, New York.
BELLIDO G.Y.	(1949) *Escvltvras Romanas, de Espana, Y Portvgal*. Madrid.
BELLIDO A.G.	(1960) *Colonia Aelia Augusta Italica* Instituto Español de Arqueologia, Madrid.
BEN KHADER A.& D.SOREN	(1987) *Carthage: A Mosaic of Ancient Tunisia*, London.
BIRMINGHAM BOTANICAL GARDENS	(1994) 'The Historic Gardens I', *Spring Newsletter*, pp.9-11.
BLAMEY M. & C.GREY-WILSON	(1993) *Mediterranean Wild Flowers*, St.Helier, Jersey.
BOERSMA J.S.	(1985) *Amoenissima Civitas, Block V,ii at Ostia: description and analysis of its visible remains*, Assen.
BOËTHIUS A. & J.WARD-PERKINS	(1970) *Etruscan and Roman Architecture*, Harmondsworth.
BOND C.J. & R. ILES	(1991) 'Early Gardens in Avon and Somerset', in *Garden Archaeology*, ed.A.E.Brown, CBA

	Research Report 78, pp.36-52.
BONFANTE L.	(1990) *Etruscan*, BM, London.
BOON G.C.	(1957) *Roman Silchester The Archaeology of a Romano-British Town*, London.
————	(1974) *Silchester The Roman Town of Calleva*, Newton Abbot.
BÖRSCH-SUPAN E.	(1967) *Garten-Landschafts-und Paradiesmotive im Inneraum*, Berlin.
BROISE H.& V.JOLIVET	(1994/1995) 'Des Jardins de Lucullus au Palais des Pincii', Bulletin de la SFAC, *RA*, pp.188-198.
CALPERNIUS SICULUS	(1961) *Eclogues*, trans. J.W.Duff, Loeb.
CARANDINI A. &	(1980) 'Excavations at the Roman Villa of "Sette Finestre" in Etruria, 1975-9 First Interim Report',
T. TATTON-BROWN	in *Roman Villas in Italy*, ed.K.Painter, British Museum, London, pp.9-43.
CARRINGTON R.S.	(1931) 'Studies in the Campanian 'Villae Rusticae', *JRS*,21, pp.110-130.
CARROLL- SPILLECKE M.	(1992) 'The gardens of Greece from Homeric to Roman Times', *Journal of Garden History*,12, pp.84-101.
CASSIUS DIO	(1961) *Dio's Roman History*, trans. E.Cary, Loeb.
CASSIODORUS	(1886) *Variae*, trans. T.Hodgkin, London.
CASTELL R.	(1982) *The Villas of the Ancients Illustrated*, reprint of the 1728 edition, New York.
CATLING H.W.	(1974) 'Archaeology in Greece,1973-74', *JHS*,94, pp.3-41.
CATO	(1967) *De Agricultura*, trans.W.D.Hooper, Loeb.
CATULUS	(1988) *Opera*, trans.F.W.Cornish, Loeb.
CIARALLO A.M.	(May 1992) 'The Gardens of Pompeii', lecture notes issued during the Discovering Pompeii Exhibition, London.
————	(1993) 'The Garden of "Casa Dei Casti Amanti" (Pompeii, Italy)', *Garden History*,21, pp.110-116.
CICERO	(1993) *Academica*, trans. H.Rackham, Loeb.
————	(1919) *Ad Atticum*, trans. E.O.Winstedt, Loeb.
————	(1928) *Ad Familiares*, trans. G.Williams, Loeb.
————	(1929) *Ad Fratrem*, trans. G.Williams, Loeb.
————	(1988) *De Legibus*, trans. C.Walker Keyes, Loeb.
————	(1979) *De Oratore*, trans. H.Rackham, Loeb.
————	(1969) *Laws*, trans, B.Radice, Loeb.
C.I.L.	(1863-) *Corpus Inscriptionum Latinarum*, vols.V;VI;X, Berlin.
CIMA M.& E. LA ROCCA	(1986) *Le Tranquille Dimore Degli Dei: La Residenza Imperiale Degli Horti Lamiani*, Venice.
CLARKE J.R.	(1991) *The Houses of Roman Italy 100BC-AD250 Ritual, Space, and Decoration*, Berkeley.
COFFIN D.R.	(1991) *Gardens and Gardening in Papal Rome*, Princeton.
COLUMELLA	(1955) *De Arboribus*, trans. E.S.Forster, Loeb.
————	(1955) *De Re Rustica*, trans. E.S.Forster, Loeb.
CORDELLO	(1986) *Ostia*, Venice.
CUNLIFFE B.	(1968) 'Excavations at Fishbourne, 1967, Seventh & Final Interim Report', *Ant.J*.48. pp.32-40.
————	(1971) Fishbourne A Roman Palace and its Garden, London.
————	(1981) 'Roman Gardens in Britain: A Review of the Evidence', in *Ancient Roman Gardens*, Washington, pp.97-108.
DAGRON G.	(1978) *Vie et Miracles de Sainte Thècle*, Bruxelles.
DAREMBERG C.H. & E.D.M.SAGLIO	(1900) *Dictionnaire des Antiquités, Greques et Romaines*, Paris.
DE CARO S.	(1987) 'The Sculptures of the Villa of Poppaea at Oplontis: A Preliminary Report', in *Ancient Roman Villa Gardens*, Washington, pp.79-133.
DETSICAS A.P.	(1973) 'Excavations at Eccles, 1972, 11th Interim Report', *Archaeologia Cantiana*,88, pp.73-80.
————	(1974) 'Exhibits at Ballots,2. Finds from the pottery kiln(s) at Eccles, Kent', *Ant.J*.14, pp.305-306.
DIODORUS SICULUS	(1952) *Diodorus of Sicily*, trans.C.H.Oldfather, Loeb.
DOWN A.	(1989) 'Exhibits at Ballots', *Ant.J*,69, pp.308-309.
DRAGOTTA A.M.	(1978) *Piazza Armerina*, Palermo.
DWYER E.J.	(1982) *Pompeian Domestic Sculpture*, Rome.
ELLIS S.P.	(1988) 'The End of the Roman House', *AJA*,92, pp.565-576.
ELLIS-REES W.	(1995) 'Gardening in the Age of Humanism: Petrarch's Journal', *Garden History*,23, pp.10-28.

ENNAÏFER M.	(1973) *La Civilisation Tunisienne à Travers la Mosaïque*, Tunis.
ERDEMGIL S.	(1989) *Ephesus [Ruins and Museum]*, Istanbul.
ESPÉRANDIEU E.	(1925) *Recueil Général des Bas-Reief, Statues et Bustes de la Gaule Romaine*, 9, Paris.
FERDIÈRE A.	(1988) *Les Campagnes en Gaule Romaine*,2, Paris.
FÉVRIER P.A.	(1975) 'Remarques sur des Mosaiques de Frejus', in *La Mosaique Gréco-Romaine II*, ed.H.Stern & M.LeGlay, Paris, pp.291-300.
FRADIER G.	(1994) *Roman Mosaics of Tunisia*, 5th edn. Tunis.
FRANCHI F.	(1992) *Rediscovering Pompeii*, Rome.
FRASER P.M. & B.NICHOLAS	(1958) 'The Funerary Garden of Mousa', *JRS*,48, pp.117-129.
FREMERDORF F.	(1956) *Das Römische Haus mit dem Dionysos-Mosaik vor dem Südportal des Kölner Domes*, Berlin.
FRERE S.	(1983) *Verulamium Excavations*, 2, Society of Antiquaries, London.
———	(1992) 'Roman Britain in 1991', *Britania*,23, pp.256-308.
FRIEDLANDER L.	(1968) *Roman Life and Manners under the Early Empire*,2, New York.
FRIENDSHIP-TAYLOR R.M.& D.E.	(1994) *Iron Age & Roman Piddington*, Interim Report for1989-1993, Upper Nene Archaeological Society.
GETTY J.PAUL MUSEUM	(1992) *The J.Paul Getty Museum guide to the villa and its gardens*, Malibu.
GLEASON K.L.	(1994) 'Porticus Pompeiana: a new perspective on the first public park of Ancient Rome', *Journal of Garden History*,14, pp.13-27.
GODWIN H.E.	(1956) *The History of the British Flora*, Cambridge.
GORGES J-G.	(1979) *Les Villas Hispano-Romaines*, Paris.
GOTHEIN M.L.	(1966) *A History of Garden Art*,1, trans.Archer-Hind, New York.
GOUDINEAU C. & Y.KISCH	(1984) *Archeological Guide to Vaison La Romaine*, Vaison-La-Romaine
GOW A.S.F.	(1938) 'The Adoniazusae of Theocritus', *JRS*,58, pp.180-204.
GRACIE H.S. & E.G.PRICE	(1979) 'Frocester Court Roman Villa, Second Report 1968-77: the Courtyard', *Transactions of the Bristol and Gloucestershire Archaeological Society*, 97, pp.10-64.
GRENIER A.	(1931) *Manuel D'Archéologie Gallo-Romaine*, Paris.
GRIMAL P.	(1969) *Les Jardins Romaines*, 2nd edn. Paris.
GUILLÉN J.I.R.	(1992) 'La villa tardorromana de "La Malena" en Azuara y el mosaico de las Bobas de Cadmo y Harmonia', *JRA*,5, pp.148-161.
HALLAM G.H.	(1914) 'Horace's Villa at Tivoli', *JRS*,4, pp.121-138.
HARDING P.A. & C.LEWIS	'Archaeological Investigations at Tockenham,Wilts 1994',(Typescript in advance of publication).
HARVEY J.	(1981) *Mediaeval Gardens*, London.
HEMSOLL D.	(1990) 'The Architecture of Nero's Golden House', in *Architecture and Architectural Sculpture in the Roman Empire*, ed.M.Henig, Oxford, pp.10-38.
HERO	(1851) *The Pneumatics of Hero of Alexandria*, trans .B.Woodcroft, London.
———	(1899) *Herons Von Alexandria*, trans.W.Schmit, Leipzig.
HEYDENREICH L.H. & W.LOTZ	(1974) *Architecture in Italy 1400 to 1600*, trans. M.Hottinger, Harmondsworth.
HILL D.K.	(1981) 'Some Sculpture from Roman Domestic Gardens', in *Ancient Roman Gardens*, Washington, pp.83-94.
HODGE A.T.	(1992) *Roman Aqueducts & Water Supply*, London.
HOMER	(1975) *The Odyssey of Homer*, trans.R.Lattimore, New York.
HORACE	(1947) *Odes and Epodes*, trans.C.E. Bennett, Loeb.
———	(1961) *Satires, Epistles & Ars Poetica*, trans.H.R. Fairclough, Loeb.
HUELSEN C.	(1890) 'Piante Inconografiche Encise in Marmo', *RM*, 5, pp.46-63.
HUNT D.	(1990) *Footprints in Cyprus*, London.
JASHEMSKI W.F.	(1979) *The Gardens of Pompeii, Herculaneum and the Villas destroyed by Vesuvius*, New Rochelle.
———	(1981) 'The Campanian Peristyle Garden', in *Ancient Roman Gardens*, Washington, pp .31-48.
———	(1987) 'The Villas at Boscoreale and Oplontis', in *Ancient Roman Villa Gardens*, Washington, pp.33-75.
———	(1993) *The Gardens of Pompeii*, 2, New Rochelle.
———	(1995) 'Roman Gardens in Tunisia: Preliminary Excavations in the House of Bacchus and Ariadne

	and in the East Temple at Thuburbo Maius', *AJA*,99, pp 559-576.
JASHEMSKI W.F.& S.P.R. RICOTTI	(1992) 'Preliminary Excavations in the Gardens of Hadrian's Villa: The Canopus Area and the Piazza D'Oro', *AJA*,96, pp.579-597.
JOHNSON A.C.	(1975) *An Economic Survey of Ancient Rome*, 2, Roman Egypt, ed.T.Frank, Baltimore.
JORDAN H.	(1874) *Forma Urbis Romae*, Berlin.
JUVENAL	(1918) *Satires*, trans.G.G.Ramsay, Loeb.
KAPOSSY B.	(1969) *Brunnenfiguren der hellenistischen und römischen Zeit*, Zurich.
KARAGEORGHIS V.	(1974) 'Chronique des fouilles à Chypre en 1973', *BCH*,98, pp.821-896.
KEAY S.J.	(1988) *Roman Spain*, BM, London.
KNIGHT J.K.	(1994) *Caerleon Roman Fortress*,Cardiff.
LAFON X.	(1981) 'A propos des villas de la zone de Sperlonga', *MEFRA*,93.1, pp.297-353.
LANCIANI R.	(1897) *The Ruins & Excavations of Ancient Rome*, London.
————	(no date, circa 1924) *Ancient and Modern Rome*, London.
LAROCHE C. & H.SAVAY-GUERRAS	(1984) *Saint-Romain-En-Gal*, Guides Archeologiques de la France,2, Paris.
LAUTER-BUFE H.	(1975) 'Zur Architektonischen Gartengestaltung in Pompeji und Herculaneum', in *Neue Forschungen in Pompeii*, Recklinghausen, pp.169-180.
LAVAGNE H.	(1993) 'Une Peinture Romaine Oubliée', *MEFRA*,105.2, pp.747-777.
LAWSON J.	(1950) 'The Roman Garden', *Greece & Rome*,19, pp.97-105.
LEE C.G.	(1981) 'Gardens and Gods: Jacopo Galli, Michelangelo's "Bacchus" and their art historical settings', PHD Thesis, Brown University, USA.
LeGLAY M.	(1981) 'Les Jardins à Vienne', in *Ancient Roman Gardens*, Washington, pp.51-65.
LENGYEL A. & G.T.B.RADAN	(1980) *The Archaeology of Roman Pannonia*, Lexington.
LEVI D.	(1971) *Antioch Mosaic Pavements*,I, Rome.
LING R.	(1990) 'The arts of living', in *The Roman World*, Oxford, pp.380-337.
————	(1991) *Roman Painting*, Cambridge.
LITTLEWOOD A.R.	(1987) 'Ancient Literary Evidence for the Pleasure Gardens of Roman Country Villas', in *Ancient Roman Villa Gardens*, Washington, pp.9-30.
LLOYD R.B.	(1982) 'Three Monumental Gardens on the Marble Plan', *AJA*,86, pp.91-100.
LUGLI G.	(1926) *Forma Italiae Reg.I Latium et Campania*,Vol.I, Ager Pomptinus, pars prima Anxvr-Tarracina, Rome.
————	(1938) *I Monvmenti Antichi di Roma E Svbvrbio*,3, Rome.
LUXORIUS	(1961) *Anthologia Latina*, trans.M.Rosenblum, New York.
MACDONAL W.L.	(1986) *The Architecture of the Roman Empire 2, An Urban Appraisal*, New Haven.
MACDONALD W.L. & J.PINTO	(1995) *Hadrian's Villa and its Legacy*, London.
McKAY A.G.	(1975) *Houses, Villas and Palaces in the Roman World*, New York.
MACKENDRICK P.	(1962) *The Mute Stones Speak*, London.
————	(1969) *The Iberian Stones Speak*, New York.
————	(1980) *The North African Stones Speak*, London.
————	(1981) *Greek Stones Speak*, 2nd edn. London.
MACROBIUS	(1969) *The Saturnalia*, trans.P.V. Davies, New York.
MAIURI B.	(1959) *The National Museum, Naples*, Novara.
MALLWITZ A.	(1972) *Olympia und seine Bauten*, Munich.
MARTIAL	(1973) *Epigrams*, trans.W.C.A.Ker, Loeb.
MEIGGS R.	(1960) *Roman Ostia*, Oxford.
MERRIFIELD R.	(1975) *The Archaeology of London*, London.
MINIERO P.	(1983) 'I materiali dell'Arredo della villa', in 'Premier rapport sur l'etude de la Villa San Marco à Stabies', *MEFRA*,95.2, pp.929-935.
MOFFETT L.	(1988) Unpublished typescript, 'Gardening in Roman Alcester', Circaea Vol.5,no.2, from Birmingham University, pp.73-78.
MOREL J-P.	(1993) 'Chronique Rome: Le Palatin (Vigna Barberini)', *MEFRA*,105.1, pp.419-434.
MORETTI G.	(1940) *Il Museo Delle Navi Romane Di Nemi*, Libreria dello Stato, Itinerai no.72, Rome.
MORTON H.V.	(1970) *The Fountains of Rome*, London.

MURPHY P. & R.G.SCAIFE	(1991) 'The environmental archaeology of gardens', *Garden Archaeology*, ed.A.E.Brown, CBA Research Report 78, pp.83-99.
MUSÉE DU LUXEMBOURG	(1983) *La Civilisation Romaine de la Moselle A la Sarre*, Mainz.
NEUDECKER R.	(1988) *Die Skulpturen-Ausstattung Römischer Villen in Italien*, Mainz.
NEUERBERG N.	(1965) *L'Architettura delle Fontane e dei Ninfei nell'Italia Antica*, Naples.
OTTEWILL D.	(1989) *The Edwardian Garden*, London.
OVERBECK J.	(1866) *Pompeji in seinen Gebäuden, Alterthümem und Kunstwerken*, Leipzig.
OVID	(1979) *Artis Amatoriae*, trans.J.H. Mozley, Loeb.
———	(1988) *Ex Ponto*, trans.A.L.Wheeler, Loeb.
———	(1976) *Fasti*, trans.J.G.Frazer, Loeb.
———	(1988) *Tristia*, trans. A.L.Wheeler, Loeb.
PACKER J.E.	(1967) 'The Domus of Cupid and Psyche in Ancient Ostia', *AJA*,71, pp.123-131.
PAILLER J-M.	(1969) 'A propos d'un nouvel oscillum de Bolsena', *MEFRA*,81.1, pp.627-658.
PALLADIUS	(1873) *Palladius on Husbandrie*, trans.B.Lodge, London.
PAOLI U.E.	(1990) *Rome Its People Life and Customs*, Bristol.
PERCIVAL J.	(1976) *The Roman Villa*, London.
ANON.	(1988) *Pervigilium Veneris*, trans.F.W.Cornish, Loeb.
PETRONIUS	(1986) *Satyricon*, trans.J.P.Sullivan, Harmondsworth.
PHILOSTRATUS	(1960) *Imagines*, trans.A.Fairbanks, Loeb.
———	(1921) *Vita Apollonius Tyana*, 2, trans.F.C.Conybeare, Loeb.
PLATNER S.B. & T.ASHBY	(1929) *A Topographical Dictionary of Ancient Rome*, Oxford.
PLINY	(1969) *Epistles*, trans. B.Radice, Loeb.
PLINY	(1952) *Naturalis Historiae*, trans.H.Rackham, Loeb.
PLUTARCH	(1948) *Plutarch's Lives*, trans.B.Perrin, Loeb.
PRESUHN E.	(1879) *Le Più Belle Parete di Pompéi*, Rome.
PROCOPIUS	(1978) *Bellum Gothicum*, trans.O.Veh, Munich.
PROPERTIUS	(1912) *Elegiarum*, trans.H.E.Butler, Loeb.
QUINTUS CURTIUS RUFUS	(1984) *The History of Alexander*, Harmondsworth.
REA J.R.	(1978) *The Oxyrhynchus Papyri*, 46, British Academy, London.
REBUFFAT R.	(1969) 'Maisons à Péristyle d'Afrique du Nord, Répertoire de Plans Publiés', *MEFRA*,81, pp.659-724.
———	(1974) 'Maisons à Péristyle d'Afrique du Nord, Répertoire de Plans Publiés,II', *MEFRA*,86, pp.445-499.
REINACH S.	(1897) *Répertoire de la Statuaire Greque et Romaine*, Paris.
RICA	(1986) *Corpus Topographicum Pompeianum, The Insulae of Regions I-V*, 3A, Rome.
RICHARDSON L.	(1988) *Pompeii An Architectural History*, London.
———	(1992) *New Topographical Dictionary of Ancient Rome*, Baltimore.
RICHARDSON R.	(1992 b) 'Does Dark Earth = Black?', *Current Archaeology*, 130,11,10, p.439.
RICOTTI E.S.P.	(1987) 'The Importance of Water in Roman Garden Triclinia', in *Ancient Roman Villa Gardens*, Washington, pp.137-184.
RIDGWAY B.S.	(1981) 'Greek Antecedents of Garden Sculpture', in *Ancient Roman Gardens*, Washington, pp.9-28.
RIVET A.L.F.	(1970) *The Roman Villa in Britain*, London.
ROSSITER J.J.	(1989) 'Roman villas of the Greek east and the villa in Gregory of Nyssa Ep.20', *JRA*,2, pp.101-110.
SANDERS I.F.	(1982) *Roman Crete*, Warminster.
SCHEFOLD K.	(1962) *Vergessenes Pompeji*, Bern.
Scriptores Historiae Augustae,	(1960) trans. D.Magie, Loeb.
SENECA	(1925) *Ad Lucilium Epistulae Morales*, trans. R.M. Gummere, Loeb.
SEYFFERT O.	(1894) *A Dictionary of Classical Antiquites*, 4th edn, London.
SIDONIUS APOLLINARIS	(1956) *Gai Sollii Apollinaris Sidonii Epistlularum*, trans. W.B.Anderson, Loeb.
SIRACUSANO N.	(1969) *La Villa Romana di Sirmione*, Firenze.
SISSON M.A.	(1929) 'The Stoa of Hadrian at Athens', *PBSR*, 11, pp.50-72.

SMITH A.H.	(1904) *The Later Greek and Graeco-Roman Reliefs, Decorative and Architectural Sculpture in the British Museum*, London.
SPINAZZOLA V.	(1953) *Pompei alla luce degli Scavi Nuovi di Via dell'Abbondanza (anni 1910-1923)*, Rome.
STATIUS	(1928) *Silvae*, trans.J.H.Mozley, Loeb.
STRABO	(1923) *Geography*, trans.H.L.Jones, Loeb.
STRONACH D.	(1994) 'Parterres and stone watercourses at Pasargadae: notes on the Achaemenid contribution to garden design', *Journal of Garden History*,14, pp.3-12.
SUETONIUS	(1991) *The Twelve Caesars*, trans. R.Graves, London.
SWOBODA K.M.	(1969) *Römische und Romanische Pälaste*, Graz.
TACITUS	(1966) *The Annals of Imperial Rome*, trans.M.Grant, Harmondsworth.
THÉBERT Y.	(1993) 'Private and Public Spaces: The Components of the Domus', in *Roman Art in Context*, Englewood Cliffs, N.J. pp.213-237.
THEOPHRASTUS	(1961) *Enquiry into Plants*, trans.A.Hort, Loeb.
THOMPSON D.B.	(1963) *Garden Lore of Ancient Athens*, Princeton.
TIBULLUS	(1988) *Elegies*, trans.F.W.Cornish, Loeb.
TOMEI M.A.	(1992) 'Nota sui giardini antichi del Palatino', *MEFRA*,104, pp.917-951.
TOYNBEE J.M.C.	(1982) *Death and Burial in the Roman World*, London.
UNDERWOOD P.A.	(1975) *The Kariye Djami*,4, London.
VAN BUREN A.W.	(1948) 'Pliny's Laurentine Villa', *JRS*,38, pp.35-36.
VAN BUREN A.W. & R.M.KENNEDY	(1919) 'Varro's Aviary at Casinum', *JRS*,9, pp.59-66.
VARRO	(1960) *Rerum Rusticarum*, trans.W.D.Hooper, Loeb.
VATIN C.	(1976) 'Jardins et services de voirie', *BCH*,100, pp.555-564.
VERMEULE C.C.	(1981) *Greek and Roman Sculpture in America*, California.
VETTERS H.	(1972-3) 'Grabungen 1971-72, Turkei', *Jahreshefte des Österreichischen Archäologischen Institutes in Wien*,50, pp.32-62.
VIRGIL	(1983) *The Eclogues the Georgics*, trans.C.D.Lewis, Oxford.
———	(1946) *Minor Poems*, trans.H.Rushton Fairclough, Loeb.
VITRUVIUS	(1962) *De Architectura*, trans.F.Granger, Loeb.
WACHER J.	(1978) *Roman Britain*, London.
WALLACE-HADRILL A.	(1988) 'The Social Structure of the Roman House', *PBSR*,43, pp.43-97.
WARD-PERKINS J.	(1981) *Roman Imperial Architecture*, Harmondsworth.
WARD-PERKINS J. et al.	(1986) Town Houses at Ptolemais, Cyrenaica: A Summary Report of Survey and Excavation Work in 1971, 1978-1979, *Libyan Studies*,17, pp.109-153.
WARMINGTON E.H.	(1938) *Remains of Old Latin*, Loeb.
WATTS D.J. & C.M.WATTS	(1994) 'A Roman Apartment Complex', *Scientific American*, Ancient Cities Special issue, pp.86-91.
WHITE K.D.	(1967) *Agricultural Implements of the Roman World*, Cambridge.
WHITEHOUSE H.	(1976) *The Dal Pozzo Copies of the Palestrina Mosaic*, Oxford.
WIGHTMAN E.M.	(1985) *Gallia Belgica*, London.
WILDRIG W.M.	(1987) 'Land Use at the Via Gabina Villas', in *Ancient Roman Villa Gardens*, Washington, pp.225-260.
WILLEMS W.J.H. & L.I.KOOISTRA	(1988) 'De Romeinse villa te Voerendaal; opgraving 1987', *R.O.B., Archeologie in Limburg*,327, pp.137-147.
WILLIAMS R.J. & R.J.ZEEPVAT	(1994) *Bancroft*, Bucks. Archaeological Society, Aylesbury.
WILSON R.J.A.	(1983) *Piazza Armerina*, London.
———	(1990) *Sicily under the Romans*, Warminster.
WREDE H.	(1972) *Die Spätantike Hermengalerie von Welschbillig*, Berlin.
WYCHERLEY R.E.	(1976) *How the Greeks Built Cities*, 2nd edn. London.
XENOPHON	(1923) *Oeconomics*, trans.E.C.Marchant, Loeb.
ZEEPVAT R.J.	(1988) 'Fishponds in Roman Britain', *Medieval fish, fisheries and Fishponds in England*, ed.M.Aston, BAR, 182, pp.17-26.

SCHEMATIC PLANS
INDICATING THE DEVELOPMENT
OF TOWN HOUSE AND GARDEN
DURING THE ROMAN PERIOD

Typical only; not to scale

A. Basic Town House with *Atrium Tuscanicum*

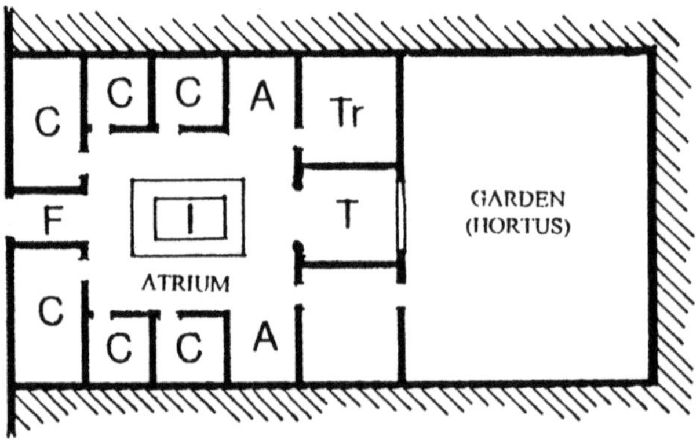

A: Ala C: Cubiculum F: Fauces I: Impluvium
T: Tablinum Tr: Triclinium

B. A Peristyle House

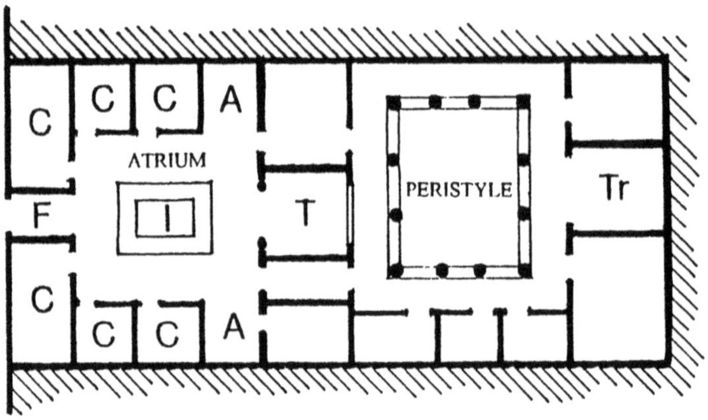

A: Ala C: Cubiculum F: Fauces I: Impluvium
T: Tablinum Tr: Triclinium

C. Later Form of Peristyle House

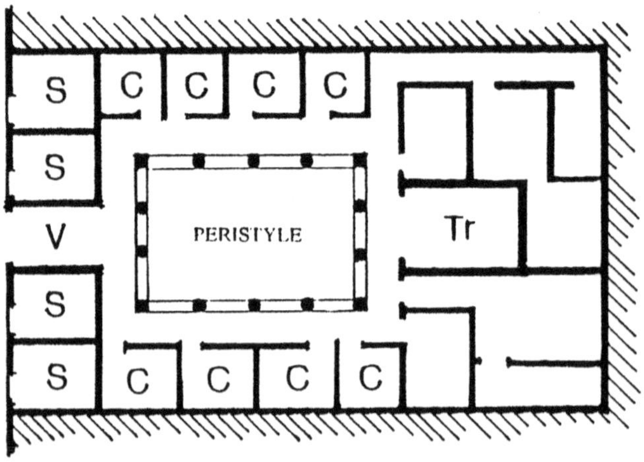

C: Cubiculum S: Shop Tr: Triclinium V: Vestibulum

Fig. 1 PLANS INDICATING THE DEVELOPMENT OF TOWN HOUSE & GARDEN DURING THE ROMAN PERIOD (L.Smith'96)

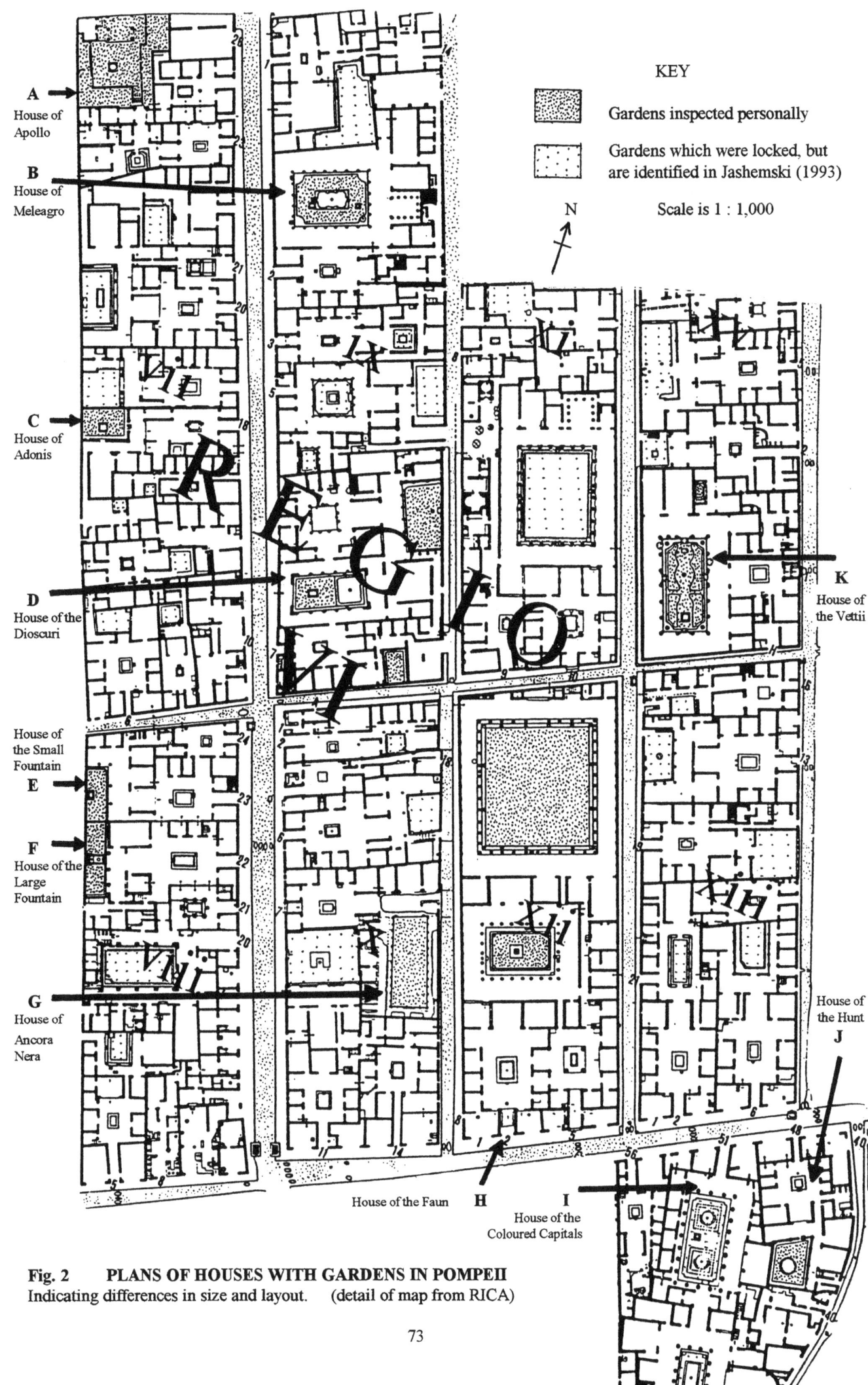

Fig. 2 PLANS OF HOUSES WITH GARDENS IN POMPEII
Indicating differences in size and layout. (detail of map from RICA)

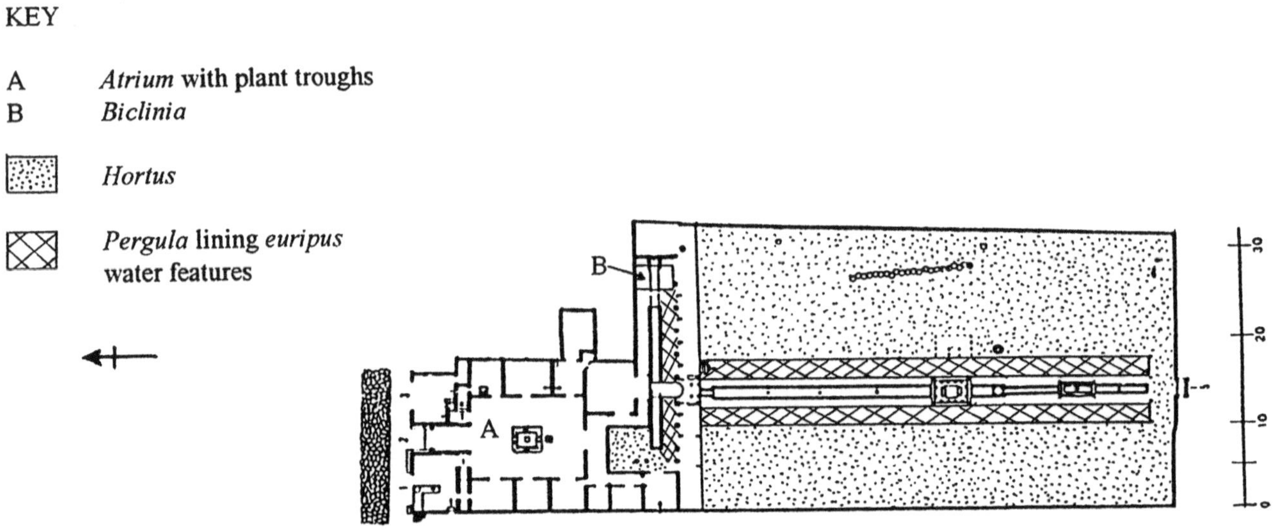

KEY

A   *Atrium* with plant troughs
B   *Biclinia*

▨   *Hortus*

▧   *Pergula* lining *euripus* water features

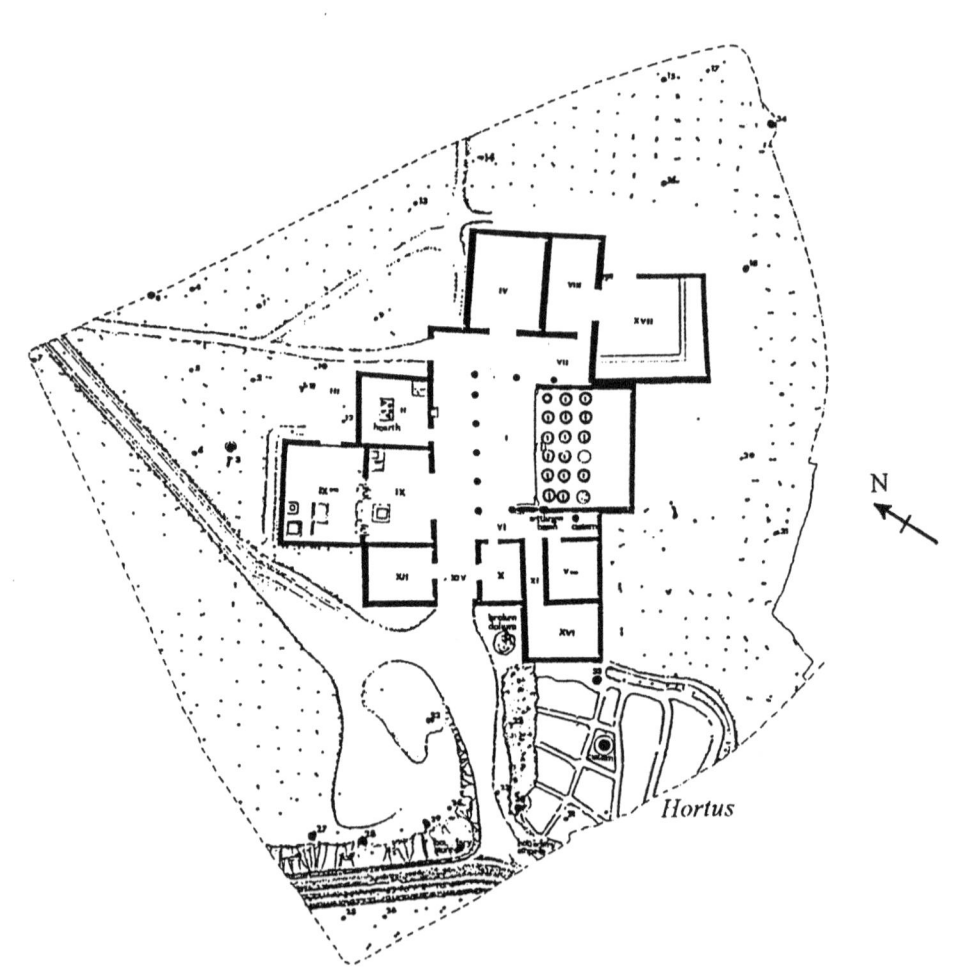

Fig. 3   PLAN: HOUSE OF LOREIUS TIBURTINUS (Pompeii,II,ii,2)   (RICA,1986,IIIA,43)

Fig. 4   PLAN SHOWING THE *HORTUS* AT A *VILLA RUSTICA*: Villa Regina, Boscoreale.
(By permission of E.S.P.Ricotti, Rome)

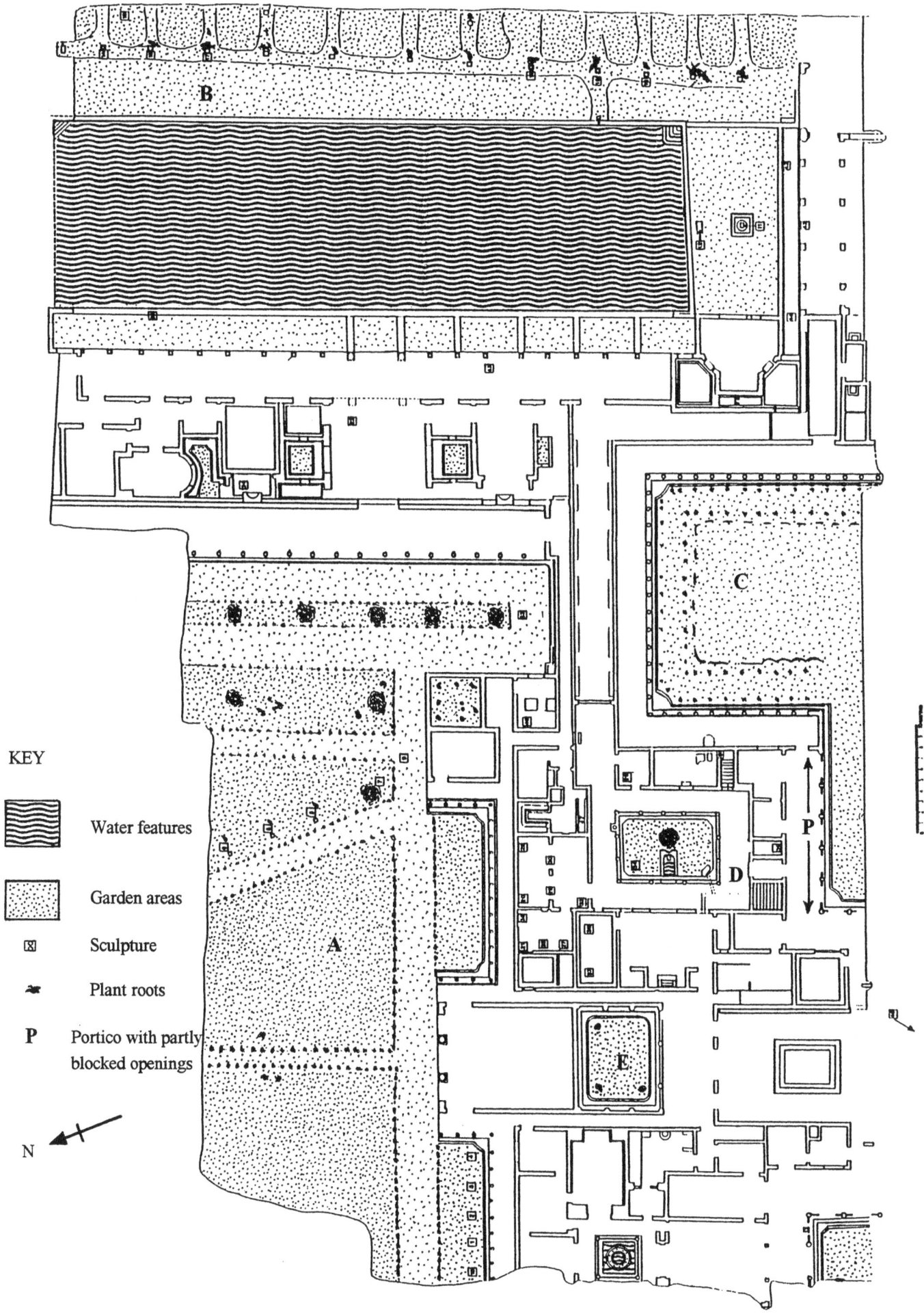

Fig. 5 PLAN OF THE *VILLA URBANA* OF POPPAEA, OPLONTIS   With findspots of plant material & sculpture.
(After DeCaro,1987,fig.2 & Jashemski,1993,plan 131. Reproduced by permission of Aristide D.Caratzas, Publisher)

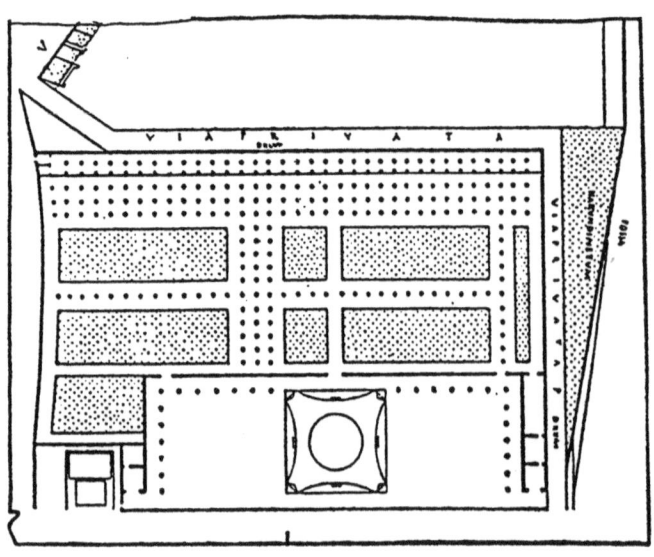

Fig. 6a MARBLE PLAN OF A FUNERARY GARDEN (Huelsen,1890,53,fig.4)

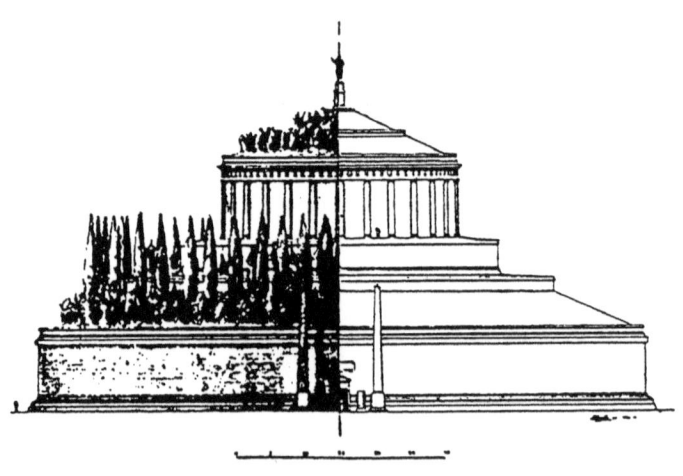

Fig. 6b RECONSTRUCTION DRAWING OF THE MAUSOLEUM OF AUGUSTUS (Lugli,1938,fig.43)

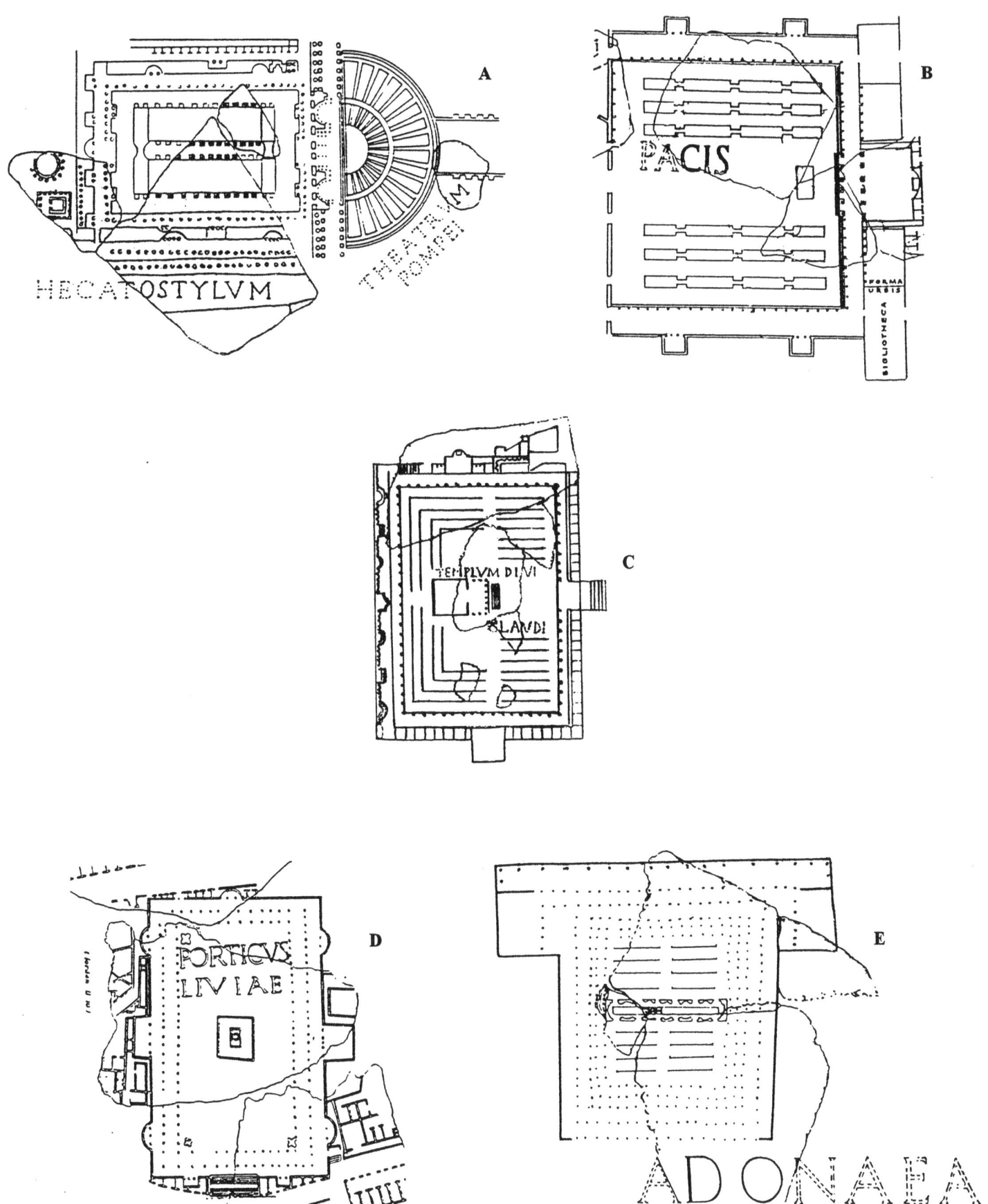

Fig. 7 PLANS OF PORTICO GARDENS FROM FRAGMENTS OF THE SEVERAN MARBLE MAP OF ROME
(After Jordan, *Forma Urbis*)

A: Porticus Pompeii   B: Forum Pacis   C: Divus Claudius   D: Porticus Liviae   E: Adonaea

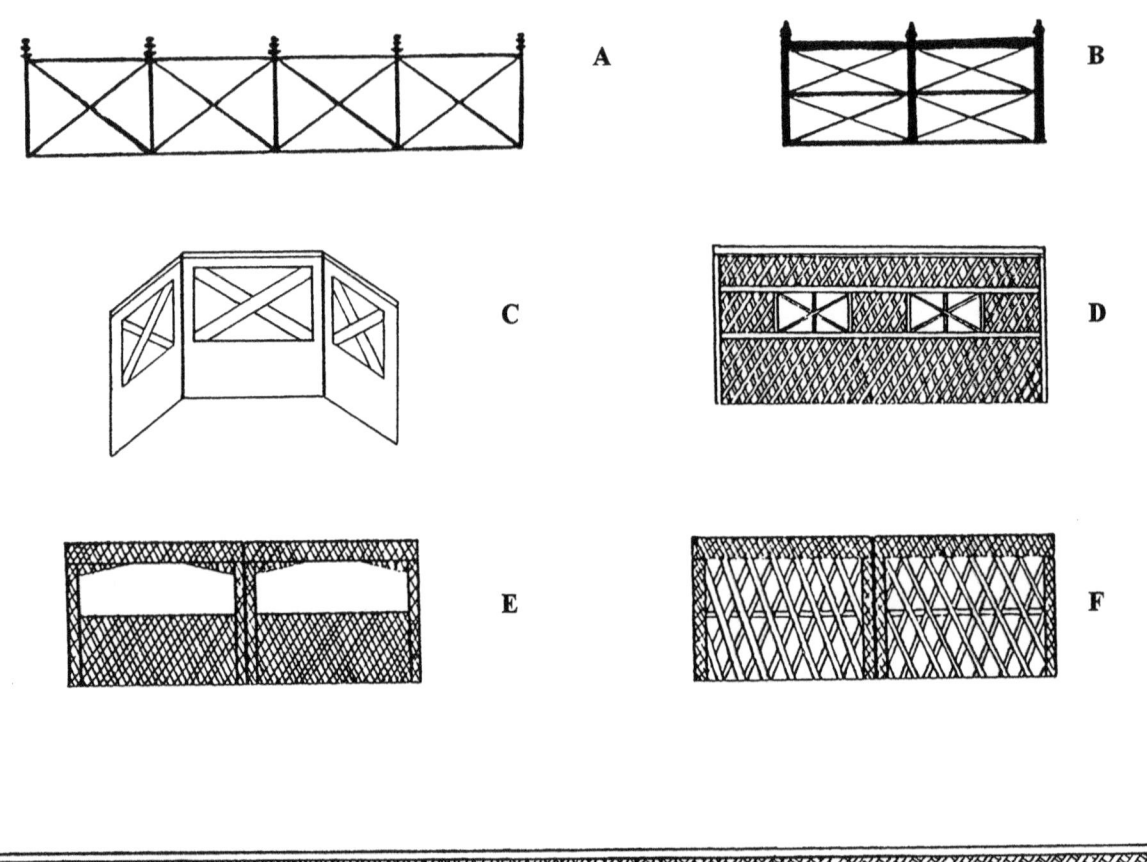
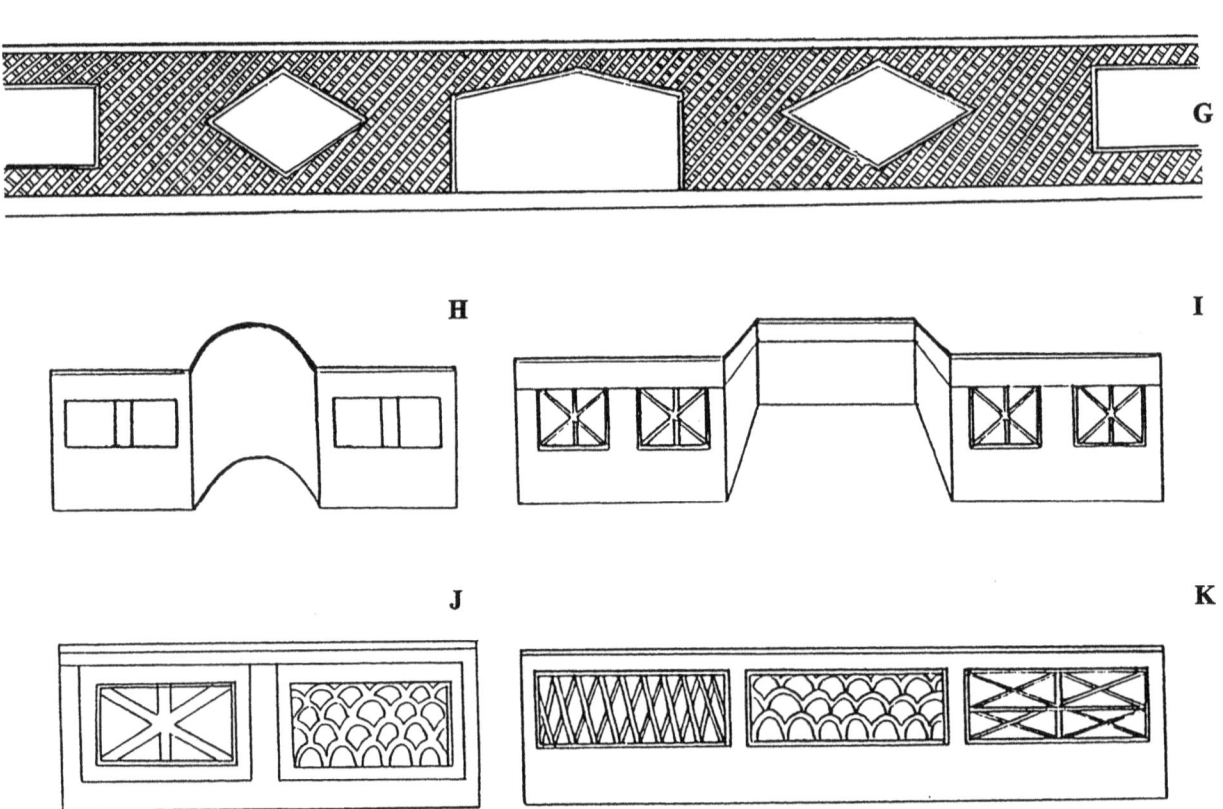

Fig. 8 DECORATIVE FENCING AS DEPICTED IN FRESCOES

KEY TO PROVENANCE
- A: Rudston Villa, Britain.
- B: Wortley Villa, Britain.
- C: National Museum Naples Inv.no.9705.
- D & G: House of the Wedding of Alexander (Pompeii, Ins.Occid.42).
- E & F: Auditorium of Maecenas, Rome.
- H & I: Auditorium of Maecenas, Rome.
- J: House of M.L.Fronto, Pompeii.
- K: Livia's Garden Room, Primaporta, Rome.

A: From Herculaneum, Naples National Museum Inv.no.9964.   (Daremberg & Saglio,1900,Vol.3,fig.3904)

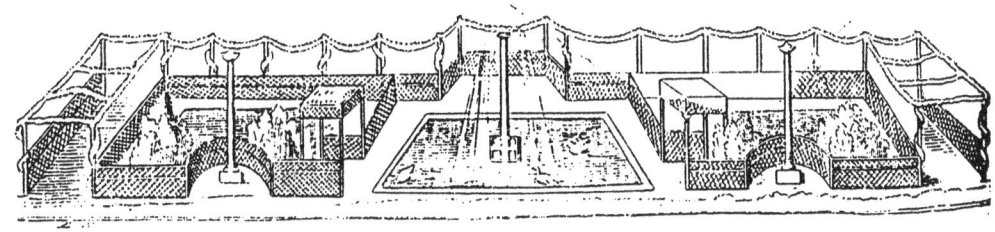

B: From the Auditorium of Maecenas, Rome   (Ibid,fig.3906)

C: From Pompeii (VII,ii,39)   (Deutsches Archäologisches Inst. neg.no.53504)

Fig. 9 MINIATURE FRESCOES OF GARDENS depicting latticework fences and *pergulae*.

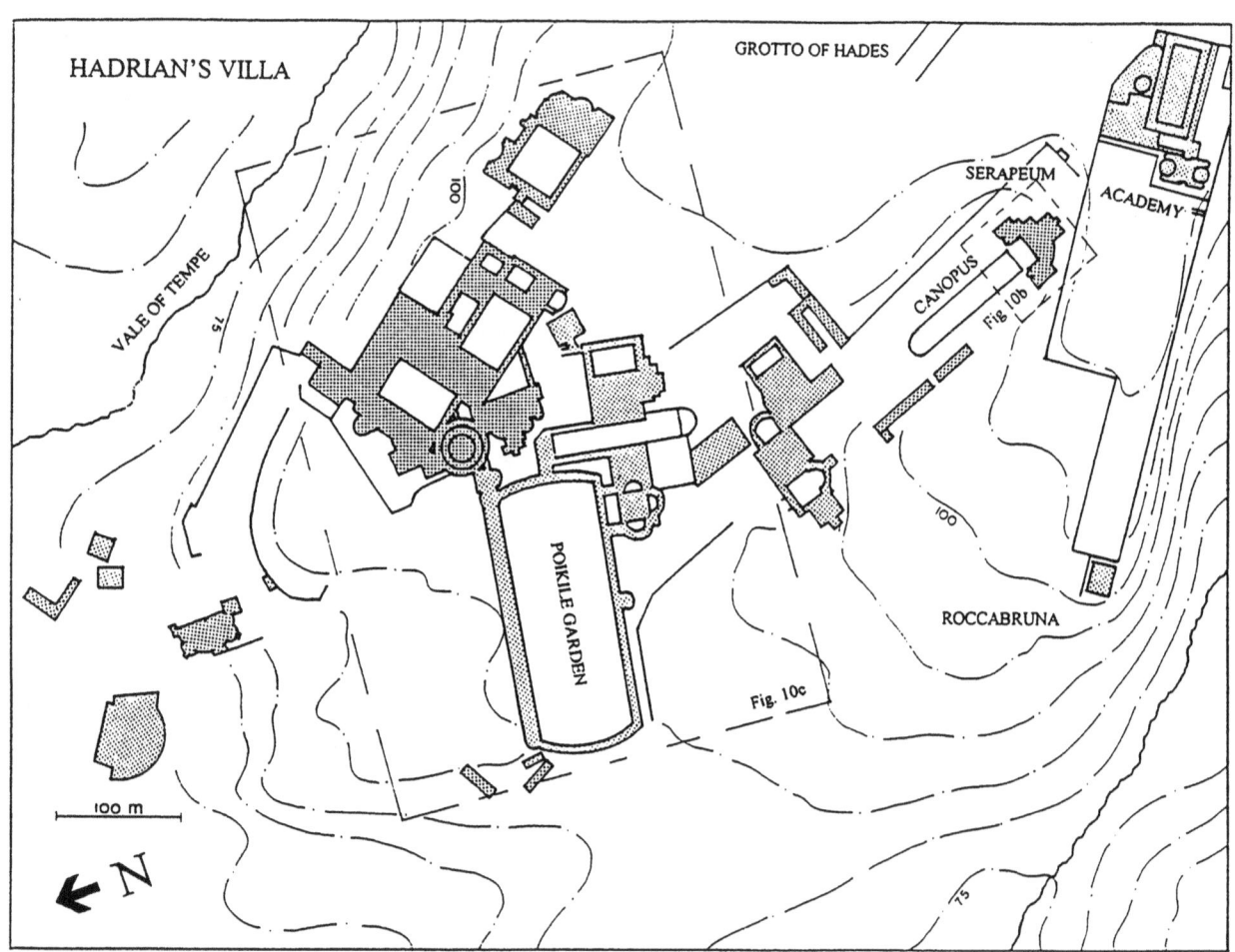

Fig. 10a LOCATION PLAN OF GARDEN AREAS AT HADRIAN'S VILLA, TIVOLI (L.Smith'96)

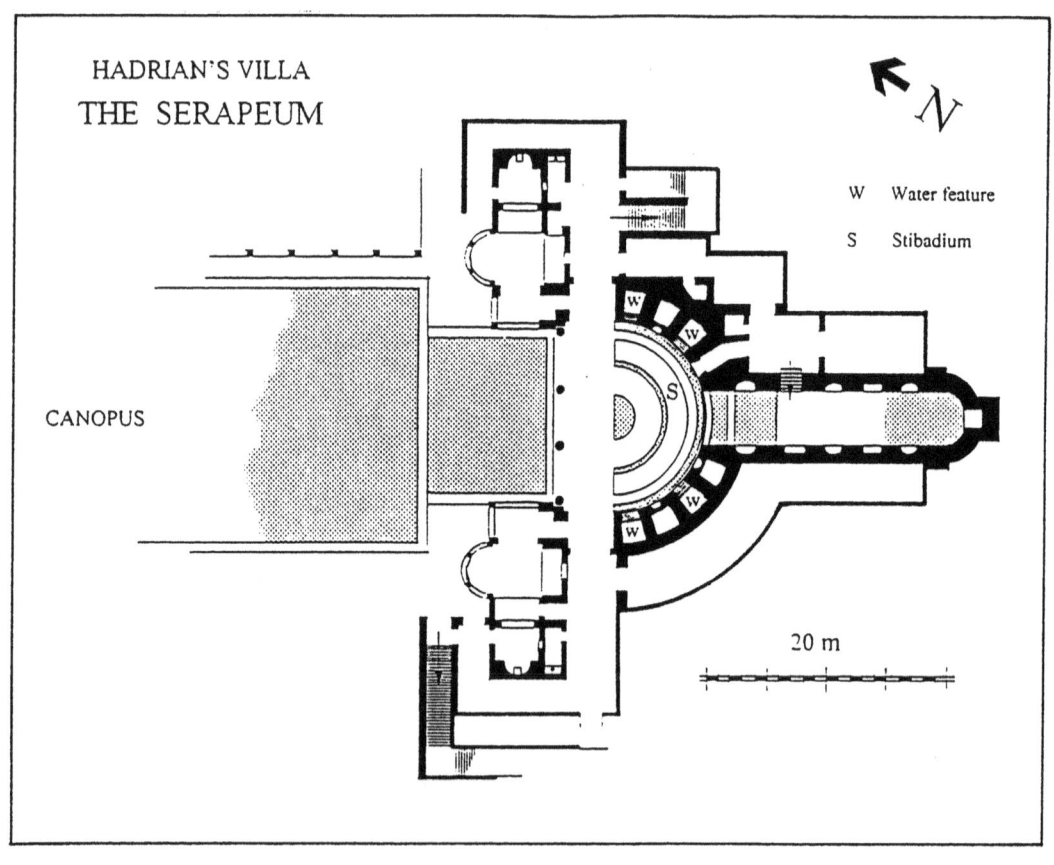

Fig.10b SERAPEUM AND CANOPUS AT HADRIAN'S VILLA, TIVOLI (L.Smith'96)

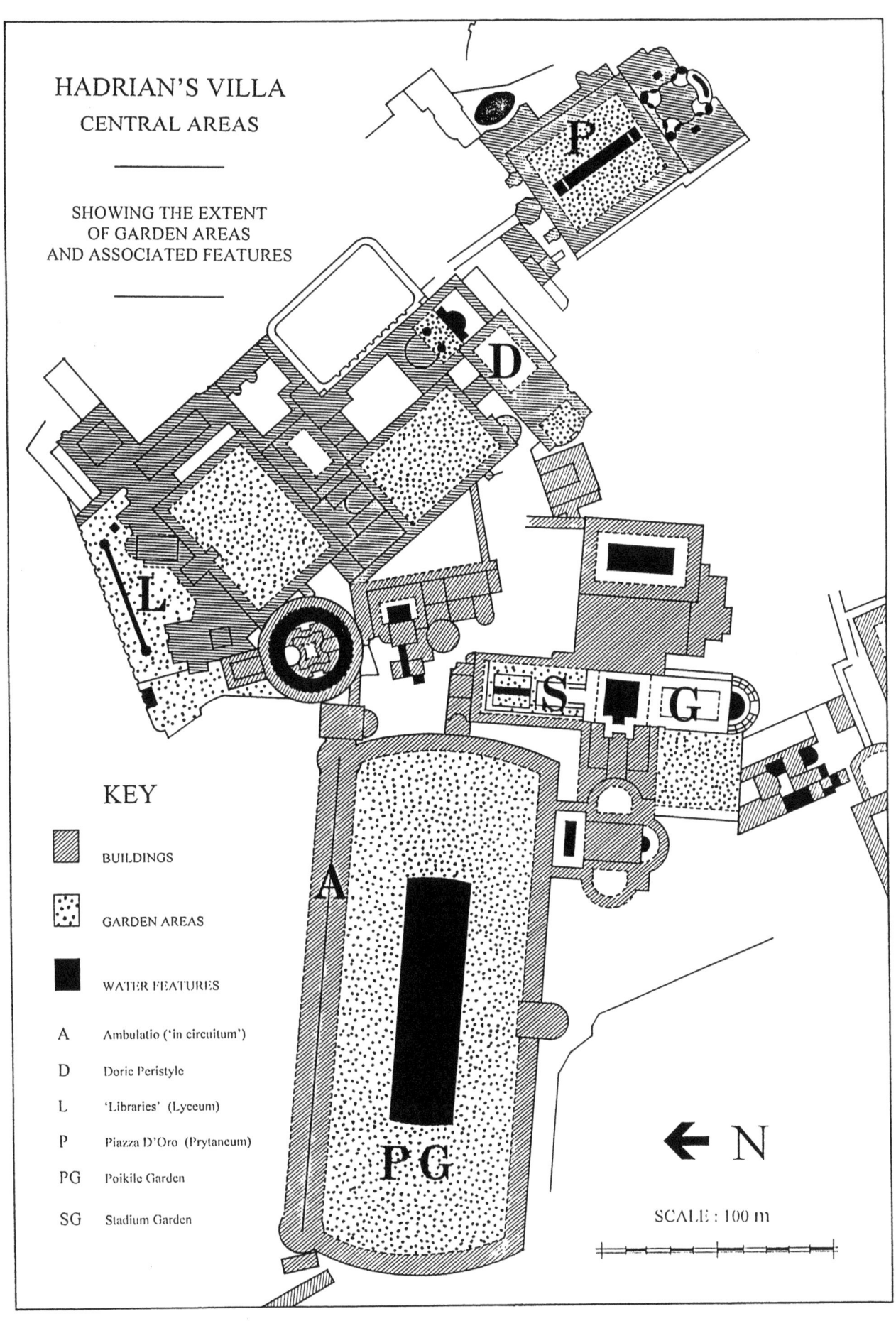

Fig. 10c   **HADRIAN'S VILLA: CENTRAL AREAS**   (L.Smith'96)

KEY

A Altar
B *Biclinium*
C Shrine
D Raised water basin
E Enclosure, possible site of thunderbolt
F *Puteal*

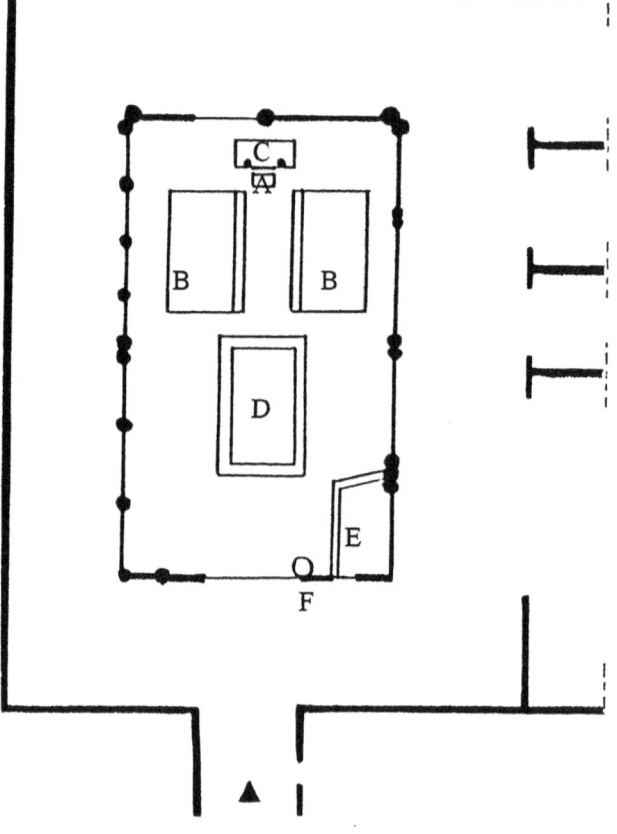

Fig. 11   GARDEN PLAN: HOUSE OF THE THUNDERBOLT, OSTIA
Showing the position of features.   (Not to scale)

Fig. 12 CROSS SECTION OF PART OF A WATER BASIN at Welschbillig, Germany.
Showing the materials used in the foundations.   (Espérandieu, 1925, 9, 416)

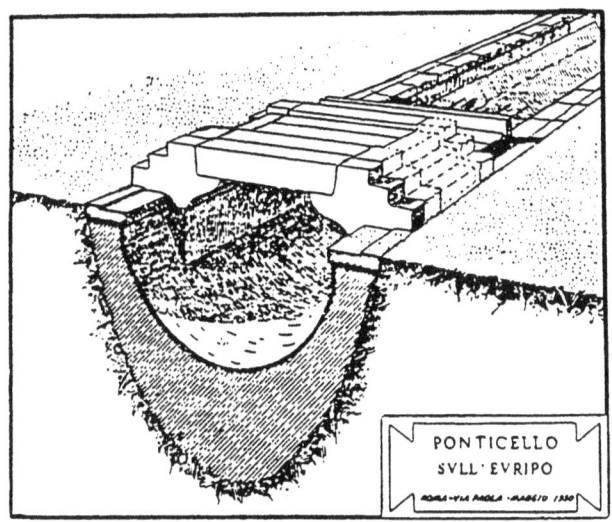

Fig.13 CROSS SECTION OF THE *EURIPUS* of Agrippa, in the Campus Martius, Rome.   (Lugli,1938,fig.27)

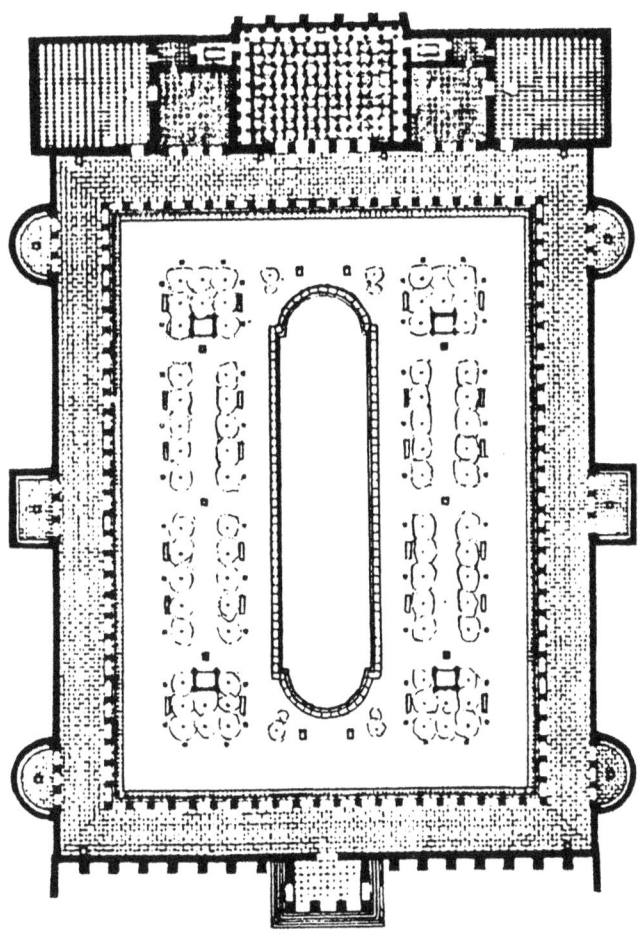

Fig. 14 TYPE C BASIN: Portico garden of the Library of Hadrian, Athens.   (Sisson,1929,Pl.21)

KEY

A   Unexcavated area under pine tree
B   Bridge with shallow arches
D   *Diaeta* or shrine

Site of exposed lead water pipes leading to basin

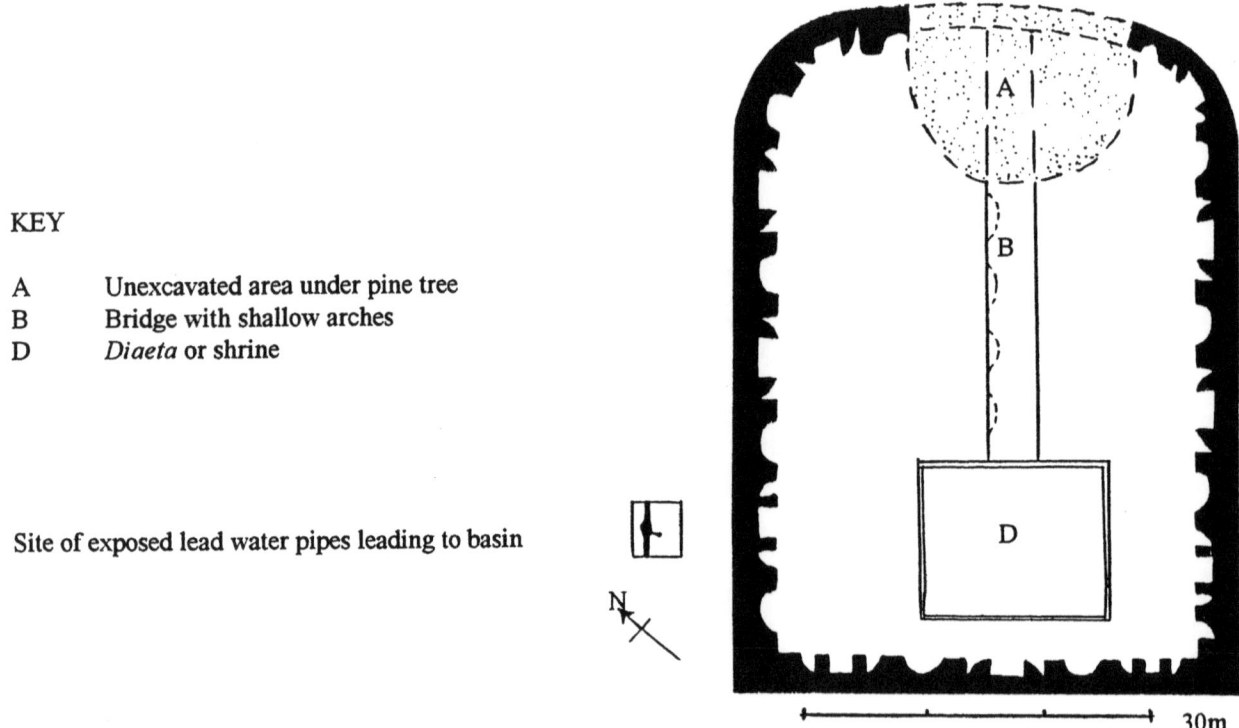

Fig. 15 TYPE D BASIN Domus Flavia, Rome. The internal walling is of an irregular shape.

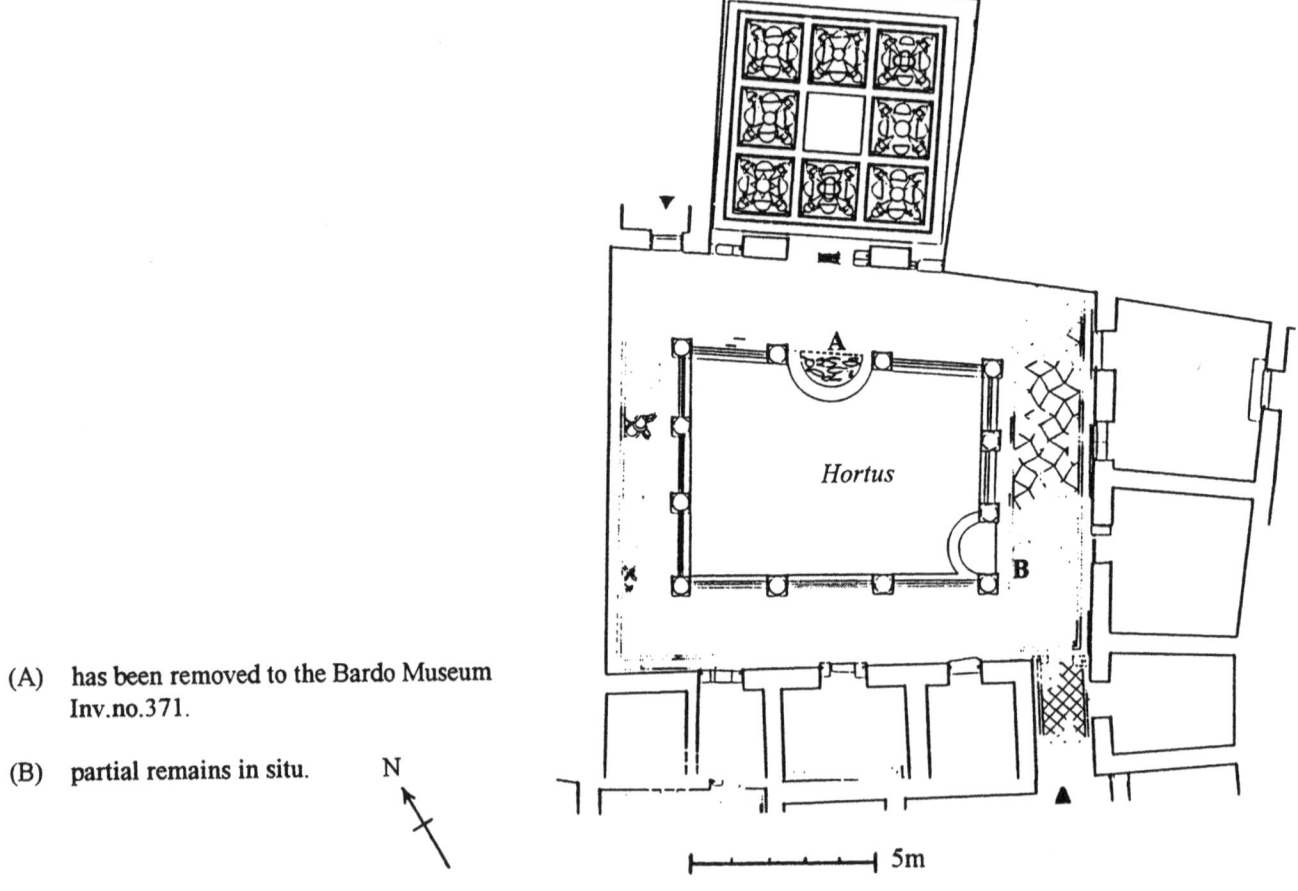

(A)   has been removed to the Bardo Museum Inv.no.371.

(B)   partial remains in situ.

Fig. 16 PLAN LOCATING TYPE E BASINS (DEMI-LUNE) House of Nicentius, Thuburbo Maius, Tunisia.
(Alexander & Ennaïfer, Vol.21, 1980, plan.10)

KEY

 Caissons containing plants

 Water

Fig. 17   TYPE F BASIN
With caissons,
House of the Water Jets, Conimbriga, Portugal.
(Alarcão & Etienne,1981,fig.1)

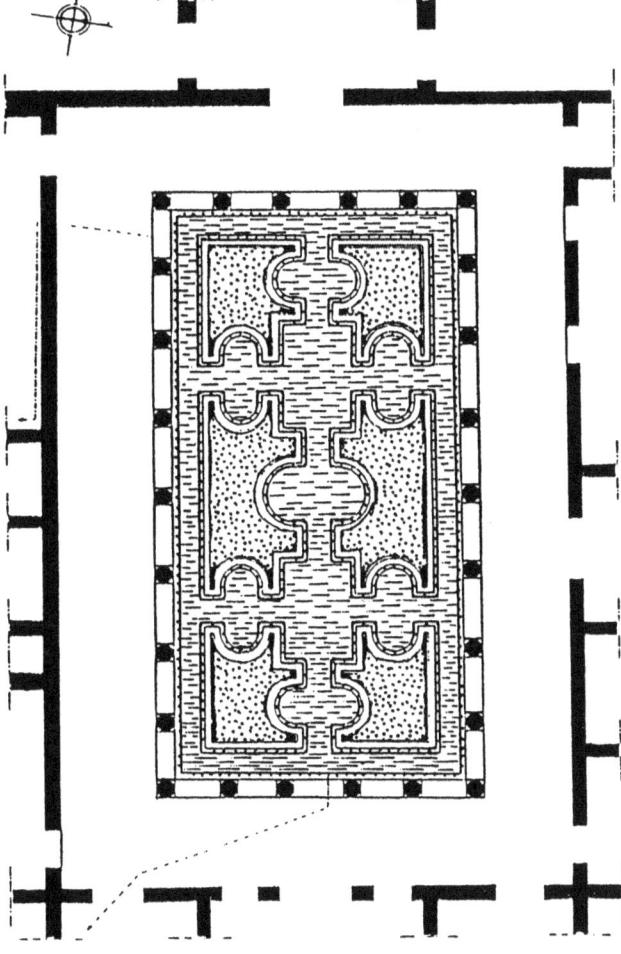

KEY

 Cultivated areas

 Water

Fig. 18   TYPE G BASIN
Variform with linked pools,
Casa de la Exedra, Italica, Spain.
(Bellido,1960,fig.32)

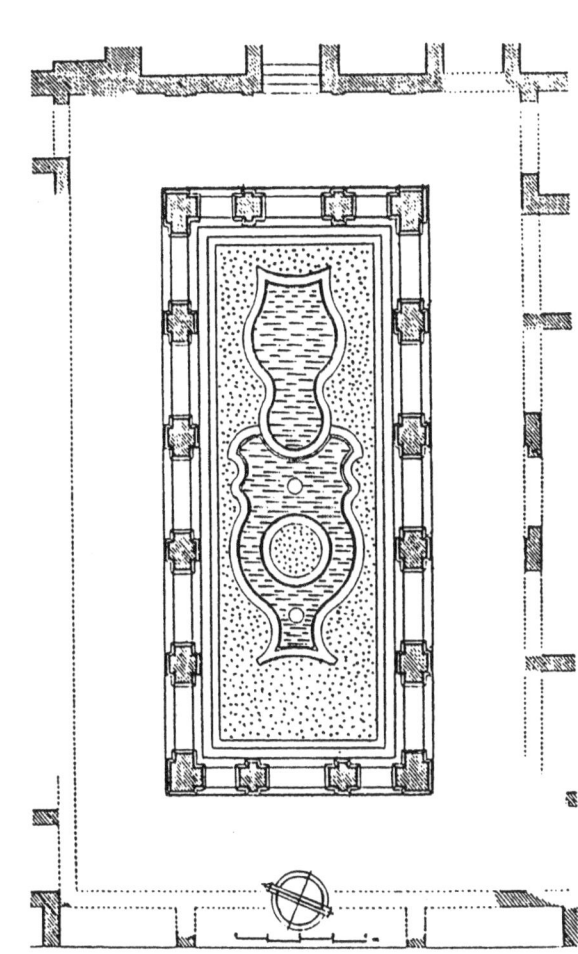

Fig. 19 MODEL OF A GROTTO From Reggio Calabria. (Neuerburg,1965,fig.9)

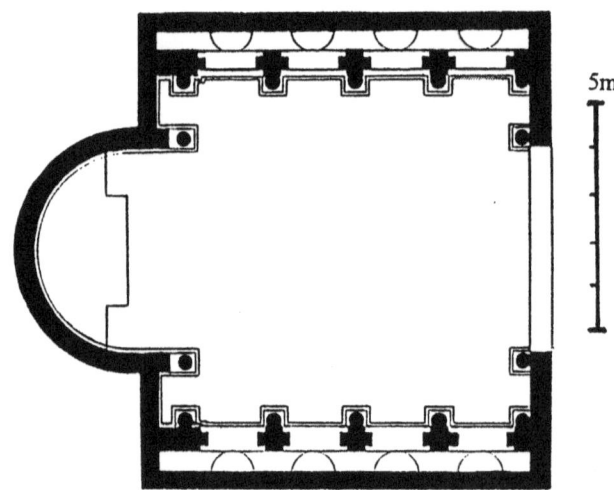

Fig. 20 PLAN OF A BASILICA TYPE OF NYMPHAEUM The so-called Villa of Horace at Tivoli. (Hallam,1914,fig.8)

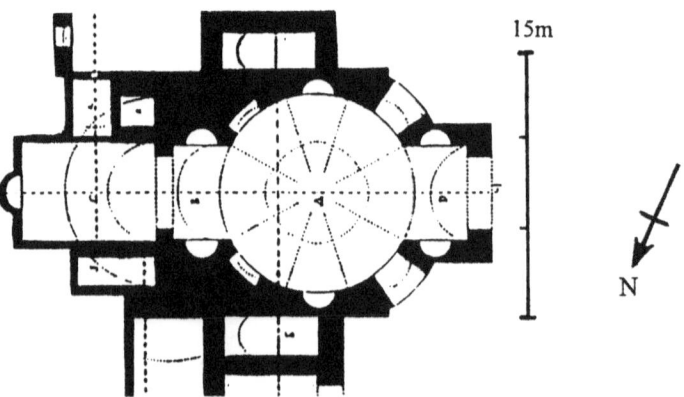

Fig. 21 MULTIPLE FOUNTAIN NICHES In the large domed hall or 'Nymphaeum' of the Gardens of Sallust, Rome.
(Lugli,1938,fig.66)

Fig. 22   FRESCO DEPICTING GARDEN STATUARY
An urn with bubble jet fountain stands between a pair of nymphs each holding a shallow dish fountain. A statue of a reclining silenus is shown above the wall. From the House of Romulus & Remus, Pompeii.   (Presuhn,1879,1,Pl.2)

Fig. 23   FRESCO DEPICTING AN URN IN FRONT OF A DECORATIVE MARBLE WALL

From the Auditorium of Maecenas, Rome.
(Lugli,1938,fig.90)

Fig. 24 PLAN AND VIEW OF THE GARDEN SCULPTURE AT THE HOUSE OF THE GOLDEN CUPIDS, POMPEII (Alinari 11994, plan after Mau)

KEY TO LOCATION OF SCULPTURE

1. Monopodium
2. Herm of Dionysus
3. Pinax
4. Janiform Herm
5.& 6. Herm of Dionysus
7. Pinax
8. Statuette of Omphale
9. Herm of boy
10. Pinax
11. Base
12. Janiform herm
13. Pinax
14. Sundial
15. Janiform herm
16. Herm of boy
17. Base
18. Boar
19. Rabbit
20. Dog
21. Herm of boy

Also there were:
5 mask oscilla
2 circular oscilla

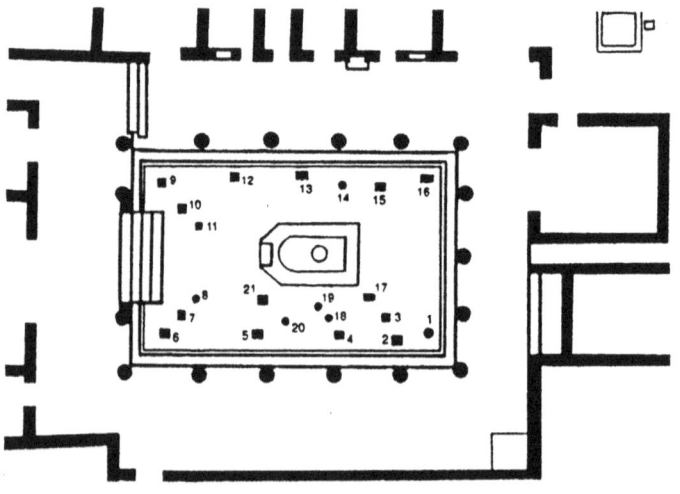

Fig. 25 PLAN AND VIEW OF THE GARDEN STATUARY AT THE HOUSE OF MARCUS LUCRETIUS, POMPEII (Alinari; plan after Overbeck,1866,fig.189)

KEY TO LOCATION OF STATUARY

1. Silenus
2.& 3. Janiform herms
4. Satyr
5. Duck
6. Deer
7. Cow
8. Draped herm of Satyr with goat & kid
9.& 10. Ibises
11.& 12. Hares
13. Group of Satyr and Pan (reverse of Pl.29)
14.& 15. Dolphins with cupids
16.& 17. Janiform herms
Also there were 5 *oscilla*

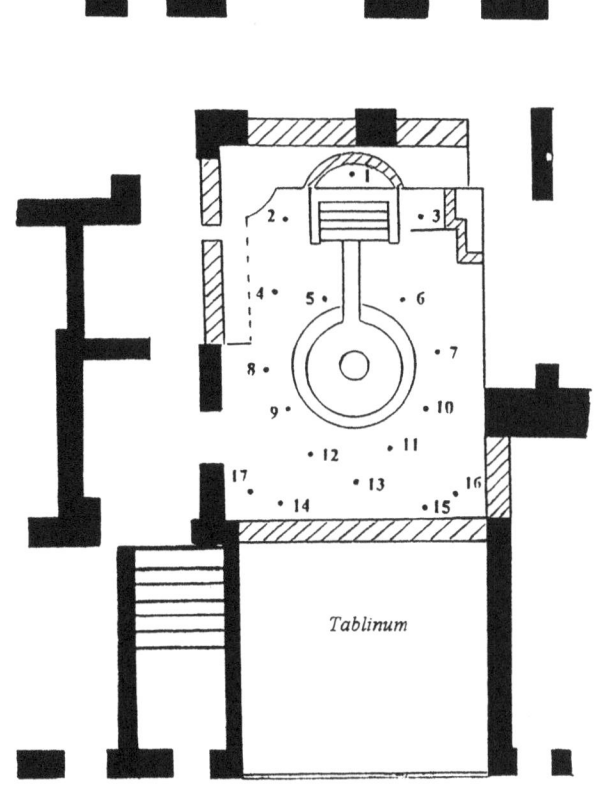

Fig. 26a BRONZE BALUSTRADE WITH JANIFORM HERMS AS POSTS Found in Lake Nemi, Italy.
(Moretti,1940,fig.48)

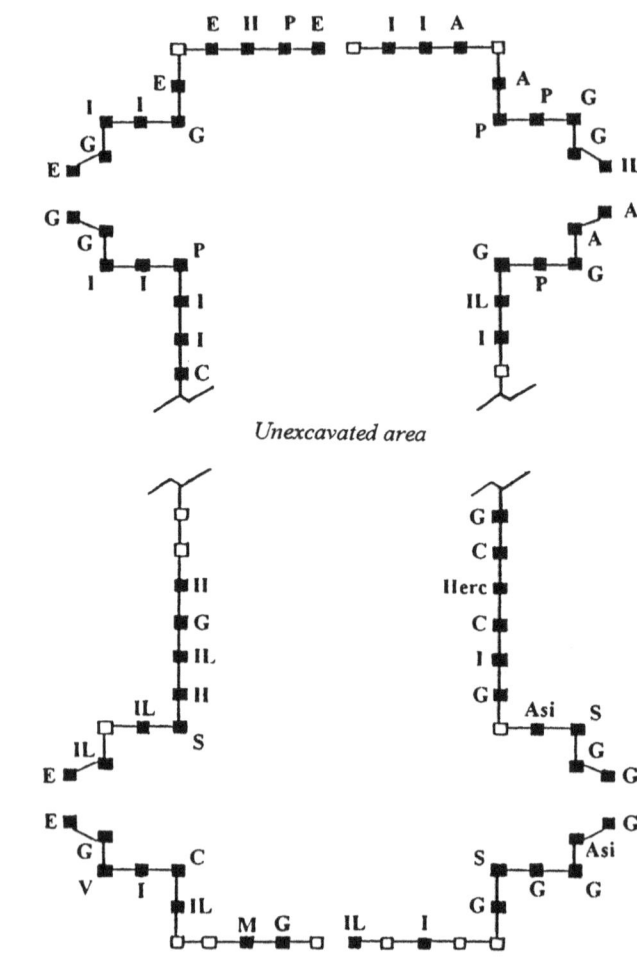

KEY TO HERM TYPES

Asi = Asiatic
A   = African
C   = Cupid
E   = Emperor or
      Hellenistic ruler
G   = Germanic
H   = Hermes
Herc= Hercules
I   = Idealised portrait
IL = Illustrious personage
M   = Mars
P   = Philosopher
S   = Satyr
V   = Venus

Fig. 26b WATER BASIN AT WELSCHBILLIG, GERMANY With herms as posts in an enclosing balustrade.
(After Wrede,1972,abb.12)

(A)   RECTANGULAR *OSCILLUM*
As depicted in a fresco, provenance unknown.
Swags of garlands hang from the *oscillum*.
Below is a shallow dish fountain basin
supported by a sphinx.
(Art Antique,1972)

(B) & (C)   MINIATURE FRESCOES
Depicting *oscilla* & urns.
(b)   circular *oscilla* (Spinazzola,1953,fig.647)
(c)   peltae *oscilla*   (NSc,1906,377,fig.3)

(D)   MASK *OSCILLUM*
Iron hook for suspension still in situ.
From the House of the Golden Cupids.
(Reproduced by permission of Aristide D.Caratzas,
  Publisher)

(E)   PELTA OSCILLUM
From Cordoba, Spain (Bellido,1949,fig.440)

A

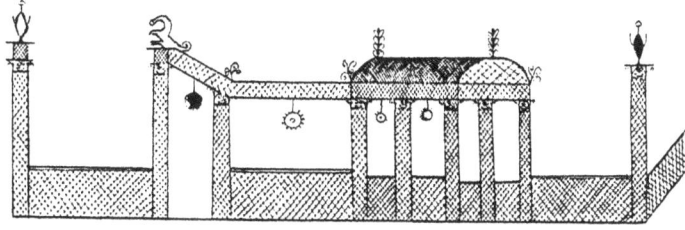

B

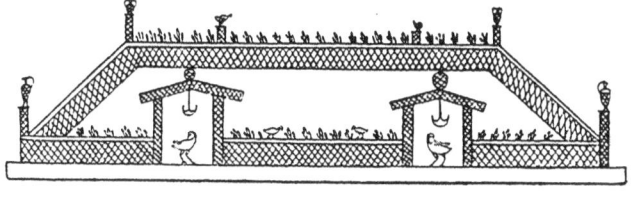

C

D

E

Fig. 27   *OSCILLA*

(A)   *PINAX* DEPICTED IN A FRESCO OF A GARDEN   Provenance unknown, now in Naples National Museum.   (Schefold,1962,fig.149.2)

(B)   MARBLE *PINAX* SET ON A POST
From the House of the Golden Cupids, Pompeii,
being no.13 on fig.24.
(Reproduced by permission of Aristide D.Caratzas, Publisher)

Fig. 28 *PINAKES*

Fig. 29   **SUNDIAL:** From the Villa San Marco, Stabiae.   (Miniero,1983,fig.16)

Fig. 30   **OWL AUTOMATA:** As described by Hero of Alexandria.   (Schmidt,1899,fig.17)

Fig. 31 *CORONARIAE*, **GARLAND AND CHAPLET MAKERS** Mosaics from Piazza Armerina, Sicily. (Dragotta, 1978)

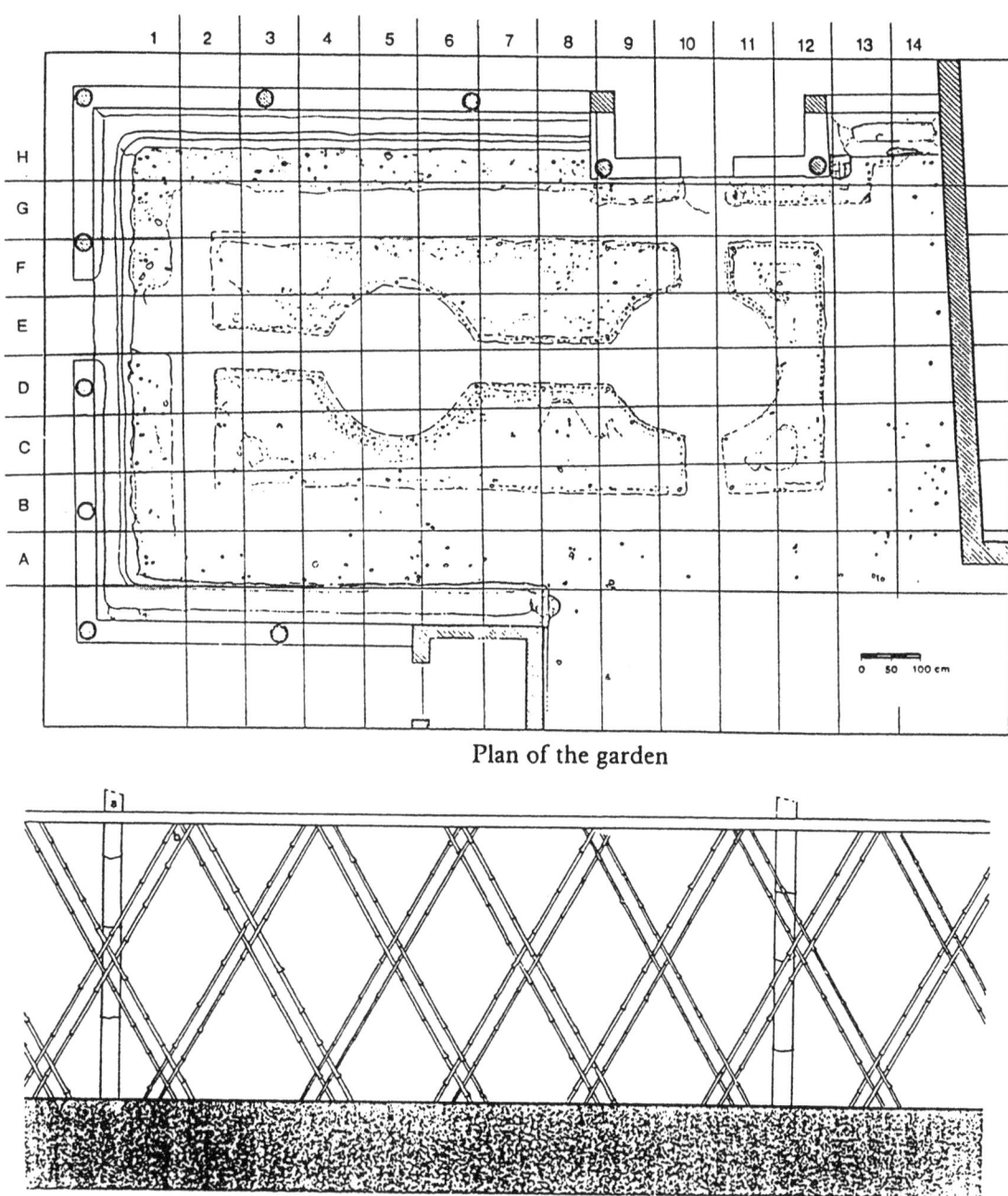

Plan of the garden

Reconstruction of the trellis which surrounded the beds

Fig. 32 HOUSE OF THE CHASTE LOVERS, POMPEII With findspots of plant material. (Ciarallo, 1993, 112)

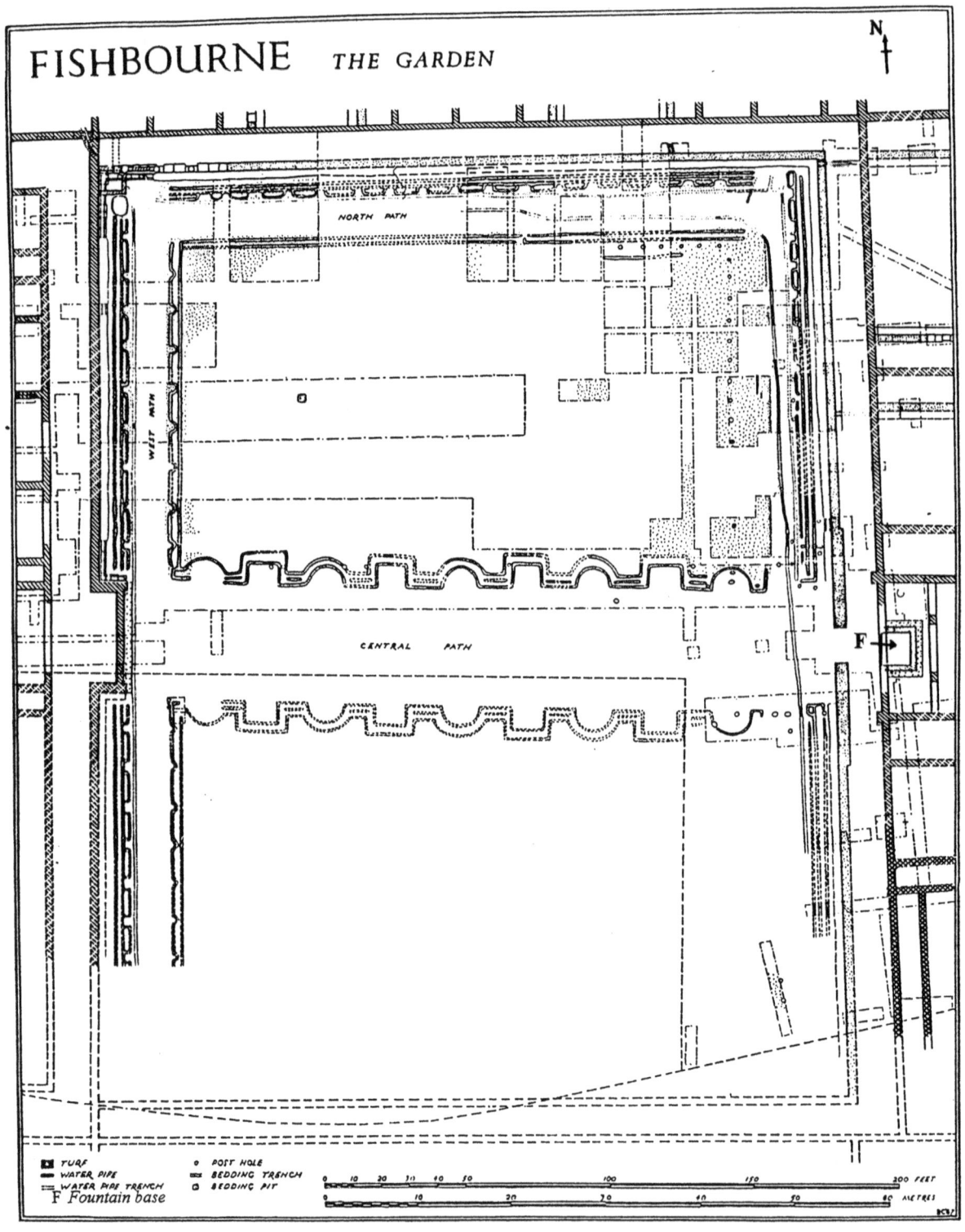

Fig. 33   PLAN OF THE GARDEN AT FISHBOURNE, BRITAIN   (Cunliffe, 1968, pl.xiv)

(A) Sowing

(B) Fetching manure

(C) Collecting fruit

(D) Grafting

Fig. 34   **HORTICULTURAL TASKS, FROM A MOSAIC RUSTIC CALENDAR**
From St.Roman-en-Gal, Gaul.   (Ferière,1988,109;44;112;111)

Fig. 35 'THE LILYGROWER', DETAIL OF THE MOSAIC FROM THE VILLA OF SCORPIANUS, CARTHAGE, now in Carthage Museum Inv.no.4.

KEY TO FIG. 36 (overleaf)

A. *Palas ligneas*, remains of a wooden spade from Chester, & iron spade shoe from South Shields, Britain (Ferdière,1988,59).
B. *Palas*, iron spade shoe, from Compiègne, Gaul (Ibid,58).
C. *Ferrea*, iron 3-pronged fork, from Compiègne, Gaul (Ibid,59).
D. *Rastrum*, 7-pronged rake, from Newstead, Britain (Ibid,58).
E. *Falx arboraria*, pruning-hook, from Villa Guiry, Gaul (Ibid).
F. *Sarculum*, hoe, from Vichy & Luzerche, Gaul (Ibid).
G. *Ascia-rastrum*, double-headed hoe, from Compiègne, Gaul (Ibid).
H. *Forfex*, shears (White,1967,119).
I. *Bidens*, 2-prong hoe, from Vingeanne, Gaul (Ferdière,1988,59).
J. *Nassiternam*, water pot, from Arles, Gaul (Daremberg & Saglio,1900,Vol.5,359).
K. Earthenware flower pot, from Eccles, Britain (Detsicas,1974,fig.8).

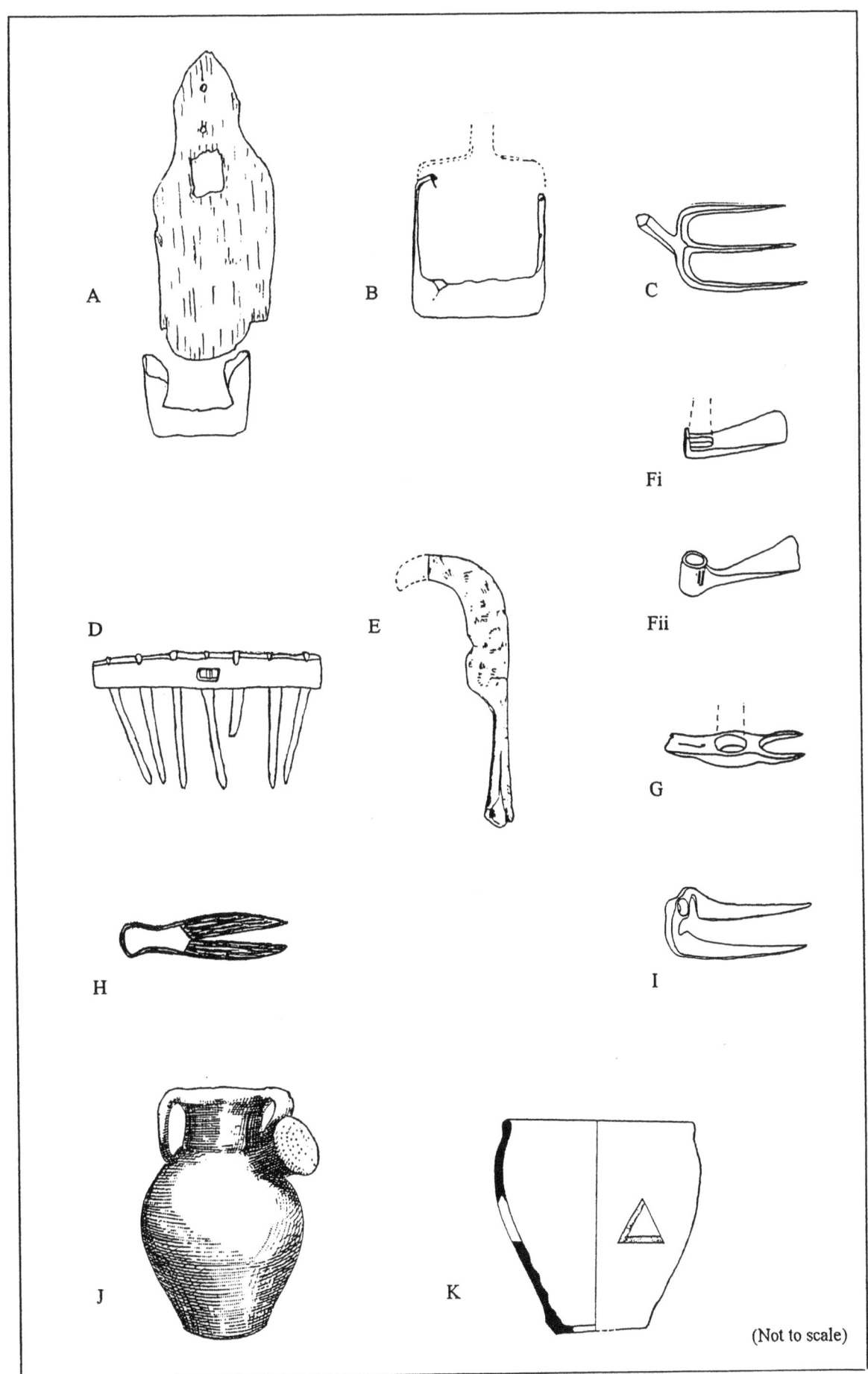

Fig. 36 HORTICULTURAL TOOLS AND EQUIPMENT   (Key on previous page)

Pl. 1   PLANTS GROWN IN RAISED CONTAINERS, IN AN *ATRIUM*   House of Loreius Tiburtinus, Pompeii.

Pl. 2   PLANT CONTAINERS IN A LATER FORM OF PERISTYLE GARDEN
House of '*Omnia tibi Felicia*', Dougga, Tunisia.

Pl. 3   FRESCO OF A *VILLA URBANA*   From the House of M.L.Fronto, Pompeii.
The garden here is composed of pathways and lawns, plus two enclosures with decorative marble walls.

From the Villa of P.Fannius Sinistor, Boscoreale (now in New York).

A *pergula* and decorative walling are placed above the grotto and fountain.

(Photographed in the Museum at Boscoreale)

Pl. 4   FRESCO DEPICTING A GROTTO

Pl. 5   HOUSE OF THE HUNT, POMPEII, with *plutei*.   A disc covers the cistern in the entranceway to the garden.

The south portico is fitted with doorways. Below is a rain water gutter with a concave quarter circle.

Pl. 6   VILLA OF POPPAEA, OPLONTIS

Pl. 7   DECORATIVE STONE WALL FROM WELSCHBILLIG, now in Trier Museum. Herms are utilized as balusters in the wall.

Pl. 8   RECONSTRUCTED PERGOLA, that will in time shade walkways on either side of a series of interconected water basins. House of Loreius Tiburtinus, Pompeii   (for plan see fig.3).

Pl. 9 *TRICLINIUM* **UNDER A** *PERGULA*, **AT VIENNE, GAUL** House in the North-East Zone (St.Romain-en-Gal).

Pl. 10 MOSAIC OF LORD JULIUS, CARTHAGE, now in the Bardo Museum Tunis.
Illustrating, botom-left, a high backed wicker chair, and in the centre of the top row is a couch, both in an outdoor/garden setting.

Pl. 11 SCHOLA FROM THE TRIANGULAR FORUM, POMPEII
The marble curved bench seat has griffin terminals.

Pl. 12 GARDEN BENCH AND MATCHING WATER BASIN, Sousse Museum.
A band of mosaic is set into the top of the basin plus the seat, back rest and front, of the bench.

Pl. 13 SUNKEN GARDEN AT THE HOUSE OF ANCORA NERA, POMPEII
Looking down to the three rusticated apses on the rear wall, the central niche contains an *aedicula*.

Pl. 14 TERRACED GARDEN AT THE VILLA OF THE MYSTERIES, near Pompeii (with cryptoporticus).

Pl. 15
PLUMBING TO WATER FEATURES
House of the Vettii, Pompeii.

Pl. 16   TYPE E, DEMI-LUNE BASIN   From Thuburbo Maius, Bardo Museum Inv. no. 1399.

Pl. 17 TYPE B BASIN (on the left, type D on the right).   Schola of Trajan, Ostia.

Pl. 18 TYPE D BASIN   House of Meleagro, Pompeii.

Pl. 19 TYPE F BASIN, with caissons.   House of the Swasticas, Conimbriga, Portugal.
(Photo by courtesy of the Museum of Conimbriga)

Pl. 20 GUTTER BASIN, along three sides of the garden.   House of the Ocean Gods, Vienne, France.

Pl. 21

A *EURIPUS* BASIN

House of Loreius Tiburtinus, Pompeii.
(View towards the *biclinium* to the rear)

Cross section

Pl. 22 ISLAND-LIKE NYMPHAEUM, of the Domus Flavia, Rome.

Pl. 23 *AEDICULA* NYMPHAEUM

House of the Little Fountain, Pompeii.
To the rear there is a garden fresco.

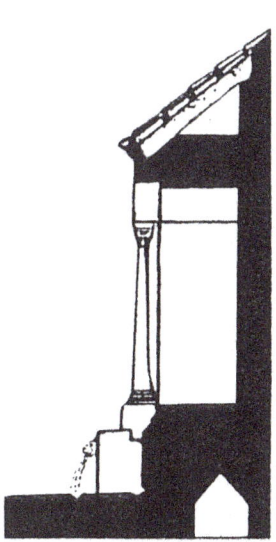

Section drawing of nymphaeum
(after Packer,1967,fig.24)

Pl. 24 FACADE NYMPHAEUM
House of Cupid & Psyche, Ostia.

Pl. 25 VENUS

Bending down to retrieve some object on the floor (the head belongs to another statue).

From the Domus Fortuna Annonaria, Ostia. Now in Ostia Museum Inv.no.123.

Pl. 26 FRESCO DEPICTING A STATUE OF MARS From the House of the Marine Venus, Pompeii. Ivy frames the scene. A mask *oscillum* is above the head of Mars.

Pl. 27 PUTTO CARRYING URN

Fountain outlet in urn.
Conservatori Museum, Rome
(Gall. Horti Lamiani,
Inv. number not known).

Pl. 28 BRONZE AMORINI CARRYING DUCK,   House of the Vettii, Pompeii.
Fountain outlet is in the mouth of the bird. To the right is a garden table, far right is a table-type water basi

Pl. 29   PAN & SATYR STATUE GROUP   fountain figures.
Water outlet in mouth of wineskin held by the satyr. Vatican Museum, Gall.Candelabri, Inv.no.2524.

Pl. 30   SILENUS & MAENAD STATUE GROUP   From the House of the Panther, Carthage.
Now in Carthage Museum, Inv.no.5.

Pl. 31 RECLINING NYMPH FOUNTAIN FIGURE urn used as a water outlet.
Therme Museum, Rome, Inv.no.121299.

Pl. 32 RUSTIC GENRE
Old fisherman, from Rome. B.M. Inv.no.1766.

Pl. 33 DRAPED HERM OF MERCURY

Found near Frascati. B.M. Inv.no.1605.
(A biro was used for scale)

Pl. 34 JANIFORM HERM HEADS of Bacchus & Ariadne.   Found near Rome. B.M. Inv.no.1623.

Pl. 35   *OSCILLUM*

Depicting Cupid sacrificing at an altar before a statue of Priapus.
From Rome. B.M. Inv.no.2458.

Pl. 36   SMALL DECORATIVE WATER STAIRS   comprising four relief panels alternating with waterstairs.
Therme Museum, Rome, Inv.no.67413-T138.

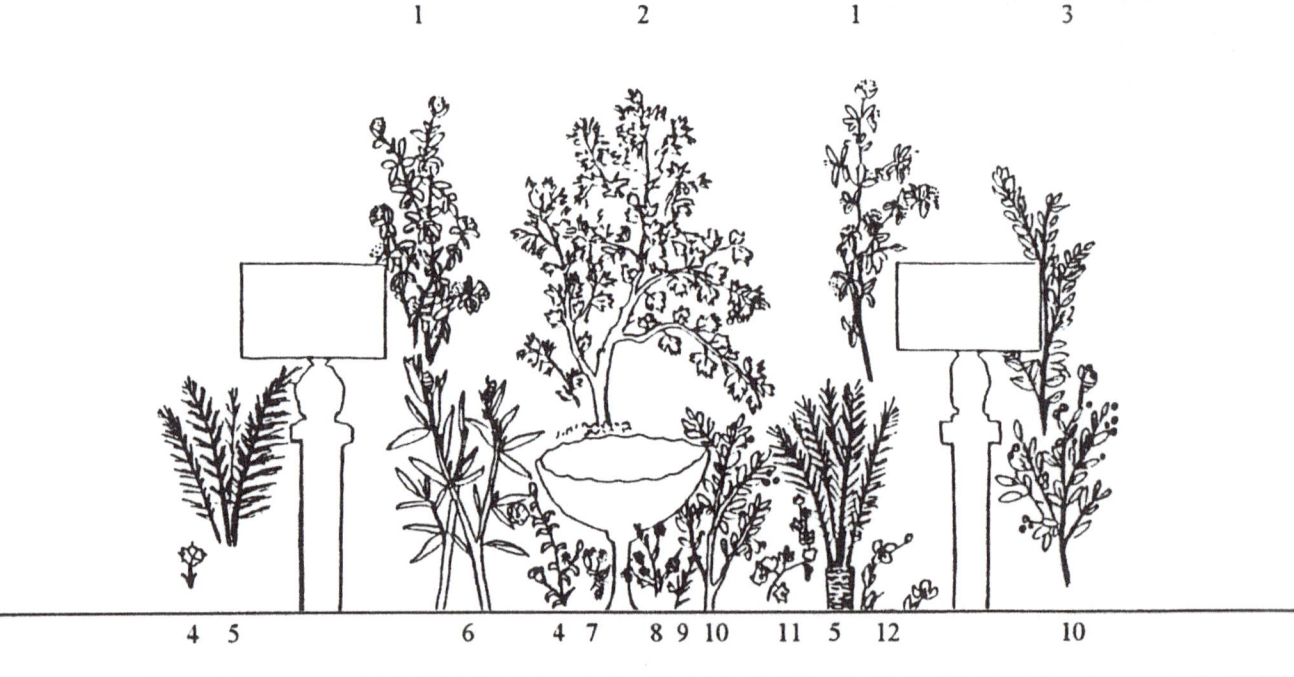

KEY TO PLANTS DEPICTED			
1. *Viburnum tinus*	4. *Rosa gallica*	7. *Anthemis arvensis*	10. *Arbutus unedo*
2. *Platanus orientalis*	5. *Phoenix dactylifera*	8. *Chrysanthemum segetum*	11. *Hedra helix*
3. *Laurus Nobilis*	6. *Nerium oleander*	9. *Vinca*	12. *Papaver somniferum*

Pl. 37 GARDEN SCENE, FRESCO FROM THE HOUSE OF THE WEDDING OF ALEXANDER, POMPEII
(Jashemski,1993,fig.2. Reproduced by permission of Aristide D.Caratzas, Publisher)

Pl. 38 FRESCO FROM THE GARDEN ROOM AT THE HOUSE OF LIVIA, PRIMAPORTA, ROME
(Garden Picture Library/Janet Johnson)   In the foreground is a lattice fence in front of a marble wall.

Pl. 39 GARDEN FRESCO FROM THE HOUSE OF THE MARINE VENUS, POMPEII
Plants from left to right are:
1. *Nerium oleander*, 2. *Artemisia* (southernwood), 3. *Rosa gallica*, 4. *Nerium oleander*, 5. *Arbutus unedo* (strawberry tree).

Pl. 40 FRESCO ON A LOW WALL AT OPLONTIS
Depicting a simple lattice fence in front of plants with red flowers, possibly the Martagon lily.

Pl. 41 ROMAN FLORA & FAUNA DEPICTED ON A PLUTEUS,   House of Adonis, Pompeii.
Left to right are: Acanthus, snake & heron, Hart's tongue fern.

Pl. 42 ROW OF FIVE TREE ROOT CASTS
    (of Plane trees)
Villa of Poppaea, Oplontis.

Pl. 43 MOSAIC DEPICTING A GARDEN TECHNICIAN, perhaps a *topiarius* or an *aquarius*.
Now in the Vatican Museum.

Pl. 44   PLANT BEDS AS DESCRIBED BY PLINY THE ELDER
A method of cultivation still in use today, e.g. at Istanbul.

www.ingramcontent.com/pod-product-compliance
Lightning Source LLC
Chambersburg PA
CBHW041704290426

44108CB00027B/2851